MW00610924

LEADERSHIP
CPR

RESUSCITATING THE WORKPLACE
through
Civility, Performance and Respect

Thank you, Charles, for being such a wonderful friend and leader!

—Ritch

Ritch K. Eich, PhD

LEADERSHIP
CPR

~

"Ritch Eich has served up an *ace* with his latest book, *Leadership CPR*. His approach to writing is similar to his approach to tennis: *leave it all on the court*. As a longtime tennis coach, I greatly appreciate the preparation, attention to detail, discipline, and valuable lessons included in Ritch's *must read* leadership book."

— DICK GOULD, Coach of 17 Stanford Men's NCAA Championship teams; John L. Hinds Director of Tennis (ret.), Stanford University

LEADERSHIP
CPR

RESUSCITATING THE WORKPLACE

through

Civility, Performance and Respect

Ritch K. Eich

Redwood Publishing, LLC
Orange County, CA

Copyright © 2018 by Ritch K. Eich.

First Edition.

All rights reserved. This book or parts thereof may not be reproduced in any form, stored in any retrieval system, or transmitted in any form by any means—electronic, mechanical, photocopy, recording, or otherwise—without prior written permission of the publisher, except as provided by United States of America copyright law. The only exception is by a reviewer, who may quote short excerpts in a review. For longer permission requests, please write to the publisher, at "Attention: Permissions Coordinator," at info@redwooddigitalpublishing.com.

Published by:
Redwood Publishing, LLC
www.redwooddigitalpublishing.com

Printed in the United States of America.

ISBN eBook: 978-1-947341-12-8
ISBN Paperback: 978-1-947341-11-1

Library of Congress Control Number: 2017961228

For information about special discounts available for bulk purchases, sales promotions, fund-raising and educational needs, or to book speaking engagements, visit the author's website at: www.leadercpr.com

Interior Design: Redwood Publishing, LLC.
Cover Design: Diane Kuntz and Michelle Manley

A selection of material in this book was adapted from some of Ritch Eich's previously published articles. The author wishes to thank the following for granting their permission to edit the articles for use in this book: Bloomberg Business (© Bloomberg LP, Reprinted by Permission.); BusinessManagementDaily.com; TheCEOMagazine. com; Corp!Magazine.com; EHS Today; Directors & Boards; FastCompany.com; Forbes.com; FoxNews.com; TheGlobeandMail.com; TheHill.com; IndustryWeek. com; The Journal of Values-Based Leadership; Leadership Excellence Essentials (HR. com); Los Angeles Business Journal (Reprinted with permission of the Los Angeles Business Journal); ModernHealthcare.com; Monster.com; Pacific Coast Business Times; PacificStandard.com; Recognition and Engagement Excellence Essentials (HR.com); SanFernandoValleyBusinessJournal.com; SigEp.org; Strategic Health Care Marketing (strategicHCmarketing.com); StrategyDriven.com; ThinDifference.com; TrainingMagazine.com; Trusteeship Magazine; Ventura County Star.

To Joan Taylor Cummings Eich

~

"The leaders who work most effectively, it seems to me, never say 'I.' And that's not because they have trained themselves not to say 'I.' They don't think 'I.' They think 'we'; they think 'team.' They understand their job to be to make the team function. They accept responsibility and don't sidestep it, but 'we' gets the credit.... This is what creates trust, what enables you to get the task done."

—PETER DRUCKER

CONTENTS

~

"No leader sets out to be a leader. People set out to live their lives, expressing themselves fully. When that expression is of value, they become leaders. So the point is not to become a leader. The point is to become yourself, to use yourself completely—all your skills, gifts and energies—in order to make your vision manifest. You must withhold nothing. You must, in sum, become the person you started out to be, and to enjoy the process of becoming."

—WARREN BENNIS

ACKNOWLEDGMENTS

Many people have encouraged me to write and have been enormously helpful over the past several years as I've tried to tackle a number of important leadership issues. In particular, many prominent editors, publishers, reporters, and other journalists, family, and friends have generously given me sage advice and motivated me to continue my efforts. They include Henry Dubroff of the *Pacific Coast Business Times*; Steve Minter of *Industry Week*; Charlie Crumpley, formerly of the *Los Angeles Business Journal* and now at the *San Fernando Valley Business Journal*; Elizabeth H. R. Gingerich, JD, of *The Journal of Values-Based Leadership*; Joe Picard and Charles Jordan at *The Hill*; Jim Kristie of *Directors and Boards*; Lorri Freifeld of *Training* magazine; Debbie McGrath and Babitha Balakrishnan of *Leadership Excellence Essentials*, *Recognition & Engagement Excellence Essentials*, and *Strategy and Planning Excellence Essentials*; and Fred Allen at *Forbes*.

Also, Connie Blaszczyk at Monster.com; Sonja Carberry, Claire Mencke, and Michael Mink at Investors Business Daily; Lynne Jordal Martin at Fox News; Jennifer Kluge and Karen Dybis at *Corp!* magazine; Lin Grensing at Human Resources Executive; Doug Sohn at American Management Association; Matt Humphrey and Lisa Ellis at Strategic Health Care Marketing; Marilyn Hertz at *The Globe and Mail*; Noah Robischon at *Fast Company*; Faisal Kaleem at *CEO* magazine; Ursula Sharp at Soundview Executive Book Summaries; Lauren Melesio at Modern Healthcare; Sarah Hardesty Bray at Trusteeship; Marianne Ratcliff, Mike Craft, Larry Ames, Tim Gallagher, and John Moore at Ventura County Star; Michael Pye, Jeff Piasky, Adam Schwartz, Laurie Kelly-Pye, Kristen Dalley, and Diana Ghazzawi at Career Press (*Real Leaders Don't Boss* © 2012 by Ritch Eich used with permission from *Career Press* c/o Red Wheel Weiser, LLC Newburyport, MA www.redwheelweiser.com), and Tess Woods at Tess Woods Public Relations.

And the person who has ensured that each of my books is so much better than had I been left to my own devices, Cynthia Zigmund of Second City Publishing. Independent journalists Mark Morrow and Amy Bentley have been invaluable colleagues and constructive critics and so helpful in the preparation of this book.

To Ross Goldberg, my unfailing friend, confidant, writing mentor, public relations guru and fellow lover of baseball, I offer my sincere thanks.

Finally, I owe a particular debt of gratitude to Sara Stratton and her superb team of talented professionals at Redwood Publishing.

I appreciate each and every one of the following individuals and organizations. I apologize profusely if I have overlooked anyone. In alphabetical order they are:

ACKNOWLEDGMENTS

Kathryn Alexander

Dotti Albertine, Albertine Book
  Design

Karen Alter

Alumni Association of the
  University of Michigan

Gary and Nancy Allbright Ames

Larry and Bunny Ames

Babitha Balakrishnan

Bob Balslev

Eugene A. Bauer, MD

Dan Beckham

Amy Bentley

Connie Blaszczyk

Laura Blodgett

Cheryl Boyes

Mike Bradbury

David A. Brandon

Sarah Hardesty Bray

Adele Brinkley

Charles Bryan

California State University,
  Sacramento, Reference
  Librarians

Sonja Carberry

John Chamberlain

Dan Coats

Mihaela Corcoa

Mike Craft

Charlie Crumpley

Custom Printing, Oxnard,
  California

Kristen Dalley

Rich DeVos

Henry Dubroff

Sarah J. Duffy

Karen Dybis

Harold Edwards

Andy Efstratis

Joan Stiles Eich

Ron Eich

Katie Elliott

Lisa Ellis

Ken Endress, Navy Facilities
  MIDLAN, PWD Great Lakes, IL

Jim Finkelstein

Jeff Folks

Dave Francis

Lorri Freifeld

Tim Gallagher

Diana Ghazzawi

Elizabeth H. R. Gingerich

Ross Goldberg

Marshall Goldsmith

Dick Gould

Steve Grafton

Lin Grensing

Paul Grossgold

ACKNOWLEDGMENTS

Kim Harper

Roger Hart

Marjorie L. Harth

Norm Hartman

Hebrew University of Jerusalem

Marilyn Hertz

Brent Hoffmann

Howdy Holmes

Kathleen Hopper

Matt Humphrey

Charles Jordan

Faisal Kaleem

Bill Kearney

John Kearney

Laurie Kelly-Pye

Verena Kloos

Jennifer Kluge

Jim Kristie

Diane Kuntz

Kate Larsen

Fran Larsen, MD

Richard G. Lugar

Michelle Manley

Shelley Marsland

Lynne Jordal Martin

Mike McCurry

Debbie McGrath

Lauren Melesio

Claire Mencke

Kathleen McKinnie

Harold "Mac" McKinnie

Jan Michelsen

Michigan State University
    Alumni Association

Michigan State University
    Libraries

Mary Minix

Michael Mink

Steve Minter

Henri Mondschein

John Moore

Mark Morrow

Isao Nishijima

Jim Noone

Mary D. Olson

Les Palm

Donald Pattison

Steve Paulus

Ora Hirsch Pescovitz, MD

Lisa Phillips

Jeff Piasky

Joe Picard

Michael Pye

Glenn Rabinowitz

M. S. Rao

Marianne Ratcliff

Noah Robischon

Sacramento State Alumni
    Association

M. Ganesh Sai

ACKNOWLEDGMENTS

Larry Salinas	*University of California, Merced*
M. Ramakrishna Sayee	*University Relations Staff*
Adam Schwartz	*University of Michigan Libraries*
Faith Segal	*Reference Team*
Kevin Sharer	*Charles Utts*
Ursula Sharp	*Kristin Utts*
Jerry Sigler	*Ghislain Viau*
Andre and Katie Binz Sims	*Antoinette Vojtech*
Doug Sohn	*Catherine Whitaker*
Jay Spurgin	*Lynaire White*
Sara Stratton	*Luann Songer Wilkinson*
John Svendsen	*Bill Wilson*
Julie A. Thomas	*Mark Wood*
Noel M. Tichy	*Tess Woods*
Brittany Torbert	*Cynthia Zigmund*

Apologia

Please also know that in this book, I have made every effort possible
to ensure accuracy and any mistakes are solely my responsibility.

~

"The purpose of life is not to be happy. It is to be useful, to be honorable, to be compassionate, to have it make some difference that you have lived and lived well."

—RALPH WALDO EMERSON

A SALUTE TO TWO NATIONAL CHARITIES

Proceeds from the sale of *Leadership CPR* will be donated to honor firefighters and police, who don't see themselves as heroes, but who often put themselves in harm's way to protect others.

The first is the nonprofit National Fallen Firefighters Foundation (www.firehero.org). Created in 1992, the Foundation honors firefighters killed in the line of duty and provides help and resources to their survivors so they can rebuild their lives. The National Fallen Firefighters Foundation also works within the fire service community to reduce the number of firefighter deaths and injuries. The Foundation hosts training events, fundraisers, an annual family day weekend, and regional golf tournaments across the country, among other events, to raise awareness and to sustain and support the Foundation's programs. The Foundation's Roll of Honor lists the names of all firefighters honored at the National Fallen Firefighters Memorial, a monument built in 1981 on federal property in Emmitsburg, Maryland.

The second beneficiary is Concerns of Police Survivors, or C.O.P.S. (www.nationalcops.org), a nonprofit organization founded in 1984 that helps rebuild shattered lives of law enforcement families through its services and programs. One of the most efficiently operated charities in the United States, with an overall score of 96 percent and a 4-Star rating from Charity Navigator, C.O.P.S. has more than fifty chapters nationwide, offering resources such as peer support, scholarships, counseling, and other benefits. Over 140 police officers are killed in the line of duty annually. Today, C.O.P.S. membership is comprised of more than 37,000 survivors, including spouses, children, parents, siblings, significant others, and coworkers of officers killed in the line of duty.

Proceeds from the sale of each of the following of Ritch K. Eich's three previous books are also being donated to important charities:

> *Real Leaders Don't Boss* (Career Press, 2012): to not-for-profit organizations caring for American military personnel who were wounded physically or psychologically in Iraq or Afghanistan.

> *Leadership Requires Extra Innings* (Second City Publishing, 2013): to the Jackie Robinson Foundation for scholarships to deserving minority students.

> *Truth, Trust + Tenacity* (Second City Publishing, 2015): to the Ronald McDonald House and several children's hospitals important to Ritch and Joan Eich and their family, including C. S. Mott Children's Hospital at the University of Michigan, Children's Hospital of Pennsylvania, Riley Hospital for Children at Indiana University Health, and Children's Hospital Los Angeles.

~

"The credit belongs to the man who is actually in the arena, whose face is marred by dust and sweat and blood; who strives valiantly; who errs, who comes short again and again, because there is no effort without error and shortcoming."

—THEODORE ROOSEVELT

NOTE TO MY READERS

In my 2012 book, *Real Leaders Don't Boss* (Career Press, 2012), I outlined eight essential characteristics of successful leaders and argued that the best leaders underpin their authority with a defined set of well-recognized values and emotionally intelligent behaviors. *Leadership CPR* follows the narrative trailblazed by *Real Leaders Don't Boss* and my two other previously published books, *Leadership Requires Extra Innings* (Second City Publishing, 2013) and *Truth, Trust + Tenacity* (Second City Publishing, 2015), and builds on themes in these books, including the following:[1]

> ❯ The characteristics and behaviors that define true leadership
> ❯ Why unquestioned trust and unfailing integrity must be every leader's "north star"
> ❯ How the most effective leaders engender loyalty through a pursuit of human connection, and why demanding workforce fealty is a short-lived power trip that always produces negative results
> ❯ How the most successful leaders balance strength and decisiveness on one side and compassion, empathy, and fairness on the other
> ❯ How leaders of the most innovative, future-focused organizations have a talent for skillful, consistent execution and an uncanny ability to "see around the corner"

In this book, you will read about the experiences of a varied assortment of leaders. I have two reasons for casting a wide net. The first is to pique interest among the most diverse possible readership I can reach, and the second is that such inclusiveness reflects my belief that, regardless of the business sector, industry, or enterprise type, the ultimate success or failure of any organization is always traceable to a rigorously defined set of ethical and behavioral benchmarks.[2] For that reason, this book explores a broad range of leadership practices in traditionally structured corporate businesses, socially and community-focused enterprises serving the arts and environmental communities, and government and public-sphere organizations, including the military.

> The ultimate success or failure of any organization is always traceable to a rigorously defined set of ethical and behavioral benchmarks.

New Pressures and Demands

The need for values-based leadership has never been more urgent than in today's hypercompetitive global marketplace with its unrelenting demands to provide greater customer value at lower and lower costs. Activist shareholders, including a new class of vocal, aggressive investors, have also become a force pushing leaders to make decisions that put profits ahead of all other concerns. This kind of pressure requires leaders to make difficult judgments. Sometimes, focusing on financial returns simply enriches one group of stakeholders while harming another; other times, demand for more returns is reasonable and correct, especially when the potential value of an enterprise is being squandered.

For example, in 2014, an activist investor, Jeff Smith, CEO and Chief Investment Officer of Starboard Value, led a charge to take control of Darden Restaurants, Inc., the parent company of Olive Garden, Bahama Breeze, The Capital Grille, and other popular restaurant brands. Smith's opening salvo in this effort was a 300-page analysis presented at a 2014 shareholder meeting, detailing why the CEO and the board were guilty of mismanagement of Olive Garden, the company's most prized asset.

Smith kept up the pressure and eventually did succeed in using his overwhelming shareholder position to fire the board and take over as Darden's CEO. In this case, Smith's analysis was correct. He refocused Olive Garden as an Italian-only cuisine and implemented other business fixes, such as stopping food waste. For example, a great many of the chain's signature unlimited breadsticks were ending up in the trash.

Profits at the chain turned around, and the company continues to give healthy returns to investors. Significantly, the chain has also seen a healthy increase in millennial dining, a promising trend considering this generation's preference for "fast casual" dining experiences and the number of Olive Garden competitors vying for the attention of this demographic.

Smith stepped down in mid-2016 from the CEO position once he felt the company was headed in a better direction, noting that his involvement in the company was "no longer as necessary" since his profitability goals had been achieved.[3]

Leadership on Life Support

In the Darden case, the activist shareholder pushed the company's leadership in the right direction. However, leaders are increasingly pushed toward transactional, bottom-line decisions that may or may not align with their basic values. Often, short-term profit wins the day over having a long-term, positive impact on a workforce or a community. The trend is worrisome, for it threatens the positive role business has traditionally played in the communities it serves.

That's why I believe that the current national political climate and the deep distrust it has engendered between ordinary citizens and their political institutions are more than just concerning. At the center of this national storm of distrust is, of course, the erratic, values-free leadership of our forty-fifth president. Since taking office, he has become known for systematically undermining long-held norms of the presidency and upending nearly every ethical and leadership standard he encounters.

Readers need not be reminded of the waves of chaos he has created nearly every day since taking office. In many ways, his presidency has been the antithesis of the values-centered leadership standards expressed in this book. As many commentators have noted, his style of leadership, so clearly devoid of ethics and truthfulness, has done great damage to our national character at home and abroad and has created an "us/them" mentality that will be hard to overcome anytime soon.

A considerable amount of the content I've chosen to include in this book was inspired by my reactions to recent actions and/or comments by this president. However, this book is by no means just a thinly veiled political commentary, on the left or the right, although I clearly have an opinion about his performance and character. The focus of this book is on leadership and on the standards that I believe ought to be timelessly upheld, regardless of the specifics of the political leaders who happen to be highlighted in this book.

To be fair, some readers may disagree with my dire assessment of his impact on traditional American values and his potential influence (positive or negative) on business. Some may even point out that he is a needed cathartic upheaval to a long record of entrenchment by the status quo, a point that is not without merit. In fact, some commentators have noted that this "disruptive innovation" is just what was needed in our society.

Disruption—Not Always a Plus

As a reminder, the term "disruptive innovation" was coined by Harvard Professor of Business Administration Clayton M. Christensen, who popularized the concept in his 1997 book, *The Innovator's Dilemma,* a book that enjoys continued popularity even twenty years later.[4] Essentially, the term describes how a new player in a business or market challenges and "disrupts" the incumbent players, such as how Uber upended the traditional taxicab business. Uber's success (and some would say its recent management missteps) has now invited its own challengers, most significantly the ride service Lyft. However, the concept of disruptive innovation is now applied to many other systems and processes, including the political process.

Yes, he has disrupted traditional alliances around the world and challenged established order, and yes, it is possible that some gains will result—although the nature of those gains and their ultimate value to U.S. interests have yet to be revealed. Richard Haass, former Republican diplomat in the George W. Bush administration and adviser to Secretary of State Colin Powell, has been the president of the Council on Foreign Relations for fifteen years. In the 2018 "Afterword" to his book *A World in Disarray,* he described President Donald Trump's foreign policy as being "based on a real misreading of the costs and benefits of U.S. leadership." Haass believes the U.S. is clearly abdicating its responsibilities in global leadership.[5]

Those who subscribe to disruption theory might point to recently announced news that a South Korea–based company plans to build a new manufacturing plant in South Carolina, a decision driven in part by Trump's threatened tariffs based on his charges of unfair trade policies. It will be largely history's job to judge if disruptive innovation theory applies in a positive way to the Trump presidency. However, the quality of Trump's often shameful, bullying leadership style is easier to examine and judge in the present moment, and that is a benchmark I use in this book.

In an article published by *The Atlantic* in June of 2017, writer John Dickerson (former host of *Face the Nation* and current co-host of CBS This Morning) cataloged the many ways he felt that Trump's inconsistent policy messaging and disregard for the truth have undermined all those who work for him. The result, Dickerson argued, is an administrative staff that "can't explain his views on climate change or defend his unverified claims on voter suppression."

Dickerson points out in his article that a "culture of undermining sends signals of disrespect … saps motivation and undermines teamwork." More importantly, he says, "these mixed signals led to the hundreds of critical vacancies that continued to exist in key government posts long after the election, since few are willing to work for an 'impossible boss.'"[6]

The Possible Boss

The eleven chapters in this book model behaviors of the "possible boss," not the "impossible boss" that Dickerson described in the above article. The *possible*, or more precisely, the *best possible* boss is a leader who inspires and engages their workforce by creating a clearly defined world of behavioral and ethical boundaries. In this best-possible-boss world, trust and integrity are unquestioned principles; diversity is celebrated; respect, empathy, and compassion are a given; leaders take responsibility for their decisions and their shortcomings without blaming others; and finding mutually beneficial, long-term solutions is always the goal of negotiation.

The eleven chapters in this book model behaviors of the "possible boss," not the "impossible boss."

Clearly, such a perfect world does not yet exist, but few would disagree that it is one to which we can all aspire. The points made in this book represent, at a minimum, incremental steps toward achieving the above leadership goals. And these steps apply to every category of leader, whether you work for a Fortune 500 company, a small nonprofit organization, or a large government agency. If you strive consistently toward realizing this "possible" leadership world, then every day that goal's horizon looms that much closer.[7]

Who Needs This Book?

Many people don't think of themselves as leaders because they don't have an impressive-sounding title—chief executive officer, executive vice president, or even manager—posted on their doors or desks. But this is a limited way of looking at leadership. I prefer to cast a more inclusive net.

My definition of a leader includes anyone with the ability to influence another person in a positive way; in the end, that's the only position of authority that really matters. By that definition, nearly everyone is a leader: mothers and fathers; brothers and sisters; colleagues, coworkers, and team members; friends, acquaintances, and even strangers. The bottom line is that whenever and however you can influence someone toward a more productive and happy life and muster the courage to act on your professed values, then you ARE a leader.

Often the most remarkable thing about the leaders mentioned in this book is how they use or misuse their authority; it is this nuance of intention that shapes the influence of leaders of all pedigrees and experience levels.[8] Unfortunately, national news headlines often highlight leaders who disregard all the leadership principles I advance. For example, Trump's pardon of controversial Arizona Sheriff Joe Arpaio. While it's true that this power of pardon is allowed under the Constitution, there were still a number of procedures set up by the Justice Department's Office of the Pardon Attorney that Trump was to follow before reaching the pardoning decision. Moving forward with the pardon was seen by some as a repudiation of the real purpose of presidential pardons and a slap in the face to the rule of law.[9]

But such overreaches of power—of which Obama, too, was arguably guilty—overshadow the humility-based approach of thousands of leaders who follow a leadership path that emphasizes helping others succeed and thrive. A recent story I read involving Secretary of Defense James Mattis is an example of this second type of leader.

Teddy Fischer, a Mercer Island, Washington, high school student, sent Secretary Mattis a text requesting an interview, and Mattis, to Fischer's surprise, responded. The details of how the high school student's text made its way to an obviously busy cabinet member are less important than the story's outcome: Mattis agreed to talk about U.S. foreign policy for a story the young reporter wanted to publish in the school's newspaper.[10]

After some consultation and coordination between school and administration officials, the teenager spent forty-five minutes on the phone with Secretary Mattis, who thoughtfully answered Fischer's questions. Again, Mattis's motivation for doing the interview is less important than the principles of leadership illustrated here, chief among them humility and making authentic human connection.

In the end, Mattis's generosity of spirit generated a far more meaningful outcome than any calculated "feel good" public relations event could produce. His time and sincere engagement with the young reporter created an empowering lesson for both the teenager and his classmates. All of the students were able to witness firsthand the rewards of courage and taking positive action, and the reporter, perhaps for the first time in his life, felt the self-affirming energy that can come only from taking a leadership position.

The Road Ahead

As noted, *Leadership CPR* follows familiar themes and pathways that readers of my other three books will recognize, but the range of topic areas is wider and more loosely connected. I have chosen this arrangement to recognize the many different ways leaders create a positive impact in their organizations and communities and in the lives of stakeholders.

In this book, you'll find examples of how leadership is demonstrated through activities as varied as supporting the arts, hiring military veterans, and extracting leadership lessons from sports heroes. You'll also see the leadership advantage gained by embracing diversity and showing compassion and respect for others. Here's the overview:

Chapter 1 – Lead With Values

The forty-fifth president's conduct in office has been the antithesis of the many laudable examples of ethical, authentic leadership to be found in every business and industry sector in America, including that of the principled leaders who serve in the public and private sectors of our economy. This chapter shows why a demanding, unyielding type of leadership can lead to disengagement in the workforce. As a counterpoint, the chapter proposes an imperturbable and calming leadership style that diffuses conflict and encourages consensus.

Chapter 2 – Show Compassion and Respect for All

Leaders who celebrate diversity, practice compassion, and treat others with respect create a powerful atmosphere for innovation and business growth. This chapter highlights some of the key ways a leader can show respect for and take advantage of a diverse workforce. It focuses particularly on the benefits women bring to a workforce, including patience, compassion, and civility. Leaders who embrace gender, racial, and ethnic diversity insist on respectful communication and approach every conflict with an empathetic ear are stronger leaders and ultimately provide a better return to their organizations.

Chapter 3 – Reward Service

Veterans make exceptional employees. This chapter discusses the organizational advantages of service in the military and other mission-driven organizations. It looks at how other countries, particularly Israel, regard the value of military service and suggests some benefits of encouraging participation in the military. The chapter also explores the positive impact that hiring former Peace Corps volunteers can bring to an organization.

Chapter 4 – Build a Better Board

A corporate board of directors plays an essential advisory role in guiding an organization toward achieving its strategic goals and meeting shareholders' expectations. This chapter examines ways that leaders can ensure this essential mission is fulfilled. It also discusses the critical need for board diversity and stresses the unique contributions that women, people of color, and younger talent bring to boards. Finally, the chapter offers ten warning signs that a board member might not be a good fit.

Chapter 5 – Invest in the Arts

The arts have long been recognized for their power to heal and keep the mental clouds at bay. Art provides a needed mental break from the occasionally suffocating strategic, financial, and operational demands of organizational life. This chapter explores how and why some of the most innovative and successful companies support the arts, both through funding external events and purchasing internal art, and why such investments pay dividends.

Chapter 6 – Trust Is Non-negotiable

Trust is a cornerstone of authentic leadership, but some leaders believe the meaning of trust is negotiable. It isn't. Whether you're leading a large organization or a small project team, this chapter offers you a set of guidelines to help you grow as a trusted, truthful leader. It makes the case that anything short of that goal threatens both your leadership and the long-term health of your enterprise.

Chapter 7 – Balance Short- and Long-Term Strategies

"Sustainability" is a term most people associate with the environment or energy sector, such as sustainable fishing, water use, or natural resource consumption. However, a growing number of social, cultural, and business enterprises are incorporating sustainability strategies into their mission statements. This chapter focuses on the steps both large and small organizations can take to shift their focus away from short-term gains and toward more sustainable business models.

Chapter 8 – Assume Responsibility

Poor leaders are quick to blame others for their problems and short-comings. This chapter discusses how failing to take responsibility undermines the respect and authority a leader must exhibit to inspire a workforce. It also points out how leaders who are not firmly committed to taking responsibility create a dynamic that undermines the long-term viability of the organization.

Chapter 9 – Seek Win-Win Solutions

Compromise and collaboration are essential to the health of enterprises (including personal relationships). This chapter focuses on dialogue, compromise, respectful conversation, and other ways to move a shared vision forward and arrive at a solution that will make all parties happy. This method is a much more effective way to run an organization—or a country—than unilateral decision making. However, a specific set of skills, along with the right temperament, is needed to be successful at crafting win-win solutions. For those who master the craft, the rewards are immense.

Chapter 10 – Look to Sports for Models and Mentors

A substantial percentage of C-suite executives have taken part in sports, some at the Olympic or professional level. This chapter discusses the many benefits of sports participation and how it builds essential leadership characteristics, such as adaptability, a keen focus on achieving goals, and calm performance under pressure.

Chapter 11 – Conclusion

A summation of all the above chapters and understanding the "DNA" of a true leader. Leaders are not born a certain way or with particular genes, but rather are formed through hard work and the dedication to living life through each of the values explained in this book.

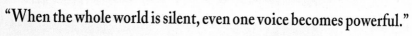

"When the whole world is silent, even one voice becomes powerful."

—MALALA YOUSAFZAI

CHAPTER 1

Lead with Values

IN THIS CHAPTER

> The Value of Great Followership

> The Cost of Tuning Out

> Learning to Follow

> My Leadership Lessons Learned

> How "Real Leaders" Behave

> The Trait Triumvirate

> Losing Faith in Our Leaders

> One Leader's Vision

> Key Concepts

INTRODUCTION

*A leadership team dominated by bullying, "my way or the highway" executives is the quickest path to a demotivated and disengaged workforce and likely business failure. As I pointed out in my 2012 book, **Real Leaders Don't Boss** (Career Press), real leaders embrace a range of emotionally intelligent behaviors that include treating everyone with respect, showing empathy and compassion, championing the success of others, and practicing humble, thoughtful communications.[11] Great leaders are also committed to a healthy work/life balance and understand the need to allot sufficient resources to teams and initiatives so as to ensure success.*

Real leaders eschew demeaning, abusive language that damages work-force morale and leads to team conflict, and, of course, they do not abide narcissistic behavior in any form. The worst bosses (those I term "ugly executives") believe their position justifies egotism and arrogance. This same self-serving conviction also gives these destructive leaders carte blanche to indulge in pathological lying, racism, and sexism and permission to disregard other basic societal norms. Such leaders create an atmosphere of tyranny that can cow, even terrify, an entire workforce.

Real leaders, on the other hand, are imperturbable leaders. They know that staying calm and focused in the middle of a crisis supports clear thinking and goes a long way toward diffusing conflict, anger, and tension. Importantly, a metered response also redirects negative energy toward more constructive solutions, which ultimately brings positive change. In a series of interviews a few days before the 2016 election, CBS's Jake Miller asked several prominent public figures about the qualities that make an effective president.

"There's a lot happening. There's a lot of voices," former Utah governor and Health and Human Services Secretary Michael Leavitt told the interviewer. "And you need a person who has the temperament … to operate in an orderly way, [who] has a history of making good decisions under fire, and can deal with it in an atmosphere where there's going to be a lot of conflicting voices and people saying unpleasant things … and [who can] respond to them in an appropriate fashion."

In the same interview series, then–President Obama pointed to three other essential qualities—discipline, vision, and a moral compass—that any future president (or leader) must have to be successful. "I think a president needs… a sense of… personal discipline," Obama noted, "in terms of doing your homework and knowing your subject matter." In absence of discipline, leaders lose track of their "overall goals," he said.[12]

The Value of Great Followership

Leaders who have never been followers risk diminishing their potential for success. As a case in point, I suspect that most of the leaders in President Trump's initial advisory team were not used to following or even listening to others. When a team has too much leadership experience and too little followership experience, chaos can ensue.

Leaders who have never been followers risk diminishing their potential for success.

As someone who grew up a privileged child in a family business, it seems as though (or is reasonable to conclude that) Trump never learned how to follow; his real estate developer father cast him as a successful business leader early on in his life.[13] After graduating from college, Trump joined his father's firm and relatively quickly took over as its head. Listening to others is simply not one of Trump's known core competencies, and this failing has probably helped create a great deal of disorder since his election.

The president's position on key national security issues, including the Syrian conflict, and America's role in NATO (to name just a couple), has shifted more than once, which may be interpreted that Trump does not consult properly with others. I strongly believe that he does receive advice from advisors (every president does); however, Trump continues to tweet at his own will and publicly criticizes anyone he pleases. As an example, he threw his own attorney general, Jeff Sessions, "under the bus" during a July 2017 interview with the *New York Times*, saying that had he known Sessions would recuse himself from the Russian election interference investigations, he would never have appointed him in the first place.[14]

The Cost of Tuning Out

Another example of failing to listen to the advice of others is Trump's attempt to ram the Muslim ban through the judicial system, only to have it blocked twice by the courts. The Supreme Court did eventually allow parts of the ban to go into effect, but not before the decision caused turmoil around the world and hardship for thousands of people.

When he failed to "repeal and replace" the Affordable Care Act (the first time), instead of seeking compromise and dialogue, he threatened to destroy the program by withdrawing government support payments, claiming the payments were government bailouts.

After the violence in Charlottesville, Virginia, it was reported that Trump again refused to listen to advice from both his cabinet and his family, who strongly recommended that he name and censure the hate groups that had descended on that city. Instead, he played to his base supporters and said the blame for the violence that killed one anti–hate group protestor lay on "both sides."

By claiming equivalency between the motives and tactics of all protestors, he ignited a firestorm of outrage. After two days of silence, during which time his staff reportedly tried to persuade him to amend his remarks, he read a statement from a teleprompter correcting this mistake, but just a few days later, he reversed and again argued "both sides" were responsible for the protest violence. This reversal drew direct condemnation from both Democrats and Republicans—Speaker Paul Ryan and Senator Marco Rubio included.[15] High-profile members of the president's business advisory council began to quit in protest, and he was forced to disband the panel, but not before tweeting insulting and vengeful comments about individual members and their businesses.

At a pro-Trump rally in Phoenix a few weeks later, he again reinforced his original comments about the Charlottesville protests, but on this retelling, he left out the controversial "many sides" qualifier and then blamed the media for not reporting his comments accurately.

Learning to Follow

I always felt I was a better naval officer because I had been an enlisted sailor first. Serving as a sailor taught me the practicalities of what it takes to get the job done. I learned how to make informed decisions and to understand the ramifications of those decisions. Most importantly, I learned the difference between leading and simply being in charge.

In four different industries, I've reported either to the chairman of the board or to the CEO, and I've also served on more than ten boards of directors/trustees, including chairing a hospital and medical center board. If given a choice between working alongside superstars in a C-suite or being an integral part of a talented team of unselfish professionals who always have your back and don't just tell you what you want to hear, the decision is an easy one. Without followers, there's no reason for leadership.

My Leadership Lessons Learned

All of my experiences, both as a follower and a leader, have given me the following insights:

> Every person in the organization has a role in its success.
> Collaboration and problem-solving are more effective than dividing and conquering.
> Being comfortable in your own skin is an asset; having an oversized ego is a liability.
> Compromise is a sign of strength; refusal to cooperate is a sign of weakness.

> If you think before you speak, people are more likely to listen.

> There is a difference between getting things done and busywork.

> It's important to know how to motivate others.

> Empathy is a powerful motivator.

> Praise in public; counsel in private.

A 2015 McKinsey survey reported that "seeking different perspectives" and "supporting others" were two of the top behaviors that effective leaders modeled. [16] Successful organizations with a positive culture typically have both effective leaders and effective followers.[17] Companies with a cadre of truly dedicated followers gain another valuable benefit: employees that "go the extra mile" to support a leader they respect.

How "Real Leaders" Behave

So, how do "real" leaders demonstrate their values to others? First, real leaders are focused on carrying out meaningful goals that make a positive, lasting impact on their organizations or constituencies. Real leaders have foresight, and their actions result in meaningful change. They act courageously to solve major challenges. They boldly seize opportunities to help others, sometimes going against their boards, customers, or even those who chose them to lead in the first place. They treat others with compassion and grace. They develop and expertly execute innovative ideas. As the late Max De Pree, the famed chairman emeritus of Herman Miller, Inc., framed it: "To be a leader means having the opportunity to make a meaningful difference in the lives of those who permit us to lead."

Real leaders are focused on carrying out meaningful goals that make a positive, lasting impact on their organizations or constituencies.

Here are three examples of leaders who I think exemplify real leadership:

> **Starbucks Executive Chairman Howard Schultz** pledged $30 million to military and veterans' causes, including the training and hiring of vets and supporting research and treatment for brain injuries and PTSD. He also committed to adding 10,000 vets and military spouses to the Starbucks payroll. Schultz has been honored as one of the business community's best and most ethical leaders and was on Fortune's 2014 list of the world's fifty greatest leaders. Early on, he offered medical insurance to part-time employees, and he has launched several environmental and social projects. When Starbucks was criticized for unreasonable employee-scheduling practices, the organization responded with an improved system.

> **University of Michigan's Carol Hutchins** is the winningest coach in NCAA softball history. Authentic, tough, and honest, Hutchins knows how to bring out the best in her team, a critical trait of real leaders. She doesn't apologize for being passionate about what she does and has instilled this philosophy in those she coaches. Hutchins knows that teams are made up of individuals who share a collective goal, as shown by her coaching style, which respects individuality.

Hutchins founded the Michigan Softball Academy in 2010, along with the program's annual "Pink Game," an event that raises money for the Making Strides Against Breast Cancer organization. Under her leadership, the Wolverines have raised nearly $750,000 for the American Cancer Society.

> **Aflac's CEO and chairman, Dan Amos**, has led the company for nearly three decades. Amos is well known not only for listening to his employees but also acting on their suggestions. During the 2008 financial crisis, he gave up his bonus and golden parachute while executives of other companies continued to reap rewards, even though their firms—and employees—were suffering. Amos has been at the forefront of Aflac's reputation for corporate citizenship, civility, and ethics, as well as its transparent approach to investor and shareholder relations. Under his leadership, the organization has contributed more than $50 million to the Aflac Cancer and Blood Disorders Center of Children's Healthcare of Atlanta and other programs around the world.

Do real leaders always make the right decisions? Of course not! Real leaders are imperfect; even the leaders I've cited. But respected and successful leaders acknowledge their mistakes, correct them if they can, and commit to making things better.

Do real leaders always make the right decisions? Of course not! Real leaders are imperfect; even the leaders I've cited. But respected and successful leaders acknowledge their mistakes, correct them if they can, and commit to making things better.

The Trait Triumvirate

Admittedly, developing extraordinary leaders who live up to the high bar we set for them is not easy. It takes more than training and experience, although both help. Nor are great leaders created by simply having mentors or role models showing the way. Real leaders are created when experience and desire combine with just the right amounts of personality and temperament.

In my 2015 book, *Truth, Trust + Tenacity*, I articulated just how these forces combine to create extraordinary leaders.[18] All three of the following characteristics are required for a fully formed leader, and each one is tightly bound with nature, nurture, and on-the-ground experience:

> **Truth:** Real leaders don't embellish facts, use half-truths, or incite followers by telling them what they want to hear. Instead, they present the facts and give workable solutions.

> **Trust:** Real leaders are not interested in dividing and conquering. Rather, they seek to unite and build coalitions. Compromise is not a dirty word or a sign of weakness; it is a sign of confidence and maturity.

> **Tenacity:** Real leaders are dogged in their determination to do the right thing. They are committed to serving their constituents, regardless of the pressures from outside forces. Their goal is to bring people together, not tear them apart.[19]

Losing Faith in Our Leaders

It is easy to see why many people have lost faith in government, corporate, and public leaders across a wide range of businesses and political affiliations. Corporate leaders often do put themselves ahead of their shareholders, their workforce, and/or the public good. Public officials often fail to think about the unintended consequences of their decisions. When forced to confront these consequences, their responses are typically slow to come and reactionary. Frequently, these officials blame others or make excuses to distance themselves from their decisions. Instead of taking responsibility, they spin half-truths that many people accept as fact.

Former U.S. Senator Richard Lugar (R-Ind.) and former U.S. Representative Lee Hamilton (D-Ind.) are prominent statesmen who modeled the kind of exemplary leadership so lacking in Congress and the White House today. Though from different parties, Lugar and Hamilton worked with each other, with presidents, and with other legislators who didn't necessarily share their points of view. They engaged with their opponents in a respectful manner, no matter how strongly they disagreed with them. They found ways to rise above party politics in order to adopt legislation for the good of the country. They were more interested in partnerships than partisanship. They energized and inspired others. Above all, they were leaders, not ideologues.

One Leader's Vision

True leaders in the corporate and political arenas think about potential problems and handle them decisively when they occur. They are not afraid to challenge, empower, and hold accountable those serving under them. They avoid micromanaging, a habit that only cripples workforce morale and bottlenecks progress. When one's rights are violated in the workplace or unfairness rears its ugly head in any organization, real leaders are "upstanders" not bystanders. They realize that South African archbishop and Nobel Peace Prize recipient Desmond Tutu was right when he said, "If you are neutral in situations of injustice, you have chosen the side of the oppressor." True leaders are focused on their customers and constituents and listen to their interests and concerns.

At the beginning of 2017, I outlined my hopes for business and political leaders in a California-based business magazine.[20] In the article, I offered ten aspirations (plus a bonus one) that I believe, if realized, would create a stronger class of leaders:

1. **Assemble world leadership:** Focus on enhancing our international influence and defense posture and strength and on the judicious use of military force. To do this, we must strengthen, not weaken, our State Department. As former Secretary of State Madeleine Albright indicated in a November 27, 2017, piece for the *Washington Post*, the State Department is deliberately being hollowed out under the Trump administration because, according to the forty-fifth president, "I'm the only one that matters."[21] But according to the Secretary of Defense, we need an

excellent State Department and can't simply rely on the military. Special attention must be given to Russia, North Korea, and China.

2. **Rebuild political parties:** Rebuild both political parties or create new ones so their positions don't reflect just those of the extreme left or right but rather those of the majority who fall somewhere in the middle. Repeal *Citizens United* to reduce the amount of corrupting money that flows into political campaigns and to prevent special interests from "buying" elections. End gerrymandering and make it *easier,* not more burdensome, for people to vote.

3. **Adapt to a global economy:** Help American workers secure new job pathways so they may better adjust to the rapidly changing world economy. Support flexible work schedules and telecommuting in order to promote work-life balance. Get more commuters off the highways with expanded rapid transit.

4. **Broaden job growth:** Remove the shackles from those willing to take well-informed risks and create jobs through start-ups. For example, reduce unnecessary regulations. We need jobs that pay a living wage, not just low-paying service-industry jobs.

5. **Respect women:** According to the 2010 census, women make up the majority of the population in the United States.[22] They should be more equally represented in organizational leadership, including C-Suites and boards, and should receive the same pay as their male counterparts. Impose stiffer penalties for those who commit crimes against women or discriminate against them.

6. **Celebrate diversity:** America is a land of immigrants, unless you're a Native American. End the nasty, coarse, and cruel treatment of those who differ from us and celebrate our diversity rather than let it divide us. Stop the incendiary rhetoric that feeds racism and further fractures American society.

7. **Honor the U.S. Constitution, especially the First Amendment:** Colleges and universities need to redouble their efforts to end campus racism and prevent sexual assaults while also reinforcing the First Amendment and refusing to buckle to student demands for safe spaces, trigger warnings, and other politically correct nonsense. Other democratic ideals spelled out by our Constitution, such as the importance of checks and balances of government and the separation of powers, must be reinforced in all aspects of society.

8. **Restore civility:** The rudeness, insults, and lies that are ruining the political realm must be reversed. Civility must be taught and restored.

9. **Accept the climate change challenge:** Find effective ways to engage and influence climate change doubters who continue to defy sound scientific knowledge. Climate change is real and cannot be ignored any longer.

10. **Modernize the electric grid and the nation's infrastructure:** All the solar equipment and wind turbines in the world won't do any good if our nation's aging grid fails to carry the power to the places it needs to go. Roads and bridges aren't going to repair themselves. And our treasured national parks system is in dire need of

improvement. Invest in America to create jobs and make an already great country even greater.

11. **(Bonus) Elevate honest and unbiased reporting:** Focus more on reporting the facts and issues and less on grandstanding for ratings. The late Gwen Ifill, who died in 2016, was known as a "reporter's reporter." She was a true journalist who eschewed the increasingly common habit of viewing journalism as another form of entertainment.

It may be hard to see the path from today's chaos and divisiveness to the better "world" I've outlined above, but if you are a leader, that's your job. You have an absolute responsibility to work toward lofty ideals. It starts by imagining a better world to strive for.

If you are a leader your job starts by imagining a better world to strive for.

Leadership the Lugar Way

Look at what people have accomplished during their lifetimes, and what you see will tell you a lot about what these people value, what they prioritize, and what they hope to achieve for society and the world.

For example, take former United States Senator Richard G. Lugar, who was mentioned briefly earlier in this chapter. A Rhodes Scholar and navy intelligence officer who represented Indiana in the U.S. Senate for thirty-six years, Lugar, now eighty-five, is continuing to leave a positive mark on his country and the world by tackling important twenty-first-century problems head-on in a thoughtful, decisive, and intelligent way.

Lugar is president of the Lugar Center, a nonprofit organization in Washington D.C., a highly acclaimed think tank that describes itself as "a platform for an informed debate on global issues," including controlling weapons of mass destruction, finding solutions to the vexing issues of global food and energy insecurity, examining the effectiveness of foreign aid, and enhancing bipartisan and effective governance. The Lugar Center's research and policy statements aim to better the debate through civil dialogue and bring together people of differing ideologies, something Lugar accomplished many times during his years in Congress, where he was among a small number of legislators who worked with presidents and other lawmakers on the opposite side of the political fence.

A Republican, Lugar served in the U.S. Senate from 1977 to 2013. He was the 2005 recipient of the American Foreign Service Association Lifetime Contributions to American Diplomacy Award and the 2016 recipient of the J. William Fulbright Prize for International Understanding. In addition, the Queen of England made Lugar an honorary Knight Commander of the Most Excellent Order of the British Empire, and President Barack Obama awarded Lugar the Presidential Medal of Freedom.

Lugar's outstanding leadership in Congress stands out for its depth and breadth. According to the Lugar Center, as the chairman of the Agriculture Committee, "Lugar built bipartisan support for 1996 federal farm program reforms, ending 1930s era federal production controls. He promoted broader risk management options for farmers, research advancements, increased export opportunities, and higher net farm income. Lugar initiated a biofuels research program to help decrease U.S. dependency on foreign oil. He also led initiatives to streamline the U.S. Department of Agriculture, reform the food stamp program, and preserve the federal school lunch program."[23]

He also co-led the effort to reduce the threat and proliferation of nuclear, chemical, and biological weapons by forging partnerships with other lawmakers to destroy deadly weapons in the former Soviet Union. He cosponsored legislation that became known as the Nunn-Lugar Program (the DOD Cooperative Threat Reduction Program), which the *Wall Street Journal* called "one of the most prescient pieces of legislation ever enacted,"[24] and some twenty-five years later, the program continues to evolve. When the Soviet Union was dissolved, approximately 11,000 warheads and missile systems above and under the sea were in Russia, Belarus, Ukraine, and Kazakhstan. With Democratic U.S. Senator Sam Nunn of Georgia, Lugar helped spearhead the securing and dismantling of weapons of mass destruction there and subsequently elsewhere around the world. The Lugar Center reports that, to date, over 7,600 nuclear warheads once aimed at the United States have been deactivated.

Finally, one of Lugar's most brilliant accomplishments is his effort to encourage lawmakers with differing viewpoints and political leanings to work together in the spirit of bipartisanship to get things done. Lugar is not shy about calling out the United States government for being divisive and dysfunctional. He wants the government to do better. As an objective way to hold members of Congress accountable, the Lugar Center and Georgetown

University's McCourt School of Public Policy developed the Bipartisan Index, a formula that measures and tracks for the public the frequency with which a member of Congress cosponsors a bill introduced by someone from the opposite party and the frequency with which a member's own bills attract cosponsors from the opposite party. The Index includes a twenty-year baseline of data for historical context. A consistently low score shows that a legislator is partisan, but a consistently high score shows a willingness to solve problems and work with the other party.

I am privileged to know Senator Lugar and truly appreciate and applaud him for being a true leader who has demonstrated that the United States government can work for all the people, all over the world. ∎

Key Concepts

> Leaders who have never been followers risk diminishing their potential for success. The president's hasty call for a Muslim ban and his refusal to condemn hate groups after an anti-hate protestor was killed in Charlottesville are examples of the chaos that results when a leader listens to no one.

> Real leaders focus on carrying out goals that make a positive, lasting impact on their organizations or constituencies. Real leaders are courageous and show foresight; their actions result in meaningful change. Real leaders boldly seize opportunities to help others, sometimes going against their own boards, customers, or even those who chose them to lead in the first place. They develop and expertly execute innovative ideas.

> Real leaders don't embellish facts, use half-truths, or incite followers by telling them what they want to hear. Real leaders are not interested in dividing and conquering; instead, they seek to unite and build coalitions. Finally, real leaders are dogged in their determination to do the right thing, regardless of pressures from outside forces.

~

"I'm not concerned with your liking or disliking me.... All I ask is that you respect me as a human being."

—JACKIE ROBINSON

CHAPTER 2

Show Compassion and Respect for All

IN THIS CHAPTER

INTRODUCTION

Hateful and inflammatory rhetoric was used as a political weapon during the 2016 presidential election to stoke fear and discontent among a vast swath of the electorate who felt they had been left behind during the long economic recovery following the 2008 economic crash. Whether intentional or not, Donald Trump's campaign gave these angry voters a set of easily identifiable targets: Muslims, Mexicans, Wall Street fat cats, government regulations, unfair trade deals, the "fake news" media, and especially East and West Coast liberals. The president grew up in the well-to-do enclave of Jamaica Estates (Queens), not the sort of louche neighborhood where people went looking for illegal drugs. One is left to wonder if that is where he learned to inveigh against the less fortunate. Still, optimistic commentators expressed hope that the newly elected president would drop his mean-spirited rhetoric and use his position to unite the country.

Sadly, this transition did not occur, and, in many ways, the president's abuse of power and divisive rhetoric have only become worse. One egregious example is his embrace of radical right-wing ideologies in the wake of the violent protests in Charlottesville, and another is when he made hurtful, seemingly racist remarks in reference to African countries during an immigration meeting with legislators earlier in 2018.

Clearly, the president's behavior does not reflect in any way my values-based leadership principles espoused in this book, and in my opinion, it has only worsened the political, social, and economic polarization in our society. Worse, such poor leadership at the top gives carte blanche to everyone below him to follow his disrespectful leadership.

In Real Leaders Don't Boss I wrote about how a respectful, calm approach helped me deal with a bully who was ready to fight me over my decision to reject a truckload of rotten peaches at the grading facility where I was working as a fruit inspector one summer. The lesson I learned about respectful communication that day is one that I have carried with me throughout my years as a leader. Sure, it's easy—and perhaps even satisfying—to take the bait of provocation and lash out at those who challenge us, but a real leader knows that resisting this response is always the better choice.[25]

Former FBI Director James Comey responded with calm, calculating reserve to his own episode of workplace harassment and bullying dished out by the president. He listened attentively to the president's request for him to drop the FBI's investigation into the Russia connections of former

National Security Advisor Michael Flynn. Then, after the meeting, Comey created a set of detailed notes about their encounter.[26][27] *Since the president fired him, Comey recently published his book,* **A Higher Loyalty.**

In this chapter, I chose the broadest possible brush to illustrate why respect and compassion for others are essential leadership values. Leaders who insist on respectful communication, who embrace diversity, and who approach every conflict with an empathetic and compassionate ear engender the strongest loyalty and engagement in their workforce, an outcome that bullying and harassment—no matter how forceful—will never produce.

Leaders who insist on respectful communication, who embrace diversity, and who approach every conflict with an empathetic and compassionate ear engender the strongest loyalty and engagement in their workforce...

Gender Diversity: More Than a Platitude

Women make up approximately 50.8 percent of the U.S. population and about 47 percent of the workforce, according to the most recent U.S. Census data. Yet, despite this percentage parity with men, women still hold substantially fewer top organizational leadership positions.[28]

Here are some recent statistics:

> 4.2 percent of Fortune 500 CEOs are women.[29]
> 15 percent of board seats are occupied by women.[30]
> 14.6 percent of executive positions within Fortune 500 companies are held by women.[31]
> 20 percent of senators in the 114th Congress are women and 19 percent of House seats belong to women.[32]

These disparities persist in the business community, despite plentiful evidence that would argue for increased participation of women and other underrepresented groups. For example:

> A more balanced workforce leads to better financial returns.
> Women-led companies often perform better than C-suites dominated by men.
> Diversity balance in the boardroom produces both financial and strategic rewards.

I've had the privilege of working with and for many outstanding female leaders who know how to get things done by artfully walking the fine line between aggressiveness and assertiveness. Aggression builds walls and does not engender respect, while respectful assertiveness builds bridges. Without exception, the successful female leaders I've worked with have achieved success through respectful assertiveness, not aggression.

The late Cleopatra Vaughns, RN, a public relations professional at Blue Shield of California, served as a good example of the importance of respect and what can happen when this quality is lacking. Ms. Vaughns took a real-world approach to her work that didn't always conform to the organization's male hierarchy. She was strong-willed in advocating for her positions, a trait lauded in men but often frowned upon in women, and she persevered despite the pushback she received. In the end, Ms. Vaughns earned a sterling reputation for enhancing the reputation of her company by working tirelessly in community relations throughout San Francisco and the Bay Area.

Over the years, I have learned countless lessons from women leaders. For example, Ora Hirsch Pescovitz, MD, former senior vice president at Eli Lilly Co., former CEO of Riley Hospital for Children, former CEO of the University of Michigan Health System, and now president of Oakland University, taught me the power of having more than one mentor in what she dubbed a "mentor's quilt." Her point was that most mentors have a specific strength and that the same mentor you use to improve your negotiating skills won't necessarily be the best to help you decide on taking a business risk.

According to Pew Research, women have a more developed ethical compass than men and are better at treating and compensating employees fairly, and as a bonus, they are often better mentors.[33] Men, on the other hand, excel at negotiation and risk-taking. Although these findings aren't surprising, having a more balanced workforce helps ensure that *all* of these skills, not just some, are maximized. It's common sense. The same attributes that make women good leaders in your customer service area also make them effective decision makers in the C-suite.

A heartening development occurred just as this book was going to edit. The World Health Organization announced that the majority of its new senior leadership team will be women. "The team represents fourteen countries, including all WHO regions," said Director-General Dr. Tedros Adhanom Ghebreyesus of the new appointments, "and is more than 60% women, reflecting my deep-held [*sic*] belief that we need top talent, gender equity, and a geographically diverse set of perspectives to fulfill our mission to keep the world safe."[34]

Here are three ways to ensure that women participate as fully in *your* organization as their male counterparts:

> ❯ Don't assume women aren't interested in the same
> opportunities as men simply because they might one day

leave the workforce to have a family. That's their decision to make, not yours.

> Establish formal programs in which men and women mentor one another equally.

> Make a commitment to champion women. Such a commitment will lead to a more balanced board and leadership team and will ultimately enhance your organization's competitive position in the marketplace.

To quote leadership legend Warren Bennis, "It is the commitment to develop and improve others' skills that distinguishes leaders from followers." Women, in general, seem to embody this commitment more fully than men do.[35]

Avoid Marginalizing

Of course, women are not the only class of workers who are held back from reaching their full potential as either team members or leaders. One of the soundest pieces of advice I can offer, after a lifetime of working with a diversity of leaders in the armed forces, health care, agriculture, and higher education, is this: Winning organizations do not marginalize any employee, no matter his or her gender, race, ethnic background, or position in the company.[36]

Winning organizations do not marginalize any employee, no matter his or her gender, race, ethnic background, or position in the company.

By marginalize, I mean to sideline employees by not encouraging them to advance, or by failing to offer the help of a mentor or career counseling. Tragically, these sidelined employees are often taken for granted due to their demonstrated dependability and productivity. When an employee feels like an unappreciated commodity, not only does the employee suffer, but the company also misses out on the full contribution of some of its best, most productive workers. To pass along some advice to those looking to find employment, my advice is to find a wide canvas on which to paint. I've often advised people searching for jobs or seeking advancement to try as best as they can to avoid working for someone who is likely to place them "in a box." I'm a firm believer in the notion that we are all different, and supervisors or managers who are prone to "boxing" someone in, or "pigeon-holing" or "typecasting" or "stereotyping" associates, severely limit their full potential.

Western Union is a perfect example of a company that treasures diversity and avoids placing their employees in a confined, structured "box." Western Union has customers worldwide, so they are unique in their celebrations, religions, education, languages, systems, and beliefs. Western Union's president and CEO says, "A multicultural understanding of these differences is required if we are to stay close to our customers.... [Y]ou need a multicultural competence simply to select the right agent for a given location, or to create the right app for a given country, one that reflects our brand in the right way. Cultural differences are complex, and therefore our business is, too." Accepting the diversity of their customer base only further strengthens the need for them to hire employees who can understand and see different ways to approach a customer versus using a pre-laid-out, boilerplate set of responses that you often get when calling into customer service hotlines.[37]

An Entertainer and Strong Leader

By most measures, Nolan Dean is an unusual leader. As cruise director aboard Oceania Cruises' luxury ship, Marina, he is responsible for keeping more than a thousand guests aboard this floating vacation destination happy and well...entertained. What makes Dean unique is that he does more than simply manage the onboard talent; he IS the talent.

Dean and his enormously talented entertainment partner, Emmanuelle Adda, who's also his fiancée, have nearly twenty years of combined experience entertaining guests around the world aboard a variety of five-star cruise ships. The popular act they offer is characterized by a fast-paced, high-energy style and includes a mixture of improv and stand-up comedy, singing, dancing, and magic tricks. It's an act that I'd challenge any other leader to follow.

When he's not on stage or behind a desk, Dean says he strives to bring the same level of engagement and commitment to excellence to his role as a leader. He says that modeling these positive characteristics from the stage and everywhere he goes across the ship to greet guests goes a long way toward engendering one of the most crucial aspects of leadership—trust. He told me he draws energy from the many positive interactions he has with guests, noting, "If the guests are happy, they return positive energy and that in turn is a motivating factor." It's a lesson from his years on the stage that he regularly communicates openly and candidly to those who report to him.

Luckily, the corporate philosophy of Oceania founder and now CEO of parent company Norwegian Cruise Lines Frank Del Rio aligns nicely with Dean's emphasis on encouraging authentic relationships and building highly functional teams. Dean said corporate leadership makes sure that the highly diverse crew made up of fifty-three nationalities always feels like an integral part of the success of the cruise line. As such, crewmember parties and plenty of opportunities to go ashore are two key parts part of the company's winning formula, as is the opportunity for career advancement within the organization. As my wife Joan and I, along with our close friends Gary and Nancy Allbright Ames (who were celebrating their fiftieth wedding anniversary), can testify, if we were to ever work on a cruise ship, this one would be our first choice! ∎

Engage, Engage, Engage

Not long ago, Gallup published a report that showed 70 percent of employees were not engaged at work.[38] According to the 2016 "Steelcase Global Report: Engagement and the Global Workplace," critical talent is squandered when employees don't feel they are taken seriously by an organization. The consequences include missed deadlines, wasted resources, lost profits, and overall organizational mediocrity.

According to Steelcase CEO Jim Keane, "Businesses need people who come to work energized, ready to generate new ideas, create new strategies, and make meaningful progress every day. They can't afford anything less. But the reality is there aren't as many highly engaged workers as organizations need. In fact, the number of disengaged office workers outnumbers the engaged, which has a direct impact on the bottom line."[39]

It doesn't take a rocket scientist to realize that employee engagement and workplace satisfaction produce positive organizational results, such as higher productivity, lower turnover, and a better bottom line. Engaged employees feel productive and happy because they have more control over their work experiences. Marginalized employees, on the other hand, feel disconnected and exhibit the lowest level of engagement.

David A. Brandon, CEO of giant toy retailer Toys "R" Us, told me, "I love to put in people who are waiting for their chance. You should never underestimate the power of people who have something to prove."

Howdy Holmes, former Indy 500 driver and current CEO of Chelsea Milling Co., the manufacturer of "JIFFY" Mix, shared the following with Joan and me during our tour of his factory: "We encourage our people to continuously better themselves, to read widely, and pursue self-improvement. We want them to constantly recalibrate their 'filing system.'"

Holmes addressed every employee we encountered during the tour by name and knew a great deal about each of his or her lives. To him (and other effective leaders) *every* employee deserves respect and brings unique needs, aspirations, and passions to the job. Consequently, he treats each one as an asset and an integral part of his extended family. Ensuring that all employees have access to opportunities for personal and professional growth is critical, not just for employees, but for the organization as well.

Six Engagement Suggestions

Sometimes, quiet and focused employees are mistaken for being complacent or lacking in initiative. Yes, individuals do have a responsibility to champion themselves, but organizations also have a responsibility to ensure that less demonstrative personalities are not alienated and continue to be hardworking and dedicated team members.

Here are six actions you can take to make sure your employees don't feel marginalized:

1. **Provide professional development for employees at all levels.** Give everyone the opportunity to learn new skills.
2. **Incorporate team feedback when evaluating employees.** Managers aren't always privy to the details of an employee's performance the way coworkers are.
3. **Give team leaders the flexibility to make changes when necessary.** Sometimes good employees are in the right company, but the wrong job.
4. **Ensure that face-to-face interactions are frequent**; you may be surprised by what you learn. Do not limit communication to e-mail or text messaging. Nothing replaces the human connection.
5. **Performance appraisals for managers and supervisors should include specific behaviors you expect them to exhibit in order to minimize marginalizing employees.**
6. **Say "thank you."** These two words are especially important during challenging times and turnaround situations where fiscal recognition and awards may be scarce. Although people don't work simply for gratitude or praise, individuals who are not acknowledged will eventually leave, taking their skills and intellectual capital with them.

Perks, such as free coffee and bagels, may be nice, but they are hardly enough. And just because Joe in accounting keeps his nose to the grindstone, that doesn't mean he's satisfied with the status quo. As humans, we want to make a meaningful contribution and to know that our efforts are genuinely appreciated. As Stephen R. Covey reminds us, "Always treat your employees exactly as you want them to treat your best customers."[40] [41]

Disrespect and Marginalization Cost *You*

Employees who are subjected to disrespect and rude behavior put in less effort and work fewer hours. They often take out their frustrations on other employees, clients/customers, family members, and even strangers. Productivity and, ultimately, profits suffer.

As noted in the introduction, the current levels of disrespect we see in public discourse are dangerously high and threaten to undermine the pillars of civil and democratic society. Much of this poisonous atmosphere can be traced to identifiable sources, such as social media sites that encourage anonymous vitriol to be posted online. Television programs, especially "reality" shows, often reward bad attitudes and disrespect. The news media, once the vanguard of civility and objectivity, is often little more than entertainment fluff with insult-flinging "opinion hosts" posing as journalists.

In my book *Truth, Trust + Tenacity*, I discuss the importance of civil discourse and our tendency to portray it as a weakness when, in fact, it is a strength.[42] It takes much more resolve to compromise and show respect than it does to be rude and unbending. Unfortunately, too many people think that superiority means they don't have to take the time to show respect toward those around them. Nothing could be further from the truth.

Rudeness affects the wider society as well, especially in today's polarized political and social environment. The following are five examples of disrespectful behavior we see far too often:

> Parents who assume store employees or restaurant servers are there to babysit or clean up after their children. Mom and dad ignore their kids' behavior and are offended when called out on it. Children who see this parental behavior

assume it's acceptable to be rude and that the rules of etiquette don't apply to them.

› People who keep you waiting for no real reason. Two of my former bosses regularly kept people waiting simply because they could. They wanted to ensure that everyone knew who was in charge.

› Aggressive drivers who weave in and out of traffic, cut you off, or text while driving—and then swear at you if you point it out.

› People who don't know how to say "thank you." How many times have you held the door for someone without any acknowledgment? Not only is it rude to ignore others' politeness, it's also a sign of arrogance. And then there are those people who feel it's beneath them to hold the door for another or to even to recognize that someone is behind them.

› People who litter, throw trash from their car window, leave the office break room a mess, and drop used cigarettes wherever they walk.

While these examples may seem inconsequential in a world with much bigger problems, they are examples we can all relate to. No one is born disrespectful, rude, or hateful—it is learned behavior.

No one is born disrespectful, rude, or hateful —it is learned behavior.

Are we such a narcissistic society that our own desires are the only ones that matter? During the most recent summer Olympics, one member of the U.S. women's soccer team disparaged the opposing team after the U.S. team's loss. Fortunately, action was quickly taken: she was suspended. The good news is that learned behaviors, including rudeness, can also be unlearned. Here are some ways to curb the habit:

> Recognize that sometimes the rude person is you. Think before you act. If you act before you think, apologize.

> Don't overreact when others are rude toward you. Let it go, walk away, don't take it personally. If you feel you must, politely call it to their attention (and then drop it).

> Finally, think more about your own actions in your daily life, especially on the job. It's demanding work to be conscious of your actions instead of simply going through the motions. Being civil is more than awareness, though; you must take responsibility for your actions and carefully consider the repercussions.

Eric Hoffer may have said it best: "Rudeness is the weak man's imitation of strength." When a colleague or stranger opens the door for you, thank him or her. Better yet, make it a point to open the door for someone next time.[43]

Remedy for Rudeness: Patience

Patience, especially among leaders, is often thought of as a weakness, but nothing could be further from the truth. Leaders who exhibit characteristics of PATIENCE—purpose, approachability, tolerance, independence, empathy, nurturing nature, confidence, and endurance— are arguably the world's best leaders. In fact, women may be naturally suited for this type of effective leadership. One study by Zenger Folkman, as reported in *Business Insider*, concluded that women are more effective leaders than men. Why? They are patient out of necessity since they had to work harder for longer periods of time.[44]

What is PATIENCE?

So, what are the basic characteristics of a leader with PATIENCE?

Purpose. Patient leaders understand that having a purpose and sticking to it over time is essential if they want meaningful change. No one illustrates this concept more than Germany's Chancellor Angela Merkel, who has been instrumental in leading her country from intolerance to tolerance while ensuring Germany is still a key player on the world stage. Merkel said, "Purpose—not the leader, authority, or power—is what creates and animates a community. It is what makes people willing to do the hard tasks of innovation together and work through the inevitable conflict and tension."[45]

Approachability. Patient leaders are open to change and understand the value of being accessible. Indra Nooyi, chairperson and CEO of PepsiCo, is known for writing personal notes to employees' parents. She understands the strength of reaching out to people at a personal level. Under her guidance, PepsiCo listened to consumer preferences and now offers more healthful products in addition to its tried-and-true staples.

Tolerance. Tolerant leaders know that intolerance stunts growth, while tolerance powers it. Hamtramck, Michigan, has the distinction of electing the country's first majority-Muslim city council. Hamtramck has had its share of problems, not the least of which is dealing with the fear that comes with change. Hamtramck's mayor, Karen Majewski, recognizes that by being tolerant and welcoming others, leaders can effect change in a positive way.

Independence. Patient leaders are independent and straightforward and, in some cases, even defiant. Rosa Parks's show of resolve on a bus fueled a movement that eventually led to the passage of the Civil Rights Act of 1964. Leadership emerges from within all walks of life and from inside of each of us; it's not reserved for CEOs or four-star generals.

Empathy. Being empathetic is a sign of seeking a closer connection with and better understanding of others. Robert Dallek, author of *Franklin D. Roosevelt: A Political Life*, when speaking recently with CBS's John Dickerson about leadership in times of crisis, told a story about FDR's legendary empathic qualities. After FDR's death, a man was standing by the railway track as the train carrying the late president's body went by. "[The] man was sobbing, and somebody said to him, 'Did you know the President?' He said, 'No. But he knew me.' Can anyone imagine... [s]omebody saying that about the current incumbent?"[46]

Nurturing Nature. Leaders recognize that everybody has great potential inside of him or her. Leaders will train and coach their employees to challenge them to tap into that potential. Great leaders will identify the goals of their employees and then set the appropriate challenges and learning experiences so that their employees can reach (and go beyond) those goals. Sarah Robb O'Hagan, CEO of Flywheel Sports and founder of EXTREMEYOU, believes that leaders can be both nurturing and tough. She says, "Leadership is not about passively waiting for the team to deliver. Your role is to hold them to the highest standards of performance while at the same time supporting their approach to getting it done—no matter how novel and unfamiliar it may be to you—and protecting them long enough for them to succeed. It's not a choice between tough versus nurturing."[47]

Confidence. Patient leaders are cool and self-assured without being cocky and conceited. Malala Yousafzai, a 2014 recipient of the Nobel Peace Prize, has exemplified this attribute since being shot, point-blank, by a would-be assassin. Exhibiting confidence and strength, Yousafzai has been unstoppable in her quest to secure educational freedom and equal rights for women around the world.

Endurance. The late Pat Summitt, the renowned women's basketball coach for the University of Tennessee, understood that thriving would take time, tenacity, and endurance. Early in her career, Summitt washed her team's uniforms herself and drove the team van. She knew breaking down the barriers of the old boys' club in college basketball would not happen quickly; she would have to endure.

We can learn many invaluable lessons by studying these leaders and how their patience led to triumph.[48]

Respect Squared

Much of the rudeness and disrespect in today's workplace and society-at-large is facilitated by technology. But an often overlooked and highly effective way to combat the current wave of rudeness is as simple and "low-tech" as pen and paper—a handwritten note.

While it's easier to send messages of recognition, congratulations, or appreciation through social media, what is often missing in those communications is authenticity and forethought. When you put pen to paper, you are forced to think about what you are writing because you can't simply hit the delete key.

The fact that it takes longer to write out a personal note also speaks volumes to the recipients. It says that you took valuable time from your busy day to write a note just for them. Not just a personal note, but a personal *handwritten* note. It's like the difference between receiving, for example, a gift of a scarf from a local department store and one that someone created especially for you. Both are thoughtful, but the handcrafted gift often means more.

To handwrite every note you send is unrealistic. However, you *can* take the time to make your messages more personal, and creating handwritten notes from time to time will remind you of the importance of what you're doing. Personal communications, including those written by hand, are still important in diplomatic circles. They should be just as important in the business world. A truly personal note of gratitude to a client, employee, supervisor, or business colleague has many benefits:

> Your note will help you stand out and be noticed and remembered in a way that more fleeting e-mail messages cannot.

> Handwritten notes come across as more thoughtful because you presumably had to carefully consider what to say before writing it down.

> A tweet, text, or e-mail can get quickly buried under a mountain of newer tweets, texts, and e-mails. A personal or handwritten message demands to be handled differently.

> Personal notes from business leaders often strengthen

employee morale, heighten productivity, improve interpersonal communication, and help retain team members who feel more appreciated, leading to reduced recruiting and training costs.

> Personal letters, including those written by hand, can have a powerful impact and move public opinion as well. CEOs like Warren Buffett and Jeff Bezos write their own corporations' annual report letters, which are widely read because they are stimulating and written in plain language, rather than corporate-speak.

Former U.S. Secretary of Defense Bob Gates wrote very personal letters to relatives of fallen military personnel, letters that conveyed a deep sense of caring to the recipient. Kansas State University head football coach Bill Snyder often writes personal letters to members of his team as well as to opposing players who were injured or performed admirably.

In the above cases, it wasn't that the notes were always written in longhand—they most likely were not—but that the authors took the time to make their communications mean something special to the individuals receiving them.

The business world could gain a lot by recapturing this lost art. The next time you want to congratulate someone for a job well done, share a project outline with your coworkers, thank your boss for giving you a raise, inspire a newly hired worker, or show appreciation to a client, make it personal. Better yet, write it by hand.[49]

Key Concepts

> Women are a powerful, largely untapped reserve of potential leaders. Organizations that marginalize women's contributions miss a terrific opportunity to increase effectiveness, productivity, and profit.

> Every marginalized employee is a lost opportunity. Winning organizations do everything possible to help all employees grow and excel.

> When rudeness and disrespect are part of your company's culture, employees are less engaged, less productive, and more likely to leave or to practice these behaviors among themselves.

> Leaders who show characteristics of PATIENCE— purpose, approachability, tolerance, independence, empathy, nurturing nature, confidence, and endurance—are arguably the world's best leaders.

> A handwritten note is often the most overlooked, but highly effective, way to combat the current wave of rudeness in both the workplace and wider society.

~

"The purpose of human life is to serve, and to show compassion and the will to help others."

—ALBERT SCHWEITZER

CHAPTER 3

Reward Service

IN THIS CHAPTER

> **Getting at the Heart of a Veteran's Resume**
> **Opportunity for a New Administration**
> **The Israeli Experience**
> **Leadership Potential in Peace Corps Service**
> **Admiral Zumwalt: A Model of Public Service**
> **Key Concepts**

INTRODUCTION

Service to others, whether via the military, the Peace Corps, or any other organization with a mission to help others, is a calling that attracts some of the best and brightest among us. Many organizations recognize the value of retaining employees who have answered this calling and are especially keen to hire these individuals. However, many businesses could stand to improve their track record in the hiring of veterans.

As someone who has served in the armed forces and worked with many veterans, I can attest firsthand to the positive attributes of military service and to why hiring veterans can help organizations thrive. Here are just some of the many positive qualities these men and women bring to an enterprise.

Veterans...

- *Know how to get things done.*
- *Exhibit a "can do" attitude and relentless passion to exceed goals.*
- *Never quit.*
- *Believe in responsibility, honor, discipline, and humility; moreover, they bring an ingrained sense of "never leave anyone behind" loyalty to an organization.*
- *Are consistent and transparent (upfront) and expect a higher standard of leadership.*
- *Strive to do the right thing.*
- *Are loyal to their country.*

I think President Reagan summed it up best in a letter he sent to Lance Cpl. Joe Hickey on September 23, 1983: "Some people work an entire lifetime and wonder if they ever made a difference to the world. But the Marines don't have that problem." [50]

In today's political climate, we could use more such disciplined leaders in the halls of Congress, especially considering that the current public approval of Congress is at historically low levels. Unfortunately, less than 20 percent of members of congress are veterans; rather, its ranks are populated mostly by wealthy lawyers—probably the least trusted class of professionals in America. [51]

The Trump administration, to its credit, has recognized the steady leadership hand that military experience can often provide. The administration's choice for Secretary of Defense (retired Marine Corps General James Mattis) was an excellent decision. In an administration characterized by chaos (as of publication no fewer than thirty-seven administration officials have either resigned or been fired), this appointment added an analytical, logistical, and operational capability to the cabinet. [52][53] *While it is perhaps still too early to predict the long-term effects of what some herald as accomplishments, the recently enacted tax cut, some easing of regulations, the pressure to bring home corporate invested monies from overseas and job growth may be helping the economy continue its nine-year boom begun in the prior administration.*

*I have lauded the exceptional abilities of veterans in some of my articles and books, especially in my 2013 book, **Leadership Requires Extra Innings**.[54] In these writings, I have stressed the point that most veterans are not afraid to roll up their sleeves and do what must be done. This exceptional quality is often overlooked by employers who fear that military experience tends to produce rigid and bureaucratic job candidates. Such stereotypes deprive organizations of the valuable leadership skills that veterans acquire during their military service. Veterans must be evaluated as individuals.*

This chapter explores the organizational advantages of military service and service in other mission-driven organizations. It includes a discussion of how other countries, particularly Israel, view military service and suggests how America might benefit from encouraging more widespread service among its citizens. I also discuss the positive impact that service in the Peace Corps can bring to an organization. The Peace Corps' leadership lessons include empathy, compassion, persevering through demanding situations, and other exemplary values that are exhibited by extraordinary, world-class leaders.

Getting at the Heart of a Veteran's Resume

America's business leaders don't always know how to read a military resume and, as a result, miss out on a great pool of men and women in their twenties and thirties with proven track records of dependability, loyalty, risk-taking, and innovation. After all, many of these individuals honed their skills by facing life-and-death situations and by overcoming staggering adversity. The military regularly produces such high-caliber men and women who also possess sophisticated analytical, logistical, and operations skills.

Even if military veterans have limited experience in a traditional office setting or lack an MBA, they usually bring strong leadership skills to the table, as well as an ability to thrive under pressure, solve problems, and function as part of a diverse team. Veterans are also taught to win, even when faced with overwhelming odds, and it's this work ethic that should place them at the head of the line.

Veterans bring strong leadership skills to the table, as well as an ability to thrive under pressure, solve problems, and function as part of a diverse team.

Unfortunately, some recruiters have preconceived notions about veterans, such as that they are inflexible, combative, and/or narrow thinkers. Nothing could be further from the truth. In my experience, not even newly minted MBAs or those with a few years' experience have the real-world awareness or the analytical skills that most veterans bring to the job. Veterans hit the ground running when they join an organization. They are used to dealing with multiple challenges and moving at a fast pace, and they are not thrown by learning something new every day. Veterans also possess another essential leadership skill: they are effective followers.

In my book *Truth, Trust + Tenacity*, I devote an entire chapter to leadership lessons gleaned from military service and discuss how military officers and senior enlisted personnel are often expected to step up and take responsibility for their actions at a far younger age than those who enter the business world directly out of college.[55]

It takes courage to steer an organization through uncharted territory and to compete with fiercer and stronger brands. It takes courage to behave ethically toward your coworkers and those you manage. It takes courage to try a new strategy or introduce a new product. Veterans possess such courage. They also know how to stay flexible in critical situations and persevere.[56]

Because of all these qualities and more, they often make the best job candidates.[57] All you need to do is learn to recognize a diamond when you see it.

To help with this "diamond finding" task, here are five ways that recruiters can interpret a military-based resume and apply a veteran's skills and competencies to a business environment:

> First, examine the various assignments the veteran has completed. If you look carefully, you'll usually see a successful track record of analyzing, organizing, and executing tasks quickly and efficiently, often with scarce resources and little oversight.

> Next, note the detail-oriented roles the veteran has performed and for whom. You will likely notice that he or she has conceived multiple strategies and employed implementation tactics in much the same way that city managers or business executives do.

> Then, scrutinize the financial assets allocated to the veteran during deployments, often involving millions of dollars' worth of equipment to operate and repair, and consider the responsibility and trust required to carry out that assignment.

> During your interview, ask about the job of leading a large contingent of military personnel and how the candidate inspired a spirit of competition and innovation among the group.

> Finally, explore how the veteran dealt with both

ambiguity and structure during his or her service and compare this skillset to that of MBAs without military service. Veterans often bring greater maturity and self-confidence as well as a stronger work ethic to the job than other candidates.

Opportunity for a New Administration

As previously noted, the forty-fifth president hired some excellent military talent for his administration, but he has left many more positions at various levels open (more than 3,000 need filling). Hiring more veterans would be a great way to fulfill a campaign promise and put the best likely candidates in a number of federal government positions.

Whether or not the administration will choose to take full advantage of this pool of qualified returning veterans remains a question as of this writing, but one thing is clear: business and public sectors in other countries—including India, China, Japan, South Korea, Canada, and the United Kingdom—clearly understand the value of military service. Perhaps Israel is one of the best examples.

The Israeli Experience

Israel's leaders place a premium on military experience and understand its value in transforming businesses. In their book *Start-Up Nation: The Story of Israel's Economic Miracle*, Dan Senor and Saul Singer note that the "capacity of U.S. corporate recruiters to make sense of combat experience and its value in the business world is limited."[58] Senor and Singer view Israel's aptitude for tapping into veterans' abilities as one reason for that nation's business success. "In addition to boasting the highest density of start-ups in the world," say the authors, "more Israeli companies are listed on the NASDAQ exchange than all companies from the entire European continent."[59]

The Israel Example

Israel has a well-deserved reputation for turning challenges into opportunity. Whether figuring out how to turn its mostly arid, inhospitable land into both the nation's breadbasket and a major exporter of farm products or establishing a nationwide electric car-charging network, Israel always finds creative and innovative ways to solve its current and future challenges.

This zeal for innovative and proactive problem solving drove the concept of building an underground hospital in Haifa, a city of 277,000 on the Mediterranean in the upper northeast region of the country. Opened in 2012, the fortified Rambam Medical Center is expressly designed to withstand the shock waves of missile and rocket attacks and the more insidious means of delivering death and destruction, including chemical and biological weapons attacks.

Haifa, as well as dozens of other cities and villages, endured a tragic Hezbollah rocket attack during the Second Lebanon War in 2006, also known as the 2006 Israel–Hezbollah War. According to official estimates, at least 4,000 missiles were fired during the month-long conflict between Israeli and Lebanese fighters.

Unlike many other "worst-case scenario" facilities built to withstand a population-directed attack, this one serves a practical purpose of being a 1,400-car garage during more peaceful times. However, if conflict does arise, the facility can quickly be converted (as quickly as forty-eight hours) into a fully functioning hospital capable of housing up to 2,000 patients.

As you might expect, such a missile-proof building had to be constructed deep underground, which meant construction took place below the existing water table and required pumping out tons of brackish water before the lowest floors could be built, a feat that required 17,000 cubic meters of concrete.[60] Such extraordinary effort was, of course, very expensive and was built with a combination of government and public support, including a $20 million gift from billionaire Israeli shipping magnate Sammy Ofer, who grew up in Haifi and died in June of 2010. Ofer, as a matter of context, was a veteran of the 1948 Arab-Israeli War and World War II serving in the Royal Navy.

To pull off the rapid transformation from a parking garage to state-of-the-art hospital, designers incorporated a complete hospital infrastructure into the plans, and construction began in 2010. Power, water and air filtration, oxygen, and all other needed components of a hospital operation are built into the six-foot thick walls. If the facility is ever needed, the conversion process will truly be a "plug in and treat" facility. It's a truly innovative approach to emergency planning. ∎

During a recent trip to Israel, I talked with many leaders, including several in the Israeli Defense Forces (IDF) and in Teva, the world's largest generic pharmaceutical company. I was anxious to visit Teva at their corporate headquarters in Petah Tikva, located on the outskirts of Tel Aviv. On my visit, I wanted to better understand how the world's largest generic pharmaceutical company was progressing, especially as they were in the midst of a multi-year restructuring plan. Once the darling of Israel's impressive corporate sector, hard times had befallen the drug behemoth. Questionable acquisitions, squeezing of profit margins by price cuts, significant debt, C-suite musical chairs (e.g., three CEOs in the last five years), inevitable supply chain challenges, and intense board scrutiny are just a few of the headwinds they were confronting. Then, in late 2017, Teva announced that about one-fourth of their workforce (that worked out to approximately 14,000 people) would be laid off, several manufacturing plants would close, some parts of their pharmaceutical business would be sold, and other efficiencies would be undertaken. [61] As this news came during the writing of my book, I am unsure what their future holds, but I do believe Teva's new leadership will weather the present storm; however, the company will probably look quite different in the future.

I also spent some time talking with Gadi Ariav, Professor of Management, Technology, and Information at Tel Aviv University's business school. Dr. Ariav offered these thoughts about the origin of Israel's success: "Two thousand years of persecution have resulted in a 'very alert' attitude and one which calls for...great vigilance, creativity, flexibility, and preparedness for imminent attacks from all quarters and more." In other words, a history of persecution has made modern Jews even more conscious about their survival, so that failure in any venture is not a choice.

Service in the IDF is a rite of passage for young people and prepares them for a productive and fulfilling future. Most Israelis from the age of eighteen, including women, must serve in the IDF. This service fosters personal achievement and national pride. Ariav told me that he was only in his twenties when he oversaw the data communication function in the Logistics Command. He noted that while he was working in this high-responsibility position and "meeting life," American kids [were spending] "extended teen-hood in fraternities and college dorms."

Military participation for U.S. citizens has only trailed off since Ariav's youth. According to the Defense Data Manpower Center, just 4 percent of the American population now serves in the armed forces. In addition, very few members of Congress or the working media or company CEOs have served in the military.[62]

I am not suggesting that we should restore the draft. Rather, I am suggesting we expand opportunities for public service. Such a policy would help Americans build personal and job skills and boost national and individual pride. Israel's reputation as one of the most entrepreneurial countries on earth comes from its embrace of innovation and risk-taking, qualities that seem to be enhanced, rather than discouraged, by military service.

Dr. Ariav summed it up this way: "Israeli entrepreneurial attitude is pretty much etched in the cultural DNA of Israelis, with a collective agreement that is reflected in some very deep Jewish traditions like a loathing of hierarchy, learning by questions, appreciation of effort and intention over results, and the belief that 'the world can be fixed.'" In other words, it's essential to be adaptable, inquisitive, change-driven, and willing to hold leaders accountable.

While our Washington D.C. is mired in dysfunctional partisanship and chaos, the State of Israel is forging partnerships among business, military, and academic institutions to create one of the largest start-up ecosystems in the world by transforming a city in the middle of the Negev desert into a cyber-powerhouse. The success of this project—economic growth through job creation and increased national security as a cyber capital—is a lesson in what can happen when seemingly disparate interests work together.

Imagine mixing Israel's recipe for balancing education, public service, and entrepreneurial success with a strong dose of the well-known American ideals of adventure, discovery, individualism, and patriotism! It all starts with a responsible and motivated workforce, which public service can help to build. As Professor Sydney Engelberg of Hebrew University and Ono Academic College, a former IDF captain, told me, "Serving in the IDF can be thought of like the bar mitzvah that occurs at age thirteen. It is a rite of passage, where all experience the essence of Israel and their personal responsibility for Israel's future."

We need a similar rite of passage into professional adulthood in the United States. By learning from the Israelis, Americans could develop a pervasive business culture of "I can and will" instead of the defeatist "I can't."[63]

Leadership Potential in Peace Corps Service

On October 14, 1960, presidential candidate John F. Kennedy arrived in Ann Arbor to spend the night on the campus of the University of Michigan on his way toward launching a whistle-stop campaign swing in the region. There were no plans for JFK to make remarks that early morning because he had not yet recovered from his debate with Richard Nixon the previous night.

Thousands of Wolverine students were waiting for Kennedy when he arrived around 2 a.m., and after he ascended the steps of the Michigan Union, Kennedy gave an impromptu speech that would later transform our nation's youth. Challenging the throngs of students to contribute a part of their lives to their country so that a free society could continue in the world, he asked, "How many of you who are going to be doctors are willing to spend your days in Ghana? Technicians or engineers, how many of you are willing to work in the Foreign Service and spend your lives traveling around the world?"[64]

A few weeks later, the president formally unveiled a proposal for the Peace Corps, a concept that had been previously advocated by Senator Hubert Humphrey, Congressman Henry Reuss, and others. In the half century that has passed since then, much has been accomplished through the creation of the Peace Corps and other volunteer service organizations that followed in its footsteps. To date, nearly 200,000 Americans have served in the Peace Corps in 139 countries.

As a point of interest, my wife Joan and I attended a 2 a.m. commemoration of the fiftieth anniversary of Kennedy's historic speech announcing the formation of the Peace Corps on October 14, 2010. We joined a large crowd of students, faculty, Regents, fellow alumni, and former Peace Corps volunteers (many of them University of Michigan graduates) on the steps of the Michigan Union to hear the comments of Peace Corps officials. Sargent Shriver, the first director of the Peace Corps, later wrote: "It might still be just an idea but for…those (University of) Michigan students and faculty."

A research team at the University of Michigan, led by Sara Konrath and Ed O'Brien at the Institute for Social Research, recently conducted a study that compared the emotional profiles of nearly 14,000 college students over a thirty-year period (1979 to 2009). The data revealed that "college kids today are about 40 percent lower in empathy than their counterparts of 20 or 30 years ago" and that "many people see the current group of college students—sometimes called Generation Me—as one of the most self-centered, narcissistic, competitive, confident, and individualistic in history."[65]

This study is surprising to many because volunteering, or what educators often call "service learning" or "civic engagement," is very much in vogue today on many elementary school, high school, and college campuses. In fact, volunteering has increased substantially across the country with the rise of many new governmental and private organizations that support service projects. All this is good news, and these efforts should be encouraged because an understanding of and appreciation of the Peace Corps service is vital to our national competitiveness. If we are to go head-to-head with other nations that emphasize service, such as Israel, it is more important than ever to have a formal and robust recognition that service is good for country, community, and commerce.

An understanding of and appreciation of the Peace Corps service is vital to our national competitiveness. It is more important than ever to have a formal and robust recognition that service is good for country, community, and commerce.

Admiral Zumwalt: A Model of Public Service

Navy reformer Admiral Elmo R. Zumwalt Jr. was a true believer in the importance of service and is an excellent example to emulate. A veteran of World War II, Korea, and Vietnam and a humanitarian in retirement, Zumwalt worked hard to reduce racism and sexism in the Navy and exemplified strength, decisiveness, innovativeness, and integrity.

In my first book, *Real Leaders Don't Boss,* I discuss how courage is one trait that must be embodied in military men and women working in leadership positions.[66] Zumwalt, the youngest person to serve as chief of naval operations, faced a multitude of challenges from within the Navy, in addition to criticism from the press and Washington pundits. He battled jealousy from other military leaders and resistance from numerous chief petty officers who disliked his reform efforts. In every instance, he courageously stood his ground and pressed forward.

Zumwalt's steadfast, humanistic form of leadership included speaking for those who often have little power to make their voices heard: blue-collar workers of all races, the middle class, neglected veterans, and the urban poor. Zumwalt would have made a great political leader for our times. He did, in fact, run for the U.S. Senate in 1976 as a Democrat from Virginia but lost to the incumbent. Had he won,

Zumwalt would have undoubtedly carried his innumerable talents from the Navy to civilian life.

But many of his achievements in the Navy had little to do with fighting or wartime skills. He treated the lowest-ranking sailors with genuine dignity and respect. He made people want to re-enlist. Through his progressive directives, known as "Z-grams," Zumwalt tried to humanize the Navy and make life better for minorities. He issued directives to set up ROTC programs at predominantly black colleges, boost black enrollment at the Naval Academy, and end sexist and racist policies. He created a Minority Affairs Office and loosened up the dress code. White sailors respected and trusted him, too.

He was also a selfless and successful leader in retirement. He helped many charities, advocated for those exposed to Agent Orange, and founded the national bone marrow registry, which seeks to match marrow donors with recipients. In awarding Zumwalt the Presidential Medal of Freedom in 1998, President Bill Clinton called Zumwalt "one of the greatest models of integrity, leadership, and genuine humanity our nation has ever produced."[67]

During a meeting several years ago with a thousand sailors in San Diego, a cook named Clarence Burris shared with Zumwalt that his wife had just died from cancer and that his three daughters now needed him. Burris pleaded for a shore assignment because his ship was about to sail. Zumwalt at once ordered a change of assignment for the cook.

As Zumwalt stood up to leave the stage, the sailors rose and cheered. A petty officer blocked the admiral's path and said, "Thank you, Admiral, for treating us like people."[68]

Key Concepts

> Veterans may not have worked in traditional offices or have MBAs, but they understand how to work with diverse groups, persevere under pressure, solve problems, turn strategy into action, learn from experience, get things done, and contribute as part of a team.

> Veterans have also been taught to win, often against overwhelming odds, because their lives depend on it. In short, veterans bring practical real-world experience to the workplace.

> Israel's requirement that most of its citizens serve in the Israeli Defense Forces creates a rite of passage for young men and women that prepares them for a productive, fulfilling future and fosters personal achievement and national pride. A similar requirement in the U.S. is not an outrageous idea. By following the Israelis' lead in this area, Americans could develop a pervasive positive business culture of "I can and I will" instead of "I can't."

> Navy reformer Admiral Elmo R. Zumwalt Jr. believed in the idea of service and worked hard to reduce racism and sexism in the Navy. He exemplified strength, decisiveness, and integrity. In retirement, he put his values to work helping many charities and human development organizations, and stands as a great example of how military experience can be used to get things done for other people.

~

"A board is never actively engaged with the daily operations of a company. That's why the catch phrase, "noses in, fingers out," is such an appropriate rubric to explain the work of corporate boards."

—THE DIRECTORS MANUAL: A Framework for Board Governance

CHAPTER 4

Build a Better Board

IN THIS CHAPTER

> Want Better Boards? Include More Women and Women of Color
> Women Don't Just *Deserve* Opportunity, They Earn It
> Younger Boards Still a Challenge
> Seek Board Members Who Break the Mold
> Ten Red Flags for Problem Board Chairs
> How to Handle Board Problems
> Key Concepts

INTRODUCTION

Corporate boards play an essential advisory role in both public and private organizations. They focus on helping an organization's leadership achieve its strategic goals as well as on meeting shareholders expectations. How boards fulfill that mission and how they choose the highly experienced men and women (mostly former CEOs themselves) to be members of their elite groups varies substantially between organizations.

Still, no matter how a board chooses its members, certain baseline responsibilities usually define the work done by boards of directors. As David H. Langstaff, the former president and CEO of TASC, Inc., said during a 2013 Aspen Institute business conference, "The role of the Board is to en-

sure that purpose, vision, and core values are in place and then to give the CEO and executive team the time and space to act responsibly."

He went on to say, "Boards must understand and support company strategies, confirm the metrics that will indicate both success and progress, and hold the CEOs accountable for performance." In addition, Langstaff emphasized that boards must "help CEOs counter the short term pressures of the market, and ensure that companies do not make short term accommodating decisions that are not in its long-term interest as responsible contributors to society."[69]

In my book **Leadership Requires Extra Innings**, I note that one way boards can fulfill their responsibility to pay appropriate attention to a company's "long-term" interests is by ensuring that their makeup is diverse, meaning that they should include women and should strive for racial and ethnic diversity. In addition, boards must work to attract members of younger generations who can "make use of the latest technologies to improve procedures and expand the organization's outreach."[70]

I also offered four principal suggestions for either evaluating your own decision to serve on a board or, if you already serve on a board, bringing new members to a board.

> When you are asked to join a board or to suggest names of board candidates, make sure the president and CEO truly intend to tap into your expertise or the expertise of the potential new board member you recommend.

> Make sure a well-developed board orientation program exists. Are newer members teamed up with more experienced board members to help them quickly grasp the mission of the organization and the member's role in it?

> Ensure that the organization's leaders intend to look "outside the box" to recruit young, bright, enterprising professionals—

including women and members of diverse racial and ethnic groups—for available board seats. Gender, racial, and ethnic diversity on boards allows for a broader perspective and leads to more creativity when solving today's complex business problems.

❯ *Finally, make sure you understand the board's role in setting organizational strategy.[71] Some boards walk a thin line between advising a company and managing its operations, but, as Peter Browning and William Sparks note in their book **The Director's Manual: A Framework for Board Governance**, the board has three principal roles: one, to ensure that the right CEO is running the company; two, to make sure that the company has a robust succession plan; and three, to ensure that the company has the right strategy.[72]*

This chapter discusses these basic board service requirements; it also discusses board diversity and the business upside of including more women on boards. Another focus of this chapter is on how to bring more innovative ideas to the boardroom through the savvy use of public relations principles. Finally, the chapter offers a list of ten warning signs that a board member might not be a good fit.

Want Better Boards? Include More Women and Women of Color

As stated earlier, women make up a higher percentage of the United States population than men and account for just under 50 percent of the workforce. Yet their representation on corporate boards—while that number has steadily increased over the last decade—is still pathetically low.

According to a 2015 Credit Suisse study of more than 3,000 global companies, 14.7 percent of boards include female members, a percentage that is 50 percent higher than it was in 2010, but still lagging.[73] Other studies cited by Catalyst, an international nonprofit organization with a mission to accelerate progress for women through workplace inclusion, confirm the Credit Suisse study results.[74] A forty-nine-country Deloitte study also mirrored these results. It concluded that women hold 12 percent of board seats. Interestingly, the same Deloitte study revealed that women *chair* only 4 percent of the boards in its survey.[75]

In Norway, women hold more than 46 percent of board seats, according to the Credit Suisse study. In France, the percentage is 34 percent, in Sweden, 33 percent, and in Italy, nearly 31 percent of boards have women members.[76] It is important to note that Norwegian law demands that boards achieve this gender diversity. One might argue that quotas result in the hiring of unqualified individuals, but that does not appear to be the case in Norway. In fact, the opposite seems to be true. The quota system has been a boon to Norwegian organizations. None of the women serving on a board is less qualified than her male counterpart, and many women are more qualified than men for the board seats they hold.

In the U.S., there are signs that some organizations have gotten the message that women make excellent board members. In fact, just recently, the Sierra Club announced that all five elected members of the Sierra Club Board of Directors are women. It is worth pointing out that when the Sierra Club was founded in 1892, it was one of the few outdoor clubs that even accepted women.

Sarah Hodgdon, Sierra Club's National Program Director, highlighted some notable advantages of women board members in a press release about the new board:

"This is a tough time to be leading in the environmental movement. We have a lot of hard decisions before us every

day and a faster pace than ever. Women are typically social-
ized to be collaborative and emotionally supportive, which
means that with a majority-female-identified executive team,
we have a group of folks who bring a lot of those skills to the
table. The powerful solidarity I feel with the other women on
our team and the support we offer each other as people and as
leaders are some of the most important factors in my success
here at Sierra Club."

Hodgdon went on to list other attributes of women executives.
She said that having women in leadership positions "leads to stronger
environmental outcomes" and engenders perspectives that "promote
improvements in energy access as well as innovative ways to combat
climate change."[77]

I often think of Shirley Chisholm, the first black woman elected
to Congress, where she represented New York's 12th Congressional
District for seven terms (1969 – 1983). When elected, she challenged
institutional "norms," and fought for rights that had, up to that point,
still been reserved for white males. Her slogan of "unbought and un-
bossed" rang true during her term—she fought to end poverty and
discrimination, protect the environment, and give women and people
of color a voice. Yet, here we are, nearly fifty years later, and it seems
we are still struggling with some of the same issues Congresswoman
Chisholm so passionately fought to fix. As of the writing of this book,
439 women have filed or expressed interest in running for Congress
— nearly twice the number of women in the same position as two
years ago, according to the Center for American Women and Politics
at Rutgers University's Eagleton Institute of Politics.[78] I hope that
this is just the beginning of a much-needed shift in both the business
and political world.

Women Don't Just *Deserve* Opportunity, They Earn It

My career in working with leaders in both private industry and the armed services has given me a unique opportunity to help advance opportunities for women as well as minorities. I've learned several lessons from both male and female leaders that can be applied to improving the placement of women on boards. If you think about it, why wouldn't you want your board to be more representative of the population at large (such as your customer base)?

Too many people still believe that a woman's primary goal in life is raising a family and that everything else is secondary. As the actress Jennifer Aniston has said, "We're seeing women through that very narrow lens. If we don't have a baby or a white picket fence or a husband, then we're useless. We're not living up to our purpose. It's shocking to me that we are not changing the conversation."[79] Aniston is correct: the conversation needs to change and change quickly.

Besides simple fairness and common sense, there are excellent organizational reasons why women should be proportionately represented on boards. For one thing, women are often more conciliatory and less dogmatic than their male counterparts when making decisions. They view compromise, a behavioral attribute sorely lacking on many boards, as a sign of confidence and strength, not weakness.

When women are at the table, organizations almost always experience greater success: better ideas surface, more workable policy alternatives are proposed, the quality of the discussion is heightened, and financial returns are stronger. The mere presence of women on a board helps to break up the "old boys club" mentality. It's time for the boys club to include more girls, period.

Unfortunately for the rest of us, women often decline board service because they believe they lack the experience. Men, on the other hand, seem willing to serve whether they have the right experience or not.

Organizations, including boards of directors, must come to understand that ability to contribute, not gender, is what matters.

> **When women are at the table, organizations almost always experience greater success: better ideas surface, more workable policy alternatives are proposed, the quality of the discussion is heightened, and financial returns are stronger.**

Here are five ideas organizations can implement to encourage women to serve on boards:

1. **Make the commitment to diversify your board.** It sounds obvious (and it is), but if you don't formally acknowledge a limitation, you can't change it. Elena Bajic, the founder and CEO of Ivy Exec, gives a simple but clear reason as to why diversifying your board is so important: "Building a diverse board isn't easy but it's vitally important. Diversity brings in new thinking, insights and perspective about consumers, markets and business practices. A lack of diversity represents a missed opportunity…a highly accomplished and diverse board—and that means more women, more people of color and a wide variety of ethnic backgrounds—is so critical, particularly today, when businesses compete on a global scale."

2. **Stop stereotyping.** Encourage women to apply for board positions. Don't assume because a woman is a parent she

isn't also interested in serving on a board. Fathers are also parents, but we rarely assume parenthood limits *their* ability to serve on boards.

3. **Many boards still run on the old model of leadership—command and control.** In my experience, women don't need to take this approach because they know how to collaborate and cooperate. If you look at how the most successful organizations operate today, it's around a platform of co-creation and collaboration, not command and control.

4. **Most of the women I've worked with have been better at multitasking than have men** (myself included), and they reach consensus faster and with less contention than most men do. Historically, women had to work harder and to innovate more, important skills to have when serving on a board. Recognize and highlight these skills by asking women to join in on the initial R&D conversations, trusting their ability to both balance the responsibilities of a current workload *and* assist in a new company launch/re-brand.

5. **Women are often told they don't have the right mix of experience to serve on a board,** or, as noted above, they may feel this way themselves. Corporate leaders need to acknowledge this fact and encourage women to acquire a greater range of P&L experiences throughout their companies.

Organizations need to pursue women purposefully for board positions, including having current board members mentor women who are interested in serving. Programs such as Catalyst Women on

Board™ encourage the mentorship and sponsorship of women for board positions.[80] Women should consider serving on a local/nonprofit board to determine if it's even something they want to do. You'd be surprised how much you can learn by volunteering on a local United Way or Chamber of Commerce board. The bottom line is that a more diversified board simply makes good business sense. I know that's the kind of board I want to serve on.[81]

It's not just about recognizing diversity for board positions; it's about recognizing diversity for all leadership roles. In writing this book, I spent hours combing through articles and quotation websites and researched to find notable quotes about leadership and development by non-white males and females, and I will admit, I came up short. It seems that most frequent quotes that exist about building a business, being a leader, taking values-based actions, or standing your ground are authored by white males. This statistic is just yet another example of the need to recognize, record, and celebrate all. ∎

It's not just about recognizing diversity for board positions; it's about recognizing diversity for all leadership roles.

Younger Boards Still a Challenge

A study released in 2017 focused on age diversity within corporate boards shows that the median age for all board members is still little changed (62.4 years old), despite general agreement that moving the age needle lower is a good idea.

The study, conducted by Board Governance Research (a private research and advisory company), was funded by the nonprofit organization the Investor Responsibility Research Center Institute. It found that few of the S&P 500 companies who took part in the research project (just 5 percent) have boards that represent a more youthful cross-section of ages. Most of these companies reported having members in their fifties, sixties, and seventies. Boards having younger decades represented among their ranks (thirties and forties) were hard to find.

The report appears to defy the logic that the considerable number of highly successful and experienced high technology CEOs that exist today would produce a corresponding number of younger board members. In fact, the study found that even among technology firms, for example, information technology firms, the median board member age is still 61.3 years old, barely one year younger than median age of S&P 500 company boards.[82]

We all know change is difficult and long-term, but now is the time to actively recruit more young adults to boards who reflect the growing and important digital dynamic, multitasking approach to the business world. Too many C-Suites are devoid of younger, idealistic, energetic, future-oriented people as many of the senior executives are in their mid 50's to 60's. The "leaders of yesterday" offer excellent advice and perspective, but companies should insist on their boards recruiting more "leaders of tomorrow."

Seek Board Members Who Break the Mold

Diversity in background and experience is also a key element for building a successful board. Although operational and strategic planning ability is an essential membership requirement, boards also need members skilled in fiscal management and budgeting, as well as in less obvious domains, such as marketing and public relations.

Diversity in background and experience is also a key element for building a successful board. Boards also need members skilled in fiscal management and budgeting, as well as in less obvious domains, such as marketing and public relations.

Although it may not be unheard of for a marketing expert to hold a board position, public relations ability is certainly unrepresented on most boards. PR is generally considered to be a "softer" skill and its impact not as measurable as that of marketing, which is traditionally linked with sales and quantitative accountability. Because of this perception, the importance of PR skills and the value they can bring to boards are often overlooked. The adage "If you can't measure it, it's not there" has unfortunately become a widely adopted misconception about the importance of PR to a company's bottom line. Although a few PR-savvy counselors have gained "seats at the table," too few boards have experienced, skilled PR practitioners filling directors' roles. This kind of omission has kept many institutions from considering how a potential scandal involving the company could bring down both the CEO and the organization.

A board needs someone who is trained in ethically protecting a company's image and experienced at putting out fires with minimal damage. Even more important, boards need someone who can help rein in and counsel executives before a crisis occurs. Highly skilled PR professionals can build effective relationships with a company's customer base and serve as a company "alter ego," connecting with the community in an unfettered way. Ensuring accurate and transparent communication and fostering good relations with the public are important PR skills that should not be ignored.

By placing seasoned marketing and PR professionals on its board, a company acknowledges the importance of reputation management. These professionals can offer sound strategic advice about building a brand, growing trusted relationships with the media, and developing competitive market strategy, including product development, pricing, and market segmentation. Few other professions bring this portfolio of skills to the board table.[83]

Ten Red Flags for Problem Board Chairs

I have been fortunate to work with many excellent board chairs in higher education, private industry, and health care. These people served as excellent role models and helped shape my views about the significance of public service, the importance of relationship building, and the value of candid performance evaluation and cogent strategy. On the other hand, there have been times when, through either personal experience or secondhand awareness, I have questioned the wisdom of choosing a specific individual for such an important job.

For example, consider what the media has described as a fiasco at the University of Virginia in the summer of 2012 under Helen Dragas, their former Rector (UVA parlance for board chair). After orchestrating a truly Machiavellian coup to oust Teresa Sullivan, the institution's popular president, Dragas found herself being forced to reinstate Sullivan in the wake of major campus rebellion and highly negative national media coverage.

Dragas later gave the newly reinstated President Sullivan, as the *Washington Post*'s Jenna Johnson reported at the time, a list of sixty-five goals, twenty-two of which had never been mentioned previously. Some of the items on the list were later found to be either impossible or illegal for Sullivan to perform. Dragas's behavior was so egregious that one professional association call the incident a "crude exercise of naked power."[84]

The UVA Faculty Senate eventually issued a vote of no confidence in the governing board (UVA Board of Visitors), which was followed by an American Association of University Professors investigation and a report that concluded, in brief, that the major breakdown in governance resulted from a failure of the board to understand the institution. To cap the incident off, the accreditation agency Southern Association of Colleges and Schools Commission on Colleges put the university "on warning," a move that could have eroded public trust in and jeopardized federal funding to the esteemed institution. As an update, in January, Sullivan announced that she would step down as UVA president. A new president, James E. Ryan, will take over in mid-2018.

A New President for UVA

In January 2017, Teresa Sullivan announced that she would step down as the University of Virginia president and asked the governing board to begin the process of finding a successor to the popular leader. Nine months later, on September 15, the UVA Board of Visitors voted unanimously to name James E. Ryan as Sullivan's successor. Ryan will begin to transition into his job sometime in mid-2018. He is currently dean of the Harvard Graduate School of Education.

Ryan, a first-generation college student, who graduated summa cum laude from Yale University in 1988, attended UVA law school on a full scholarship and graduated first in his class in 1992. Since joining the UVA School of Law Faculty in 1998, Ryan has earned a reputation as a popular teacher and received the All-University Teaching Award in 2010. In 2011, he received the Outstanding Faculty Award from the State Council of Higher Education for Virginia.

Ryan will be the ninth UVA president when he takes over the leadership reins from Sullivan in 2018. He is known to be a measured and universally liked educator whose modest background, commitment to the power of education to change lives, and intrinsic belief in the value of helping others would seem to make him a perfect match for the venerable educational institution. ∎

Because of this situation and others like it, I have developed a list of the top ten reasons for *not* selecting someone as board chair:[85]

1. Forgo anyone who is a consummate controlling micromanager.

2. Be skeptical of those who are unabashedly political in nature.

3. Examine extremely carefully any candidate who pursues his or her own agenda at the expense of others or the organization.

4. Beware of those who enjoy working in covert or clandestine ways.

5. Avoid considering those who crave greater power or influence or simply wish to add another notch to their ego belts.

6. Disregard persons unable or unwilling to distinguish between the policy authority of a board and the executive authority of the president in carrying out policy.

7. Steer clear of those who may be very interested in being the CEO or president.

8. Pass over those who set unreasonable expectations of others.
9. Reject outright anyone you fear may set up the CEO or president to fail.
10. Rebuff anyone who deceives, bends the truth, or knowingly lies to suit his or her needs.

If a board chair exhibits one or more of these characteristics, a board risks the possibility that it might be plunged into considerable chaos under this member's supervision. Such turmoil might result in departures of talented employees, unwanted board angst, major hits to the organization's reputation, and, ultimately, severe financial losses.

Putting together a list of guiding principles for board and board chair behavior does not need to be exhaustive, but it should, at least, include the following:

> Board members should be given instruction on proper ethical behavior, including avoiding conflicts of interest.
> The fiduciary expectations of board service transparency should be emphasized along with the need for members to build cordial, helpful, and constructive professional relationships with the president/CEO and key constituencies.
> Objective measurement of board members' performance, including that of the board chair and CEO, is another key structure to have in place.

How to Handle Board Problems
So, what do you do if the sitting board chair exhibits problematic traits?

Unfortunately, most boards of directors, trustees, regents, or visitors are reluctant to act quickly or courageously, favoring instead a "take it slow" posture. Such inaction often enables and allows the situation to grow worse. Boards must be willing to take decisive action. Removal of problematic individuals, while painful to all involved, eventually leads to restoration and renewal.

Limits of a Board's Responsibility

The story of Olympic Gymnastics team doctor Larry Nassar is tragic and shocking. Nassar was found guilty of sexual abuse under the guise of medical treatment. Not only has Nassar permanently tainted the lives of 265 girls and women, he also brought disgrace upon the U.S. Olympic Committee and Michigan State University (MSU), where he served as an osteopathic physician.

In 2015, the public became aware of this scandal when USA Gymnastics finally cut ties with Nassar. Since then, many have rightly questioned who amongst the top Olympic and university leaders actually knew about Nassar's criminal behavior. It's a line of questioning that parallels that of the forty-eight-count conviction of Penn State University coach Jerry Sandusky in 2012, where there had been many rumors and even formal inquiries about Sandusky's behavior.

While lawsuits have piled up against Nassar, MSU, and the U.S. Olympic Committee, and many in leadership positions have acknowledged their direct and indirect culpability (all eighteen members of the U.S.A. Gymnastics committee have resigned), the debated question is revisited again and again: where does responsibility begin and end?

In my view, boards should feel a special responsibility to act as a watchdog for employee safety and ensure that bad behavior is uncovered wherever it may exist. I've served on many boards and while I think most board members genuinely care about all who are part of the organization, few board members push for specific and effective ways to monitor and protect their organization from abuse.

I am not suggesting that a governing board should be charged with knowing where all the bad actors are at all times, but they can ensure the CEO and his or her executive team are constantly reinforcing the desired culture and empower each employee to be an UPSTANDER and not a BYSTANDER! Hospital boards, boards of media companies, entertainment industry boards, university boards, small and large company boards, non-governmental boards, all must take steps to ensure employees feel emboldened and fully supported if they report a suspected abuse.

Michigan State University and every college in the land should have taken a lesson from the Penn State University scandal by launching university-wide discussions to figure out if abuse was occurring and encourage speaking up. One must ask: where was the moral leadership in these cases? Boards have a legal, fiduciary and, I would argue, human and ethical responsibility, to be vigilant. They must be proactive and ask tough questions, even where it may feel uncomfortable.

Of course, there are many reasons boards may fall short on their responsibilities. Too often, boards are not ethnically diverse, and don't usually include enough women and young members. Sometimes board members serve on too many boards and as a result, members aren't always focused enough on broader issues. In addition, sometimes the behavior of star performers is overlooked as long as they are bringing value (greater prestige, soaring profits, or philanthropic dollars) to the organization.

However, such practices are not organizationally sustainable. Maintaining the highest level of integrity and care for the entire workforce from the top to bottom is an expectation EVERYONE must share, including the governing board whose responsibility includes overseeing the CEO or president and his or her executive team. ∎

Too often, boards are not ethnically diverse, and don't usually include enough women and young members.

Key Concepts

> Even though women make up about 50 percent of the workforce, their corporate board representation is pathetically low. That status is an unfortunate miss because women and minority members bring creativity to the boardroom and strengthen collaboration among members in ways that contribute directly to an organization's bottom line.

> A majority of board seats are filled by former CEOs and other C-suite members who bring years of operational planning and fiscal management experience to the boardroom. However, organizations should consider board members with "softer" abilities as well, including public relations and marketing. These professionals can guide the messaging and public profile of the organization in ways that pay real dividends, especially during challenging times that threaten a company's image and reputation.

> Reject a board chair if you believe the candidate is a micromanager or if he or she is too political, secretive, power-seeking, disrespectful of power and protocols, and/or focused on being the company's CEO or if he or she sets unreasonable expectations or has untrustworthy

service motives, an agenda, and/or a tenuous relationship to the truth.

› Make the effort to recruit younger people to join your board as they can provide knowledge to build a better tomorrow as well as provide a new perspective on what the "leaders of tomorrow" will be receptive toward.

"Every child is an artist. The problem is how to remain an artist once he grows up."

—PABLO PICASSO

Invest in the Arts

IN THIS CHAPTER

> **Art That Inspires, Sells, and Promotes**
> **Make Art an Inside Job**
> **Creative Thinkers, Please Apply**
> **Artist as Model**
> **Key Concepts**

INTRODUCTION

A few years ago, a novelist, Alexander Chee, told an interviewer that his favorite place to write was on a train, and he mused that if Amtrak offered a residency program for writers, he would be the first in line. Chee's remark sparked a flood of social media responses, all agreeing with him that a train-writing residency was a fabulous idea.

A senior member of Amtrak's social media team noticed the flurry of online activity created by Chee's suggestion and was so intrigued that she formally floated the idea to Amtrak management. Soon, the suggestion was transformed into an actual train residency for writers, and Chee was indeed one of the first in line to apply for it.

As you can imagine, the first invitation elicited an enthusiastic response. In fact, 16,000 writers of all types applied for the residency: an all-expenses-paid train ride across America in a private sleeper car with nothing to do except write and watch the changing American landscape passing by your own private window—sharing the view always optional.[86]

According to Amtrak's website, the residency (it is now on hiatus) was intended to "allow creative professionals who are passionate about train travel and writing to work on their craft in an inspiring environment." Amtrak offered its resident writers round-trip train travel on one of its long-distance routes, along with meals in the dining car and use of a sparsely equipped private sleeping roomette with a desk, a bed, and an all-important window.[87]

Even if the Amtrak residency program is not revived, it likely brought huge returns to Amtrak, given the recent difficulty the system has had in selling the relevancy of long-distance train travel. Clearly, the residency was a public relations bonanza that appealed to the public's nostalgic ideas about train travel. But more importantly, it gave those advocating for enhancement of our national rail system, including train-loving voters, an engaging story to tell when arguing with Congress about Amtrak funding levels.

Of course, Amtrak is not the only organization that actively supports writers and artists. Both Autodesk, a multinational Silicon Valley software company, and the ubiquitous social media giant Facebook have supported similar programs. The point is, the savviest companies realize that supporting the arts is a sound business decision.

In this chapter, I explore why support for the arts—through both external contributions and purchases within your organization's own walls—is an investment worth pursuing.

Art That Inspires, Sells, and Promotes

In my book *Truth, Trust + Tenacity*, I recount how Edsel Ford, the son of Henry Ford, hired Mexican painter and muralist Diego Rivera to travel to Detroit in the early 1930s and paint a series of frescoes called

"Detroit Industry" in an interior courtyard of the Detroit Institute of Arts (DIA).[88] The paintings that Rivera produced based on his observation of laboring workers at the Ford River Rouge Complex in Dearborn, Michigan, are now a designated National Landmark. As an aside, in 2015 my wife and I, along with her sister, Cecily, and her husband, Ralph Wood, visited the DIA to see a special exhibition sponsored by Bank of America featuring many works of Diego Rivera and Frida Kahlo. Clearly, the original investment is still paying dividends.

Ford's commission is part of a long and continuing tradition of business's support for the arts through the purchase or display of iconic sculptures, installations, paintings, photographs, tapestries, drawings, and other forms of art. Many companies, including Progressive, JP Morgan, Chase, Abbott Laboratories, Baxter, Deutsche Bank, UBS, Bank of America, and others, have extensive art collections. Some collections even rival or exceed those held in museums.

But the value of owning such art is more than investment value, although this aspect cannot be discounted. Many of these company-owned art pieces are regularly loaned out for exhibitions and retrospectives of an artist's work. When this happens, the public, the sponsoring museum, and the company are rewarded in diverse and valuable ways. Of course, not all companies can afford to buy a Picasso or a Rodin to loan out and reap this corporate benefit. And that's okay. Supporting the arts at any level pays big rewards, in and out of the workplace.

In 1967, philanthropist David Rockefeller created the national nonprofit Business Committee for the Arts (BCA) to encourage businesses to support the arts. Since that time, the BCA has expanded to include a yearly award, cosponsored by its partner, Americans for the Arts, that recognizes the top ten businesses of all sizes for exceptional involvement with the arts.

The BCA also sponsors surveys with its partners. According to a survey conducted by the BCA and the International Association of Professional Art Advisors, "82% of employees said that art was important in the work environment, and 73% percent said their view of the company would change if the art were removed."[89]

The importance of art in the training of medical students also has been well documented. Universities such as Harvard and Yale require medical students to tour art galleries as part of their art appreciation classes. The goal is to help them hone their observation skills and become more flexible thinkers who can make better diagnoses.[90]

The melding of arts with other disciplines is common in programs such as the Stamps School of Art & Design at the University of Michigan. The arts faculty conducts a wide range of research projects in conjunction with scientists, doctors, information architects, climatologists, and others to solve real-world issues.

Make Art an Inside Job

The arts have long been recognized for their power to heal and keep the mental clouds at bay, and they may provide just the break your team members need to clear their minds of the sometimes suffocating strategic, financial, and operational demands of organizational life. A 2016 study published in the journal *Art Therapy* showed that after just forty-five minutes of free-form art without instruction, nearly 75 percent of the participants had lower cortisol levels, often referred to as the stress hormone.[91]

Art is more than aesthetic. It has a positive—and powerful—physiological impact on the brain. Fine and performing arts have been used in health-care programs around the world to help reduce blood pressure while improving patients' focus as well as their outlook on their jobs and on life in general.

The arts may provide the break your team members need to clear their minds of the sometimes suffocating strategic, financial, and operational demands of organizational life.

Bringing art into the workplace is one way an organization's leadership can improve the well-being of an entire organization. Art stimulates creativity and thoughtful observation. It can combat tunnel vision in the decision-making process and, importantly, help make a sterile work environment feel more inspiring. Clients of your business may also react positively to thoughtfully displayed artworks, and this benefit might just improve the health and success of your business.[92]

Steelcase, the global leader in office furniture, has long understood the interrelationships between art forms, design, functionality, creativity, and workplace efficiency. If you want to see one of the most effective blends of art, architecture, and business success, visit the Steelcase corporate headquarters in Grand Rapids, Michigan. The entire business environment delights the senses. Robert Pew, the former board chairman of Steelcase, felt so strongly about the impact of art that, during the construction of Steelcase's new corporate headquarters in the 1980s, he oversaw the acquisition of hundreds of pieces of art that were integrated into the building's design.

The works, including those of James Rosati, Dale Chihuly, and Andy Warhol, remain at the organization and are exhibited in the company's offices around the globe.

This is no big shock, considering that Pew and his partner, Frank Merlotti Sr., the former president and CEO, were leaders who believed in—and practiced—the ideals of humility, generosity to employees, and cooperation, while delivering quality and value to customers.[93]

Amazon has also started to transform their workspaces in order to provide unique workspaces for their employees, which they hope will inspire creativity and innovation. After nearly six years, they have built a forest as part of their Seattle headquarters, complete with a bird's nest, more than 400 species of tropical plants, and a cascading waterfall. When asked to describe the decision to build this alternative workspace, Amazon's vice president said, "We asked ourselves what was missing from the modern office, and we discovered that that missing element was a link to nature." This space will allow employees to remove themselves from the typical desk and/or cubicle space and connect with nature, which research has shown can increase performance on creative problem-solving tasks by 50 percent, as well as that adding plants to office settings can increase productivity by 15 percent. Multiple studies have also linked greater daylight with improved worker health, productivity, and ethical behavior. I believe this is only the beginning of what we will see done to transform the standard workplace. As more and more companies begin to see the value in creativity and support "outside of the box" thinking, our standard workplaces of desks and cubicles will slowly fade away.[94]

Art Contest Launched an Iconic Brand

The Kellogg Company used some shrewd marketing and an art contest more than a hundred years ago to ensure that customers kept buying one of its most popular and iconic cereal brands, Kellogg's Corn Flakes. According to the company's website, "W.K. Kellogg believed that if people tried a superior product, they would keep buying it. To ensure that consumers would continue to seek out his products, he [Kellogg] distributed free samples of his Corn Flakes and then followed up with advertising in magazines and on billboards. Kellogg also held a children's art contest, selecting the best entries for use in Kellogg advertisements." *Kellogg's Funny Jungleland Moving Pictures*, the first free cereal premium ever produced, was distributed to consumers in 1909.[95] ∎

Here are five simple suggestions for integrating the arts into your own workplace:

1. **Include music in your workplace.** The Nordstrom department stores were once known for their pianist-in-residence. The pianist was hired for the benefit of customers, but store associates gained equal benefit. Take a cue and install a music system for the lunchroom or a conference room and set up a good playlist to run. Ask your team what type of music they prefer and incorporate their ideas. Some executives may like classical music while others prefer jazz or rock. Choose music with broad-based appeal so that all teams can enjoy some music during their workday or lunch hour. The result will be a more relaxed and refreshed team, which often translates into more effective problem solving.

2. **Plant a small garden outdoors or on a patio.** If you have the funds, consult a landscape expert to create a soothing Zen garden, or better yet, ask employees for their own ideas. Be sure to include tables, chairs, and benches so that employees can enjoy their lunches there. Don't have any outdoor space? Transform a patio, a sunroom, or a lunchroom by adding beautiful plants, potted trees, and flowers. Place plants throughout the workplace. Add statuary from the local garden store and a water feature, such as a fountain. The result will be a calmer team that is better able to focus. And don't be surprised if teams start meeting regularly in the newly installed garden.

3. **Create an art gallery.** Consult a local gallery owner or artist to help bring in paintings, sculptures, professional photography, or other pieces of art for display the way many hospitals do. If you don't have the budget to purchase pieces, invite local artists, art students, or even employees to display their works on a rotating basis in the hallways at your place of work. Chances are the artists will be thrilled: you get a rotating gallery and they get free exposure. It's a win-win for everyone.

    You can also ask a local foundation or art school to help you acquire donated art. The result will be a less-sterile environment that will inspire your team and may even elicit conversations between team members viewing the art, conversations that wouldn't have otherwise taken place.

4. **Take your team to see a live performance.** Try a dance troupe or a play. Check the local newspaper listings or go

online to find a production that fits everyone's schedule, and make a day of it. Even if some team members complain that they can't afford the time away from the office, I assure you that nearly everyone will appreciate the break and will come back refreshed and ready to solve problems.

5. **Hold a staff meeting in an art space.** Take your team to a local museum, art gallery, or arboretum. Keep the meeting to a few hours and allow everyone to enjoy the venue afterward. The off-site setting alone will reduce anxiety and encourage people to participate more than they would have back at the office. Surrounded by an inspiring setting, without office distractions, chances are they'll contribute more.

Business is inherently stressful, especially for those in leadership positions.

Steelcase's Frank Merlotti believed that office environments either promote mental health and competitive excellence or deprive workers of both. He taught me that chief executives must expect excellence of themselves and their employees, and they must also check their teams for burnout and mental malaise. In fact, Merlotti insisted his own team always take their full vacation time, for renewal purposes. Bringing in the beauty, splendor, and restorative power of the arts is certainly worth the return you'll see on your investment.[96]

Creative Thinkers, Please Apply

Parents today are right to worry about future employability when they counsel their children about their choice of a college major. Math, science, and computer software engineering are much more reassuring bets for the future than English, anthropology, or art. While that's a correct assessment of the jobs landscape in general, that doesn't mean that the latter degrees are considered worthless in the corporate world. In fact, increasing numbers of business leaders recognize the value of a liberal arts or arts education. Here are some benefits to hiring an artist:[97]

> **Tenacity**—Artists have "staying power," discipline, and doggedness that enable them to overcome many different challenges.

> **Mental acuity**—Artists have an ability to reason, conceptualize, decipher problems, and come up with tangible solutions.

> **Cooperation and teamwork**—Artists know how to collaborate and pool resources.

> **Innovation**—Artists originate, create, invent, and introduce new ideas.

> **Independence**—Artists can work without supervision and know how to be productive on a regular basis.

> **Self-confidence**—Artists have a sort of presence honed in the trenches, whether acting in front of an audience, singing in a choir, painting a mural, being a lead dancer, or performing in a marching band. They also know how to "pitch and sell" an idea.

Liberal arts majors (and arts majors for that matter) bring a set of sought-after talents, including critical thinking, complex problem-solving ability, and intercultural aptitude.[98] A recent online study conducted among 318 employers by Hart Research Associates, a Washington,

D.C.-based public opinion research firm, found that some of the skills potential employers value most are innovation, critical thinking, ability to solve complex problems, ethical judgment and integrity, intercultural skills, and written and oral communication skills.

A job candidate with a specific, needed skill that is underpinned by a broad liberal arts education may outshine other candidates who have only field-specific knowledge. The study even showed an employer preference for these more broadly educated job candidates. According to the study, "Few [of the employers] think that having field-specific knowledge and skills alone is what is most needed for individuals' career success."[99]

> **A job candidate with a specific, needed skill that is underpinned by a broad liberal arts education may outshine other candidates who have only field-specific knowledge.**

Business owner and author Lisa Phillips wrote about the power of the arts and their ties to leadership skills.[100] She noted that an arts background is a very good platform for leadership for the following reasons:

> ❯ Confidence and ability to take command of a stage, deliver a message, make a presentation, and perform in front of an audience
> ❯ Problem solving and the ability to reason, understand, and overcome failure

> ❯ Perseverance not to quit but instead to see challenges through and find solutions
> ❯ The ability to collaborate

For the record, Howard Schultz, executive chairman of Starbucks, holds a BS degree in communications; Andrea Jung, former Avon CEO, graduated from Princeton with a degree in English literature; Michael Eisner, former Walt Disney Company CEO, has a degree in English literature; Richard Plepler, HBO chairman and CEO, holds a BA in government; Carly Fiorina, former Hewlett-Packard CEO and U.S. presidential candidate, attended Stanford University and has a BA in medieval history and philosophy; John Mackey, Whole Foods CEO, dropped out of the University of Texas, where he was pursuing a degree in philosophy and religion; and Susan Wojcicki, YouTube CEO, attended Harvard and graduated with a BA degree in history and literature. So, the message is, if you or your son or daughter has decided to pursue a liberal arts degree, all is not lost.[101]

Apple's Steve Jobs often spoke of the connection between technology, the humanities, and the arts.[102] In 2010, when introducing the iPad, he said, "It's in Apple's DNA that technology alone is not enough. It's technology married with liberal arts, married with the humanities, that yields the results that make our hearts sing." In fact, according to Jobs's biographer Walter Isaacson, after Jobs dropped out of college, he audited classes in calligraphy and music as well as physics and electronics. Many of Apple's most talented engineers have been accomplished musicians or have taken part in some other art form.[103]

Joseph M. Cahalan, Xerox's former vice president of communication and social responsibility and now CEO of Concern Worldwide U.S., a global human rights organization, has said, "Arts education aids students in [developing] skills needed in the workplace; flexibility, the ability to solve problems and communicate, the ability to learn new skills, to be creative and innovative, and to strive for excellence." Those, too, are encouraging words for arts and liberal arts graduates and the companies who hire them.

Verena Kloos, known prominently for her work as the president of BMW Design Works, established her design consultancy practice, Verena Kloos Strategic Design Consulting, in 2014 with the ambition to bring her deep knowledge and expertise in strategic design to a wider audience of clients and customers. The company stands for design thinking at its best: improving the business through a fluid, interactive process aimed at creating or refining your most precious company asset—your unique strategic identity. At the intersection of design, technology, and strategy consulting, Verena Kloos Strategic Design offers their customers a highly tailored approach, delivering tangible results for long-term success. As an aside, when I established the CLU Corporate Leaders Breakfast speaker series for the business communities in Ventura, Santa Barbara, and Los Angeles Counties more than a decade and a half ago, I had Verena attend as a keynote speaker, and she didn't disappoint. In fact, since that time, many female executives have followed her lead in addressing record-breaking-sized crowds. She is yet another advocate for creativity in business.

Clifford V. Smith, former president of the General Electric Foundation, said, "GE hires a lot of engineers. We want young people who can do more than add up a string of numbers and write a coherent sentence. They must be able to solve problems, communicate ideas, and be sensitive to the world around them. Participation in the arts is one of the best ways to develop these abilities."[104]

And former Secretary of Education William Bennett said, "The arts are an essential element of education, just like reading, writing, and arithmetic … music, dance, painting, and theatre are all keys that unlock profound human understanding and accomplishment."[105]

Placing value in the arts is not limited to workspaces and traditional companies. Hospitals are also taking part. The Lucile Packard Children's Hospital at Stanford has transformed into an interactive and nature-focused children's playground. The team there has found that creating a space where kids feel comfortable improves their recovery time and also makes it easier to prepare them for upcoming surgeries and procedures. The hospital is almost the exact opposite of a traditional hospital—it is full of color and sculptures; it has play areas and interactive walls; each floor is equipped with a beautiful patio so that patients and their parents can go outside whenever they please. It's meant to feel less like a hospital and more like a nurturing, normal, environment.[106]

Artist as Model

Great artists make you *think*. The late Norm Hines was one of those artists. His creativity, skill, and quiet leadership drew people to him. Hines was strong physically, bright, athletic, warm, big-hearted, and multifaceted in his interests. He was savvy, a builder of consensus, and the antithesis of a quitter. Those qualities, as well as his artworks, made him a lasting leader in the art and education communities.

After I was honorably discharged from the United States Navy in 1970, my wife, Joan, and I decided that I should accept the position of assistant dean of admissions at Pomona College in Claremont, California. When I arrived, Norm Hines was already on the staff of the admissions office, and that's how we met.

Although I stayed in this position for only two years (I accepted a fellowship to pursue my PhD at the University of Michigan in Ann Arbor), I liked and admired Hines very much. I thoroughly enjoyed working with him and learned much about private higher education and art from him. Hines had a most admirable work ethic and a quiet steadiness about him. He possessed an engaging smile and a kind demeanor. He was self-confident but never arrogant. Importantly, he was also well grounded with a clear north star to guide him.

Hines was a builder of character as well as sculpture. He expected his family and friends to persevere, never to give up, always to find another way, and to dig deeper to accomplish an important goal. He taught his art students the same lesson. I suspect that part of his drive for excellence was developed earlier in his life when he was a superb multi-sport athlete in both prep school and college. Hines had high expectations of himself and others. Although he died in May 2016 at the age of seventy-seven, his character, drive, warmth, spirit, and discipline continue to inspire me.

Hines lived the quintessential life of an artist after retirement, finding inspiration for his works in the scorching California desert, where he had a studio, and in the tropics of Fiji. For a dozen years after he retired, Hines and his wife, Marjorie L. Harth, Emerita Professor and director of the Pomona College Museum of Art, split their time among Claremont, the Anza Borrego desert, and a small island in Fiji where the couple owned property.

Hines started doing ceramics and then moved to sculpture. In his work, he used a wide variety of materials, including granite, marble, bronze, metal, and wood. His projects ranged from smaller works, such as bronze platters and culinary knives, to the massive environmental sculpture Caelum Moor in Arlington, Texas, that made him nationally known.

Caelum Moor was Hines's biggest and perhaps most important art project. It was a five-acre work made up of huge, thought-provoking carved stones that blended art and the environment with ancient history and offered visitors a place of reflection and self-discovery. Caelum Moor was one of the largest environmental sculptures in the nation, and art critics nationwide raved about it. The site, which included a lake, a waterfall, and an amphitheater, became the location of annual Highland Games as well as private events and concerts.

"It was a passion for me," Hines told the *Los Angeles Times* in a 1986 article as he explained how he spent months in a quarry 200 miles from Arlington, cutting, carving, and polishing 550 tons of Texas pink granite. The finished work evoked images of Stonehenge and similar megaliths that dot the British Isles. Caelum Moor—giant, evocative, and unique—was an instant hit when unveiled with much fanfare in 1986 and became a local landmark.[107]

Unfortunately, eleven years later, in 1997, the sculpture was dismantled and put into storage with a promise that it would be reinstalled at another park. The city of Arlington did keep its word, and twelve years later, with Hines's guidance, Caelum Moor was reinstalled at a park next to the Texas Rangers ballpark and the Dallas Cowboys stadium. This site didn't resemble a moor, and Hines wasn't able to design the site the way he did the first time, but he told *Pomona College* magazine that he was happy his work was in public view once again.

Hines was an inspiration who displayed all of the characteristics that attract companies to artists. Eminently flexible, disciplined, and optimistic, he rearranged the stones for the new location, and, true to his stellar character, he stayed humble about his once-famous work's rebirth. Hines told the magazine, "I see this as a new beginning for Caelum Moor, not as the end of anything."[108]

Key Concepts

> Organizations that buy art and support artistic endeavors gain more than investment value. Many company-owned art pieces are regularly loaned out for exhibitions and artists' retrospectives, and when this happens, the public, the sponsoring museum, and the company are rewarded, each in their own way.

> Art stimulates creativity and thoughtful observation. It can combat tunnel vision in the decision-making process and help make a cold, sterile work environment feel more inspiring.

> Artists and liberal arts graduates bring to an organization many positive characteristics, including tenacity, mental acuity, innovation, self-confidence, and a cooperative, team-oriented mindset.

> Norm Hines, an artist who created one of the largest outdoor sculptural installations ever displayed in the United States, exemplified all of the characteristics that attract businesses to artists.

~

"Of all the properties which belong to honorable men, not one is so highly prized as that of character."

—HENRY CLAY

CHAPTER 6

Trust is Non-negotiable

IN THIS CHAPTER

> The Impact of a Dishonest Leader
> Building a Culture of Trust
> Ten Ways Leaders Can Earn Trust
> Keeping Public Communications Honest
> Key Concepts

INTRODUCTION

Leaders without the trust of their workforce—or their department, division, team, or even their small working group—have practically no chance of success. As much as I dislike such sweeping generalizations, this is one I must endorse. In fact, in my 2015 book, **Truth, Trust + Tenacity,** *I gave the word* trust *top billing, right after the word whose abuse is the root cause of nearly all distrust in the workplace and elsewhere—truth.*

A steady stream of lies, half-truths, and misrepresentations of the truth is sadly the hallmark of the current political environment. So much so that both the **New York Times** *and the* **Washington Post,** *two news sources that the president has repeatedly called fake news outlets, began tracking his record of lying as a service to their readers. Although any published accounting of this administration's truthfulness—or lack thereof—captures only a snapshot in time, the current level of presidential prevarication is truly distressing.*

*According to the **Washington Post**, the president has made well over two thousand false and misleading claims as of March 2018. To ensure its own information accuracy, the **Post** rates the president's lies on what it calls a Pinocchio scale from one to four, beginning with a One Pinocchio rating (showing dishonesty by a shading of facts) and ending with Four Pinocchios (the telling of absolute falsehoods). Importantly, each of the president's claims is meticulously and objectively challenged with documented fact.[109]*

*The **New York Times** has taken a daily calendar approach—on days of sunshine, the president didn't tell a public lie, and on days of no sunshine, the president did tell public lies. What this accounting reveals is equally devastating: with few exceptions, according to the **Times** every time the president speaks in public he repeats past, often widely discredited, falsehoods or adds new lies to the list.[110]*

The Impact of a Dishonest Leader

As I noted in the introduction to this book, a president's dishonesty worsens the current political climate and further divides an already dangerously divided and disenfranchised populace. In such an environment of distrust, it is difficult for even the most trustworthy and honest leaders to avoid being affected by the credibility malaise blanketing the American psyche. With a workforce unlikely to give leadership the benefit of the doubt, the integrity margins that leaders must walk are razor thin. As Aesop framed the matter some 2,500 years ago, "A liar will not be believed, even when he speaks the truth."

History has shown us that a number of our former American presidents have concealed the truth from the American public. Deceiving the public has been an unfortunately consistent trait throughout much of presidential history. The Vietnam War leading up to and including the end of the war in Indochine; the Pentagon Papers; Bill Clinton…

you can pinpoint a number of times when the president at the time engaged in deception. Some of us aren't able to call it that and instead use the term mistruths, false or misleading statements, or unintentional fibs—I believe because we don't want to actually believe that there was a level of dishonesty involved. We'd rather believe it was a mistake. However, it has been argued that our president is in a "class by himself" in regard to his lies. Texas A&M's George Edwards argues that Trump "tells more untruths that any president in American history."[111]

To illustrate how far the honesty bar has fallen in our nation's capital, I am reminded of a story I heard President Ulysses S. Grant's biographer Ron Chernow tell in his book *Grant*. One day a visitor came by the White House to see Grant. "And Grant in his office hears the White House usher telling [the visitor] that the President is out of the office. Well, when the stranger leaves, Grant pops out of the office and says to the usher that, 'You should have said that I was otherwise engaged... I don't lie for myself, and I don't like people lying for me.'"[112]

Whether you're leading a large organization or a small project team, this chapter offers you a set of useful guidelines to ensure that you keep your position as a trusted, truthful leader.

Building a Culture of Trust

One of the critical lessons I've learned in life—and it extends beyond the workplace—is the importance of trust. This concept may seem trite in the days of "I got mine, go get yours," but if you dependably treat people the right way, you will get the results you want. This idea is especially true in business. In fact, the most important responsibility of a business leader is to create a culture of trust throughout the organization. Being trustworthy means more than just keeping your word; it includes reliably embodying the values of the organization.

For example, great leaders show appreciation for every job that is done well, regardless of whether it's in the C-suite or the mailroom. Without leaders who demonstrate through their actions as well as their words what the company is all about, trust is an organizational value that will always be in short supply.

If you dependably treat people the right way, you will get the results you want.

In a culture of trust, executives and managers set the tone for the kinds of behaviors that will and will not be tolerated. To do so, they must model desired behaviors and respond appropriately to rule-breakers by showing zero tolerance for disrespectful behavior, abuse, discrimination, backbiting, and bullying. Allowing such traits to flourish will destroy morale, diminish productivity, damage the company's reputation, and encourage dedicated employees to leave.[113]

During my professional career, I've worked with a wide range of businesses and public and private organizations, including universities, hospitals, and the armed services, on the importance of trust, integrity, and transparency and what can happen to a leader's reputation when any of these traits is missing or tarnished.

Character and reputation are inseparable from trust. I always emphasize to clients that *character* defines who you are, what values you hold dear, where your moral compass lands, and how you will respond when tested by conflicting ethical principles. Character dictates whether you do the right thing when no one is watching. Character also determines the principles and beliefs you will endow to future generations. In short, character is who you are.

Character and reputation are inseparable from trust.

Reputation, by contrast, describes how you are seen through the eyes of others. Judges of reputation include community leaders, donors, legislators, the business community, competing businesses and organizations, the media, and any other group with whom you or your organization interacts. In *Truth, Trust + Tenacity*, I discuss how real leaders not only *embrace* the traits of trust, integrity, and transparency, but also *act* on them.[114] As the old saying goes, "Talk is cheap."

Character and reputation—the result of a record of trust—make up the heart and soul of all organizations, and these traits are especially impactful in academic institutions. Once reputation is shattered, it can be difficult to regain. Here are some lessons about keeping a reputation built on trust:

> **A good reputation goes hand-in-hand with *brand*.** Brand is the promise an organization makes to all of its customers and stakeholders. You can't hire a consultant to clean up your brand; it needs to happen organically and over time. Strong, positive reputations are not created through clever slogans or expensive online campaigns.[115]

> **A good reputation is built on a foundation of trust.** Trust is something that neither a marketing committee nor an executive team can simply choose to establish. A person doesn't wake up one morning and say, "Today I am going to be trustworthy." Trustworthiness is determined by others. Reputation is built and nurtured over time. As Michael Josephson of the Josephson Institute of Ethics said, "Of all

of the ethical principles contained in the idea of character, trust is the most complex and the most fragile."

›   **Leadership is most visible at the top.** Yes, leaders make mistakes, but if they are truly ethical and really care, so will everyone under their leadership. New leaders must allow time for trust to build in a workforce, based on transparency and ethical practice.

Trust and integrity mean doing the right thing even when it's unpleasant or costly. Those who practice trust and integrity don't lie or deceive—ever. They are sincere, candid, and forthright, and they are faithful to their promises and to those they serve.

This is the kind of integrity that Senator John McCain of Arizona, a Republican, showed when he literally got up from his bed in a hospital where he was being treated for brain cancer to cast the deciding vote to kill his own party's legislation to replace the Affordable Care Act. Senator Mazie Hirono of Hawaii, a Democrat who is also battling cancer, showed up as well in order to vote against the bill. Both McCain and Hirono clearly understood that the nation was at a crossroads and that it was time to demonstrate what standing by your principles looks like. Perhaps such courage will inspire others in both parties to stand up for what they believe.

Now, here are ten ways that a business and its leaders can earn trust:[116]

Ten Ways Leaders Can Earn Trust

1.   **Lead by example.** Embody the qualities you expect to see in the people you lead and deal with. You want your workers and peers to be honest, so be honest in all of

your business dealings. You want your employees to be hardworking, so set that example and stop taking long lunches or leaving the office early. Model the traits you want others to show, such as integrity, kindness, creativity, inventiveness, and industriousness.

2. **Be humble.** Don't expect anyone to care about where you went to college or your past successes. Plenty of business-people went to top universities and graduated with honors, and plenty more have won awards from chambers of commerce and other organizations. Braggarts are boring and turn people off. Get over yourself. Self-promotion and publicity stunts are obvious and obnoxious and can damage your reputation.

3. **Show your commitment every single day.** Work alongside the people you lead. Work longer and harder than they do. Climb into the trenches and get your hands dirty occasionally. If you manage a warehouse, manufacturing plant, or factory, get off the phone, get out of your office, and visit the production floor on a regular basis. Talk to employees, get to know their names, ask them how things are going, and give them a hand if needed. Ask them if there are any glitches that need correcting.

4. **Help people succeed and advance.** Promote your staff. Help your employees gain exposure and give them opportunities for development and advancement. Great leaders let their teams shine and are confident enough not to need the spotlight.

5. **Be a teacher or mentor.** People will leave your business to pursue other opportunities unless they see an investment

is being made in their future. Focus on employees who are bright, hardworking, dedicated, reliable, and creative, and who have skill sets that you don't, or who show potential. Mentor them at work and support their participation in programs that allow them to earn a new skill certification or degree. Identify an area in your business where mistakes are permissible (i.e., won't seriously jeopardize the company). Perhaps, for example, the company needs a newsletter created. This endeavor might provide an opportunity for an employee with a passion for creating, marketing, and writing to step outside of their normal role and experiment. If they make a mistake, it doesn't throw your firm into the trenches, but rather opens the door for a teaching opportunity. Fear of trying must be driven out of the workplace, for it too often paralyzes employees, and as a result, neither the company nor the employees will grow.

6. **Strike a balance between delegating and being hands-on.** Excessive delegating indicates an opting out of responsibility; micromanaging, on the other hand, deflates employees and tells them that you don't value their judgment. Find the middle ground.

7. **Encourage creativity.** Take chances to encourage new ideas. Teach people how to take calculated risks, and then let them test their wings. Don't punish failure. Learn from mistakes. A leader must create a setting where there is a full vetting of ideas, where everyone is expected to provide suggestions, and where no idea is necessarily wrong.

8. **Communicate your expectations.** People want to know what is expected of them, so they can work to meet

or exceed expectations. Help your employees succeed by being clear about their roles, responsibilities, and deliverables.

9. **Reward success.** If you run a small business, thank those who do a good job by giving them a personal handwritten note, a lunch out, or a gift card. Large businesses should have an employee recognition program to honor individual successes on a regular basis. People want to be acknowledged for a job well done and appreciate being called out for respect in front of their peers.

10. **Build coalitions and maintain civility in all business dealings.** The "divide and conquer" approach doesn't work in the private sector or in government. Nothing gets done that way. Civility and compromise are essential. Many people think that if you compromise, you're weak. Nothing could be further from the truth. Leaders who compromise show that they are strong enough to put others before themselves and to go out of their way to understand a differing point of view.

Keeping Public Communications Honest

A major aspect of forging a trustworthy reputation is good public communication, which often involves building a relationship with the press. Throughout Sean Spicer's short tenure, the president's former press secretary showed what can be argued as a great level of disregard for even self-evident truth. He regularly repeated outrageous lies that ranged from the size of Trump's inauguration crowd to other claims easily disproven by a simple Internet search. It could certainly be argued that it seemed as if he often chided and berated his press audience when the media didn't accept his falsehoods. His performances even inspired a popular Saturday Night Live skit and became rich fodder for late-night comedians. If there is a lesson in Spicer's six-month tenure, it is "what not to do" when serving as a press officer.

A major aspect of forging a trustworthy reputation is good public communication.

After Sean Spicer left the podium, Trump brought Sarah Huckabee Sanders to the position. She came to the job seemingly more polished and is the first mother to serve as the White House press secretary. Unfortunately, her job under Trump remains much the same as Spicer—continuing to discredit the news media. An article in the *Washington Post* argued that Sanders was perfectly cast for this role—she declines to answer the media's questions, she gives nothing away, and she continues to support the idea that the media is "fake news."[117]

As a former public affairs officer in both the naval reserve and the private sector, I understand the challenges of being a conduit between the press and your organization. However, if there's one lesson I've learned in my professional life, it is that credibility, respect, and integrity are paramount. Without these qualities, reporters will always second-guess you, and you will have difficulty getting your message heard.

The press secretary to the president of the United States is charged with communicating the commander in chief's message through the press to the American people and to our allies around the world. Our founding fathers sought to ensure that no one, including the president, would ever hold absolute power. Freedom of the press plays a major part in guaranteeing that our country stays a democracy.

Christiane Amanpour, chief international correspondent for CNN, recently offered a moving reminder of this in a CNN op-ed piece titled, "Amanpour: No free press, no democracy." She pointed out that many journalists die every year in an effort to shine the light of truth on corruption, deceit, and injustice, though these brave men and women are not typically memorialized as heroes. "Remember that anywhere in the world," Amanpour points out, "only the truth we [(the press)] fight for guarantees freedom." [118]

When Mike McCurry was press secretary to former President Bill Clinton, he used his dry sense of humor, combined with a genuine interpersonal style and a high degree of cooperation, to enable him to succeed in his position. He told me that his goal was always to give the press honest, credible information and that he worked assiduously within the White House to get key players, including the president, to level with him. As a result, McCurry never felt as if he had been blindsided, not something Spicer could really say.

If you want to get your message out, it is important to work *with* the media outlets you use for communicating your message. You cannot expect the media to listen to you if you are not perceived as credible, respectful, or honest. However, if you embrace the following points, you will likely enjoy a productive relationship with the press as well as your constituents:

> **Be consistent.** Just because you do something every day doesn't mean you're being consistent. If press briefings or press releases are perceived as unreliable or chaotic, your message will never be heard. Recent White House press briefings have been inconsistent in messaging and haphazard in presentation. According to Bill Wilson, a

former naval reserve public affairs captain and television newsman with many decades of experience, if you want your message to be heard, consistency is essential. Get your facts—and your story—straight.

> **Be empathetic.** If you've been in someone else's shoes, you'll have a better understanding of the challenges they face. As a former newsman and company CEO, Wilson understood how the media worked and, as a result, could empathize with media people, even if he didn't always see eye-to-eye with them. While not every press secretary or public affairs officer has the kind of experience Wilson does, everyone *can* show respect for journalists by recognizing that they have a job to do and try to put themselves in the reporters' shoes.

> **Respect your audience.** Press people are on the front lines and consider it their mission to uncover the truth. News also happens to be big business. Breaking stories *sell*, and that's why media people tend to be dogged and persistent. According to Wilson, it's not your role, as press liaison, to do a reporter's job for him or her, but it is important to be responsive and honest. If not, your reputation will suffer. Respect the needs of the media, and they will generally respond in kind.

> **Be honest.** Dealing with the media can be challenging and frustrating. According to Larry Ames, former Boston Globe assistant sports editor and author of the book *Never Dull*, being open in all matters is critical: "Honesty, quickly delivered, is all you ever need to know." When the media knows you're being up-front, even if it's to say that you can't comment on something, your honesty leads to trust. Trust is essential in any relationship.

> **Learn from your mistakes.** Everyone messes up—it's part of being human. Learning from our miscues, though, makes us better at what we do. Don't let a mistake linger, hoping it will just disappear. Own up to it, correct it, and move on. And do so quickly! The media will respect you for it and understand. After all, they also make mistakes. Continuous learning is important in working with reporters.

Jim Noone, the managing director for Mercury, a high-stakes public strategy firm, and the former manager of government relations for ITT Corp. in Washington, D.C., as well as a retired naval reserve public affairs captain, has said before that it is important to cooperate with the media. When I asked him to speak to the subject for my book, he told me, "The media should be treated with respect as an independent check on our institutions, including the U.S. government, the Department of Defense, and the Navy. Put differently, the news media are the eyes and ears of the citizens."[119]

Trusting the Media: An Important Lesson

When treacherous fires ripped through Ventura, Santa Barbara, and Los Angeles Counties in December of 2017, residents of those counties were reminded just how important relying on and trusting the news media can be. As people were trying to navigate the streets, they turned to technology and various apps to show them which streets were shut down, which were at a traffic standstill, and which were still open for driving.

Over the years, technology has slowly replaced real news and real reporters, but the devastating fires proved technology has not yet replaced human judgment. The *New York Times* reported, "Reporters have spent days navigating people home and keeping them out of harm's way, with guidance beyond the turn-by-turn. Where a road might appear open on an electronic map, it might in reality be under a miasma of smoke too painful for breathing. A side street may seem passable, but just out of sight, a fire could be barreling down."[120]

Throughout the several years that the exceptional Mary Olson, the general manager of the award-winning NPR station KCLU radio (88.3 FM Ventura County, 102.3 FM and 1340 AM Santa Barbara County, 89.7 central coast, and 92.1 FM San Luis Obispo) reported to me, I was constantly reminded how thousands of southern Californians relied on regular news updates from skilled KCLU reporters working close to courageous firefighters, police, and other first responders in the fields, towns, valleys, and mountains under siege in our region. What would we do without public radio? ∎

– 108 –

McCurry feels that relationships with the media, by definition, are adversarial but can also be amicable and professional. Hostility only breeds more hostility. Everyone I've spoken to on this topic insists that having a supportive organization behind your efforts is essential to working with the media. An organization that has a combative relationship with the press will find it difficult, if not impossible, to achieve its goals. And if the person at the top of the organization has a hostile view of the press, even the best press secretaries or public affairs professionals in the world will find it difficult to succeed at their jobs.

The media and the press secretary don't have to be the best of friends; in fact, they shouldn't be. There needs to be a respectful amount of distance to ensure fair reporting. But real leaders, including press secretaries, understand the value of the media in communicating with clients, constituents, and even those who may have opposing points of view.

According to Norm Hartman, a business pioneer in media training and crisis communication, as well as an award-winning broadcast journalist, there is an obligation that arises out of the presidency to answer questions from the press, unless personnel issues or matters of national security prevent him from doing so. Author of "The Media and You—A Basic Survival Guide," distributed worldwide by the Centers for Disease Control and Prevention, Hartman has trained countless industry executives for interviews with *60 Minutes*, *The Today Show*, *Dateline*, *Nightline*, CNN, CNBC, *The Wall Street Journal*, and many other media outlets.[121] It's simple, he says: "When you trust the people you work with—and they trust you—you'll be better able to get your message out."[122]

Key Concepts

> The most important responsibility of a business leader is to create a culture of trust throughout the organization.

> Your reputation is decided by others, not by you. It is based on your character, as revealed through your behavior.

> Integrity means doing the right thing, even if doing so is difficult or unseen by others.

> If you are tasked with external communications—if that means communicating with the press, community and business leaders, or stockholders—you must show the highest levels of credibility, respect, and integrity. Without these unquestioned characteristics, you will always be second-guessed and have difficulty getting your message heard.

My grandfather, Harvey Eich, Yuba County Treasurer and my father, Wilton Eich, holding me on a visit to Bodie, California, where my father was born.

Bodie is a 19th century gold mining (ghost) town nestled in California's Eastern Sierra Nevada Mountains and is now preserved in a state of arrested decay. Bodie State Historical Park attracts thousands of visitors each year. *Photo courtesy of Norm Hartman*

Marysville Little League All-Star team, I am in the second row, fourth from the left.

First Presbyterian Church of Marysville, CA. April 1950, I am in in the front row, fifth from the left.

The Marysville Merchants, a semipro baseball team, was the first baseball team to fly on a plane to a game. Twelve of the team's players took the plane called the Freisley Falcon on a forty-five-mile flight to get from their hometown of Marysville to Woodland, California. They unfortunately lost the game but made history nonetheless. My family was a part of that team—my grandfather, Harvey Eich, was the manager (he is the man standing behind the dog at the far right above), three of my great uncles (Allan, Byron, and Warren Eich) were players, and my father, Wilton Eich, was the batboy. *Photo Credit: Community Memorial Museum of Sutter County*

Me as vice president at St. Joseph Mercy Hospital (Health System), Ann Arbor.

Tennis

My high school tennis team picture – I served as our team captain.

USS Amherst (PCER-853). The first ship that I received orders to report to was the USS Amherst. Interestingly, it was built by Pullman Standard Car Manufacturing Company, Chicago and it was launched a month before I was born in 1944. She participated in the WWII landing on Leyte, helping with recovery and transport of survivors and casualties; then in the assault on Luzon and later in the Okinawa campaign. The patrol craft escorts were often referred to as seagoing ambulances. The Amherst was one of thirteen commissioned and after she was retired, she was transferred to the South Vietnamese navy.

Me in my navy uniform, 1992. *Photo Credit: The Decks Ran Red,vva.homestead. com/mil_ Hist_WWII_PCE_Rs.pdf; and www.navsource.org/ archives/12/02853.htm*

Me standing (left) with a World War II Pearl Harbor survivor, alongside the USS Carl Vinson (CVA 70), September 2, 1995 in Honolulu.

We are part of a
Navy-Marine Corps team.
My wife, Joan,
is the rock of the family.

Left: Navy enlisted family housing, which was typical of the 1940s/1950s. Joan and I lived in Foss Acres enlisted family housing – long since razed, but was similar to this photo. *Photo Credit: source unknown*

Left: U.S. Marine Major (then Captain) Geoff Eich in front of his Harrier "jump- jet."
Right: Navy Lieutenant Ted Eich (then Ensign) at the USS Arizona Memorial at Pearl Harbor.

Eich family photo – Bader School, Ann Arbor, 1983. *Front row:* Joan Eich and Ted. *Back row:* Ritch and Geoff. Funny story about this – we had all been doing yard work that day and completely forgot about the photo appointment.

Joan and me with two of our grandkids at Nationals Park in Washington, D.C., meeting with Nats Manager Dusty Baker on September 10, 2016.

Dusty and I talking in the Cubs dugout at Wrigley Field when Dusty managed the Chicago Cubs. The Eich family is proud to call him a good friend.

Joan

Joan & Ritch in Jerusalem.

Me with our first "grand dogs." These were our sons and daughters-in-laws' dogs. The one on the left as was a beautiful golden retriever and the one on the right was a beautiful Labrador retriever. Here they are pretending to be interested in me but really eyeing my toast (that they eventually got).

Joan and me at the Farmers Insurance Open, La Jolla. For the past two decades, Joan and I have enjoyed serving as volunteer marshals at over a dozen major PGA Tour stops, including Pebble Beach and the Arnold Palmer private course at La Quinta. Helping to ensure such events are successful is important because many local community charities benefit from the proceeds of these golf tournaments.

50th high school reunion group photo of four friends and me, from left to right: me, Les Palm, Gary Ames, Dave Francis, Malcolm Morgan.

The Medical Center Relations Team at Riley Hospital for Children, Indiana University School of Medicine and University Hospital (now IU Health).

Joan and legendary Detroit Tigers baseball broadcaster, Ernie Harwell, enjoy a moment together at the dedication of the George "Sparky" Anderson Field in Ullman Stadium in Thousand Oaks, California.

One of our favorite persons: Tom Brokaw. Joan and I met him in his NBC Office in New York when he was the anchor on NBC Nightly News. This photo was taken at the Ronald Reagan Presidential Library in Simi Valley more recently.

Joan and me showing Eich Associated website in the background.
Photo taken by Juan Carlo, Courtesy of Ventura County Star

Geoff, Nancy, Mary, and Ted Eich at Ted's graduation from George Washington University School of Law, spring, 2007.

The Eich grandkids at a get together in 2017.

A cousin and two grandsons having fun in Hawaii.

Eich and Sun family members at the Maui Aquarium.

If there is such a thing as a "natural leader," my brother Ron, pictured here in his Cub Scout uniform with me, fits the bill. As kids, everyone gravitated to him in the neighborhoods. His organizational savvy and "people skills" were formed early in Marysville, CA. A superior student, he received a four year scholarship to the University of California, Berkeley and completed his MBA soon thereafter at Cal. Armed with his business degree and commissioned as an army officer, he was soon hired by IBM and spent the next thirty plus years working for Big Blue. After he retired, he got his broker's license and sold real estate in Mendocino for several years. Ron and his wife, Joan Stiles, met at Berkeley, have three grown children, Shari, Brian, and Keith, and they all live in Colorado– I couldn't have had a better role model!

The Ronald McDonald House of Western Michigan (located in Grand Rapids, MI) where I served on the founding board of directors. The Ronald McDonald House of Western Michigan is a strong organization and continues to serve close to 500 families annually. *Photo by Craig VanDerLende*

This sculpture is on display in Indianapolis and was designed and built by artist Greg Perry in 1994. The official name is "Landmark for Peace" and is meant to honor the contributions of both Martin Luther King, Jr., and Robert F. Kennedy. The sculpture is made of metal that was salvaged from melted guns given back to the Indianapolis Police Department as part of a firearms amnesty program. Joan and I both worked in Indianapolis for about a decade, seeing this statue many times. The park is aptly named "Martin Luther King, Jr. Park." *Photo courtesy of Joan Cummings Eich*

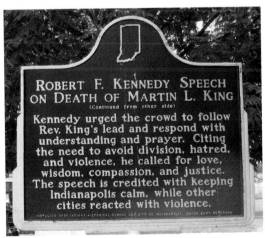

On April 4, 1968, Robert Kennedy was in Indianapolis as part of his presidential campaign when he received the news that Dr. King had been shot and killed. While his team advised him to not make a speech, he stood up and addressed the crowd, just near the spot where this memorial stands. The key point here is that Kennedy displayed a real act of courage by speaking that night, without regard for his own safety. Many believe this helped keep people in the City of Indianapolis from rioting, which was occurring elsewhere in other major cities across the U.S. *Photo courtesy of Joan Cummings Eich*

A beautiful, snowy Michigan State University campus scene along the Red Cedar River where Joan and I met in 1967. *Photo courtesy of Michigan State University Archives and Historical Collections*

The historic 10-10 tie in Spartan Stadium in November 1966 between Michigan State and Notre Dame was the hardest-hitting football game I ever attended. I met Joan in a campus class the following year. *Photo courtesy of Michigan State University Archives and Historical Collections*

President John F. Kennedy first proposed the concept of a "Peace Corps" on the steps of the Michigan Union well after midnight on October 14, 1960. Years later after receiving my Ph.D from the University of Michigan in 1977, I was honored to serve on the alumni association board of directors. *Courtesy of Michigan Photography, University of Michigan*

Wolverine football team gathers with their famed "winged" helmets. *Courtesy of Michigan Photography, University of Michigan*

The CSU campus above – Sac State has more than 3,500 trees that shade the main campus. *Photo courtesy of California State University, Sacramento*

The Guy A. West Bridge links Sac State (CSU, Sacramento) to the Campus Commons by spanning the American River. Guy West was the first president of the institution. California State University, Sacramento was the first of my three alma maters, and the university stimulated me to strive for excellence in athletics, academics, student government and my fraternity. I remain grateful to several faculty members, administrators, coaches and fellow students. *Photo courtesy of California State University, Sacramento*

A photo of the Bridges Hall of Music (often called "Little Bridges") at Pomona College. The campus is beautiful and Joan often referred to it as "our Camelot." *Photo by Mark Wood, courtesy of Pomona College*

My first job after completing my active duty navy commitment was at Pomona College in Claremont, CA where I was assistant dean of admissions. This is Harwood Court, where Joan and I served as faculty residents from 1971-1972. *Photo by Mark Wood, courtesy of Pomona College*

Carol Tomlinson-Keasey Quadrangle with the statue "Beginnings." Carol was a lifetime educator who first saw the future University of California, Merced space when it was farmland. She served as the university's founding chancellor until 2006 subsequently retiring. *Photo courtesy of the University of California, Merced*

The University of California, Merced campus where I later served on the founding board of trustees for the university foundation under the incredibly inspirational leadership of the founding chancellor, "Carol T-K." (Also mentioned above.) Being part of a dedicated and delightful team of university and business leaders charged with creating the first research university of the 21st century in the heart of San Joaquin Valley farmland under Carol Tomlinson-Keasey's leadership was an amazing experience. Not only are its faculty striving to reverse consistently low levels of education in the valley but administrators are ensuring every campus building is LEED certified. *Photo courtesy of the University of California, Merced*

~

"Sustainable development is the masterful balance of meeting our needs today without jeopardizing future generations' ability to do the same."

—UNITED NATIONS (1987) World Commission on Environment and Development

CHAPTER 7

Balance Short- and Long-Term Strategies

IN THIS CHAPTER

> **Short-Term Focus—Not a Sustainable Strategy**
> **Global Market Needs Adaptive Leadership**
> **Rebels Required**
> **Sustainability Leaders**
> **Sustainability Requires Creativity**
> **Safety Is Not an Option**
> **Key Concepts**

INTRODUCTION

Sustainability is a term most people associate with environmental or energy practices aimed at preventing depletion of a natural resource or biological ecosystem, such as sustainable fishing, farming, water use, or forestry. However, for at least the past decade, the scope of the term has evolved, and a growing number of social, cultural, and business enterprises are incorporating sustainability strategies into their mission, vision, and policy statements. In many ways, sustainability is less of a choice these days and more of a business survival tactic.

Siemens, an iconic German firm known for its power generation and transmission systems as well as medical diagnosis systems, is one of thousands of multinational companies that have adopted this mindset. Siemens has applied sustainability tenets throughout its far-flung operations. In 2017, a Toronto-based magazine published by the research firm Corporate Knights put Siemens at the top of the Global 100, an annual list of the most sustainably run companies in the world. In addition to an ambitious plan to achieve carbon neutrality by 2030, Siemens is pushing a range of innovative initiatives designed to enhance the operational sustainability of its core business and its business partners.

According to the Corporate Knights website, sustainability is a core enterprise responsibility of every business. "Civil society, governments and the private sector" the website notes, "all have a pivotal part to play in the decades to come" to ensure a more sustainable future.[123] As validation for this statement, Corporate Knights points to the wide range of sustainability initiatives evidenced by the 4,000 companies it researched to produce the final Global 100 list.

Sustainability is also being used in the financial industry. Storebrand, a Norwegian pension and insurance company, incorporates sustainability factors into its fund selection process. The company uses what it calls the Storebrand Standard to score potential investment funds. The rating system is designed to screen out "companies with poor environmental records, a history of human rights violations or corruption charges, [or] production of tobacco or weapons."[124] A low sustainability rating is a red flag for invest-ment managers.

The tendency of U.S. businesses to focus on short-term gain is one of the most common complaints—and worries—expressed by both private- and public-sector business analysts. Although many U.S. companies have gotten the sustainability message (about 20 percent of companies evaluated for the Global 100 were U.S.-based), there is much room for improvement.

This chapter focuses on the steps, both large and small, that organizations can take to shift their focus away from short-term gains and toward a more sustainable business model.

Short-Term Focus—Not a Sustainable Strategy

I am a firm believer in capitalism, but capitalism cannot thrive if we focus on short-term profits at the expense of long-term sustainability. While there's no question that for-profit businesses exist to make money, focusing solely on this goal often produces the opposite effect.

One company that appears to understand sustainable growth is the J.M. Smucker Company. Profitable for more than 100 years, the organization aims for sustainable growth and reasonable expectations. Very little attention is paid to quarterly results. Smucker's approach enables the company to harness its efforts toward successfully integrating new products rather than chasing marketplace trends to meet quarterly expectations.

Compare the Smucker approach to the short-term-profit approach that damaged the brand of banking giant Wells Fargo. By setting unreasonable expectations for its employees, the company encouraged (even forced) cheating and illegal behavior. In the end, this shortsighted strategy resulted in the dismissal of more than 5,000 employees and led to congressional hearings on the company's practices. Ultimately, the CEO was forced out, thousands of customers were lost, including the state of California, and a once trustworthy brand was tarnished.

The behavior of the Wells Fargo employees who cheated customers cannot be condoned, but for me the buck always stops at the chief executive's desk. It might seem like an obvious point, but when a company sets unreasonable and inflexible short-term goals, managers and front-line employees feel compelled to cheat, lie, and manipulate facts in order to meet those goals and keep their jobs. Because most organizations are performance-based, there is a built-in temptation to do whatever is necessary to hit the goal numbers, even if those actions are unethical or illegal.

Unreasonable performance expectations affect not only business leaders and their executive team members, but also the entire organization, its shareholders, and employees. Performance-based compensation should not be designed to encourage employees to engage in dishonest or illegal behavior out of fear of losing their jobs.

> **Unreasonable performance expectations affect not only business leaders and their executive team members, but also the entire organization, its shareholders, and employees.**

Peter Drucker has said, "Effective leadership is not about making speeches or being liked; leadership is defined by results not attributes."[125] To that statement I would add the following refinement: the difference between a genuine leader and a boss is that a leader understands that *reasonable* results are what lead to long-term growth.

What can organizations do to encourage more sustainable business practices? Here are several recommendations:

> ❯ **Stop focusing on quarterly results.** There is no good argument for basing your future on Wall Street's short-term expectations. Focusing on quarterly profits, for example, is not good for consumers, employees, or shareholders. If Amazon.com had done that in its early years, it would never have survived and thrived the way it has.

> ❯ **Drop unreasonable expectations at all levels, starting with the board of directors and shareholders.** Expecting organizations continually to outperform the previous quarter

just doesn't make sense. Peaks, valleys, and plateaus occur naturally and are not necessarily cause for panic.

> **Develop performance plans that include realistic goals and involve the entire organization.** For example, when Continental Airlines offered employees a bonus of $65 for every month their on-time arrival record was surpassed, the company saw a huge improvement in performance. The amount of the bonus was obviously insignificant, but no employee wanted to risk being the weak link, and all employees could clearly see the impact they could make. The goal was reasonable, so it worked.

> **Reward people for doing their jobs well, not just for exceeding goals.** Be sure bonuses and incentives are not structured in such a way that they leave employees feeling defeated before they even start.

> **Offer resources.** Don't expect employees to support you if you don't support them. Wells Fargo demanded that its employees meet unreasonable goals without providing the resources to meet those goals ethically. Howdy Holmes, CEO of Chelsea Milling Co. and a leader I often cite for real-world examples, told me that he makes a point of developing sensible, fair goals with his team that they can exceed while feeling fully engaged. He believes leaders need to lead, not control. This can sometimes be tricky in a system that often puts leaders in a position of controlling others instead of being a resource to them.

It's not rocket science: treat people well, give them the resources they need, don't micromanage, focus on long-term results, and you'll be more likely to thrive. Foster an environment of cutthroat competitiveness and short-term results, and you and your organization will eventually crash and burn.[126]

It's not rocket science: treat people well, give them the resources they need, don't micromanage, focus on long-term results, and you'll be more likely to thrive.

Global Market Needs Adaptive Leadership

The nationalistic promise to "Make America Great Again" was a campaign slogan in the 2016 presidential campaign that resonated with a large segment of our society who believed the claim that global trade agreements and policies were the exclusive reason that their jobs (largely manufacturing ones) had been eliminated. Unfortunately, the idea that we can somehow turn back the hands of time to a simpler, less technology-driven manufacturing era is folly, even if it were possible to defy the natural order of the universe.

As Thomas Friedman, the *New York Times* columnist and best-selling author, pointed out in a November 14, 2017, *Times* article, the global climate is changing in ways that go far beyond the weather. We're also going through a "climate change" in globalization—from an interconnected world to an *interdependent* one—and in technology, as AI and robotics reach radical new levels of sophistication. While countries like China are incorporating these evolving realities into their national vision for the future, current U.S. leadership is touting outmoded forms of energy and wall-building as its strategies. As Friedman points out, every effective leader should be starting his or her day asking questions such as, "What world am I living in? What are the biggest trends in this world? And how do I align my country [or my company] so more of my citizens get the most out of these trends and cushion the worst?"[127]

As the world continues to evolve, so must those who want to get ahead. Blacksmiths were replaced by auto mechanics, and mechanics are now reinventing their careers as cars become more computerized and vehicle repair becomes more technology-based. And now, with the emergence of Elon Musk's leading-edge Tesla automobile, a battery-powered, self-driven car that could revolutionize the industry, car mechanics may soon face another career transition choice. Experts have started to write about the shifts they see in our current and ever-evolving job market and have deemed this era as one of the "nonlinear career"—workers no longer want to spend their entire lives sitting at the same desk. As Mike D'Ausilio, managing director of human resources at JPMorgan Chase, wrote, "When you think about the ways the market keeps changing—the disruption, the speed, the digital desires of people to do everything on their phone—this is going to create skill sets we didn't necessarily look for in the past.... [There] are going to be skills five, ten years out that don't even exist yet."[128]

Friedman again hit the nail on the head when he said in a different *Times* piece, "My generation had it easy. We got to 'find' a job. But, more than ever, our kids will have to 'invent' a job."[129] In other words, innovation and adaptation are now essential for survival in a global economy.

Take, for example, Limoneira, a 124-year-old Santa Paula–based international grower of citrus, avocados, and other crops. It has adapted and diversified over the years to become a major global agribusiness and not merely a grower of farm products. With approximately 10,700 acres of rich agricultural land and real estate properties and water rights in California and Arizona, Limoneira has diversified its board of directors to include more than just men and agriculture experts.

This forward-thinking approach is part of the company's mission to "preserve and promote its tradition, heritage, and legacy in agriculture, community development, and stewardship to maximize value for its shareholders."[130] The company has a simple stewardship goal of leaving its resources—land, water, environment, and community—in better shape than when it acquired them. Such stewardship gives the company and its employees a common purpose while enhancing Limoneira's prospects for long-term sustainability.

Don't Be Afraid of Technology

It's hard to embrace all the constant updates and developments in the tech world. It seems social media, one way or another, touches every aspect of our businesses, our lives, and our relationships. Leaders embrace this change rather than shy away from it. They recognize that this doesn't mean impending doom but rather represents a fresh, new generation of opportunities. The explosive growth of social media, especially in the business and marketing world, shows us that there is a new set of human behaviors driving business.

How we communicate and make decisions is now greatly influenced by the digital world. In a recent Nielsen survey, only 33 percent of consumers said they trust paid advertisements, but an *incredible* 92 percent trust peer recommendations.[131] That means if somebody blogs or tweets or writes a Facebook post about you, your company, your service, you name it, their followers are watching, reading, and making silent decisions about you, your company, or your service, without you even knowing it. As business leaders, we have to learn new techniques, adapt to new processes, or be flexible to different ways of doing things. Embrace this as you set out on your path to leadership. Remember to adapt and recognize the importance and influence of social media and technology. ∎

Workers today must also grow and adapt. Multiple sources, including Forrester Research and the Bureau of Labor, tell us that most people will average between ten and fifteen jobs during their lifetime, and it is rather unlikely that anyone will spend their entire career in one field.[132] In exploring this further, a McKinsey Global Institute study found six sectors that are expected to account for most of the job growth going forward: health care, business services, leisure and hospitality, construction, manufacturing, and retail.[133]

According to the study, layoffs today are more likely to be permanent, and new jobs that are created in the aftermath of layoffs will likely be in different industries. If you're in business services today, it's quite possible you may transition into health care services at some point. Manufacturing jobs have become more automated, meaning many traditionally trained manufacturing professionals will end up moving into other industries.[134]

Much of this change, of course, is just the natural order of business; therefore workers today and in the future will need to be flexible and adaptive to this ever-evolving employment landscape. Leaders cannot afford to resist this change either. They must embrace it. Consider this thought from Warren Bennis, the pioneering leadership scholar and author: "Leaders must encourage their organizations to dance to forms of music yet to be heard."

Change is just the natural order of business; leaders cannot afford to resist change.

Rebels Required

A rebellious attitude toward stale and outmoded business practices must be cultivated. Isn't it true that today's rebels often become tomorrow's leaders and heroes? Think about our nation's Founding Fathers and those who stood up to the British during the Revolutionary War. At the time, George Washington and his cohorts were called rebels, agitators, and even traitors. But these same men and women went on to found a new nation and become its leaders and revered heroes. Rosa Parks followed in this tradition. Her small act of defiance on a public bus in Montgomery, Alabama, led to a bus boycott that propelled the civil rights movement forward.

The French have a term for such "troublemakers," too. *Garagistes* was originally used in the Bordeaux region of France to denigrate small-lot wine makers who refused to follow the rules. The word now refers to a full-fledged movement that has led to the production of some of the best wine in the world. *Garagistes* has become synonymous with rule-breakers, pioneers, renegades, and mavericks.

Often in business, innovative ideas, products, and services are the best way to move an organization forward. To do so means leaders must be willing to take risks and implement changes that others may not like or will actively oppose. By our own nature, humans are resistant to change. History has proven time and time again, however, that most people get over it.

Leadership writer William Deresiewicz, author of *A Jane Austen Education*, put it this way: "For too long we have been training leaders who only know how to keep the routine going. Who can answer questions, but don't know how to ask them. Who can fulfill goals, but don't know how to set them. Who think about how to get things done, but not whether they're worth doing in the first place."[135]

Sustainability Leaders

In 2015, Pope Francis did something that might qualify him as a long-view leader: he openly supported the idea that global warming is real and human-caused and that it threatens the very existence of us all. Critics questioned why Pope Francis was delving into politics and science, but he was correct to do so.

Climate change will affect how future generations live and will force them to adapt to its negative effects. Human actions, from rapid industrialization to deforestation to the use of fossil fuels and harmful agricultural practices, have contributed to global warming and other forms of environmental damage. These activities, plus many others, will stretch our increasingly limited resources, especially if the population continues to grow, and will hurt most the poor in the developing world. The Pope's message in his encyclical is that all people worldwide have a shared responsibility for taking action by using less and reusing more.

To make this happen, those with the means to implement environmental protection measures and sustainable business practices must demonstrate enlightened, vigorous leadership. Leaders in government, the military, industry, and business need to step up their game. Celebrities and faith leaders can help, too, because they can influence millions of people. Executives and board members from industries such as oil, energy, and manufacturing—which have traditionally fought stricter environmental regulations—will have to abandon the tired old mindset that calls for them to resist any moves that compromise profits. That sort of outdated thinking will alienate customers who increasingly support eco-friendly businesses and shun companies with bad environmental records.[136]

Some business leaders have shown early leadership in incorporating more sustainable business practices. Ray C. Anderson, whose carpet company, Interface, was the first company to achieve 100 percent sustainability, is a good example. Anderson proved that sustainability made sense for business by growing profits even as he took steps such as developing a process for recycling old carpets, pioneering a leased carpet program, incorporating the work of indigenous peoples, switching to solar and other alternative energy sources, reducing water use and contamination, and achieving net negative greenhouse gas emissions.

Other companies known for their success in sustainability include Unilever, Patagonia, Nestlé, Marks & Spencer, Nike, GE, IKEA, and Puma. Unilever made news worldwide when it created a Sustainable Living Plan. The company has decreased energy use, reduced waste via recycling and efficiency drives, and lowered carbon emissions by one-third in its manufacturing operations through the use of cleaner technologies and greater efficiency. Toy company Lego has committed to investing $150 million over the next fifteen years to make its plastic building blocks more sustainable.

Unilever's CEO, Paul Polman, told a group of sustainability specialists from NGOs, government, academia, and business gathered at Unilever's London headquarters in 2015, "In a volatile world of growing social inequality, rising population, development challenges and climate change, the need for businesses to adapt is clear, as are the benefits and opportunities. This calls for a transformational approach across the whole value chain if we are to continue to grow. Consumers are recognizing this, too, increasingly demanding responsible business and responsible brands. Our experience is that brands whose purpose and products respond to that demand—'sustainable living brands'—are delivering stronger and faster growth."[137]

Sustainability Requires Creativity

If you were placing an employment ad for a manager who was an "original thinker," whom would you choose to interview for the position? Your leading candidate might be someone like Indra Nooyi, PepsiCo's prescient chairwoman and CEO, who boldly took her company's products beyond what many people now view as unhealthy drinks and junk food snacks. As the leader for the past eleven years of the iconic American brand, Nooyi dared to acknowledge that junk food and soda are fattening and bad for your health. She vowed to offer healthier products as well as improve the healthfulness of the bad ones by lowering their sugar and salt content, among other changes. Considering that many people still love soda and junk food, regardless of their negative health implications, her disciplined risk-taking enabled PepsiCo's revenues to reach $66.7 billion and profits to reach $6.5 billion in 2014.

The CEO of "JIFFY" Mix, Howdy Holmes, mentioned earlier in this chapter, is a former professional Indy car driver as well as a fourth-generation head of a multinational business. His forward-thinking leadership style and management approach helped to bring his family's traditional baking mix company into modern times. He wasn't afraid to shake things up at his company when he took over in 1987. He stepped outside of the company's—and his own—comfort zone to make major organizational changes, such as adding non-family members to the board, bringing in talented, experienced senior managers, involving employees more in business decisions, and seeking new mechanical and accounting systems. By keeping his finger on the pulse of America's evolving health concerns and eating habits, Holmes also took the bold step of debuting a new vegetarian corn muffin mix in 2014.

Today's business world demands original thinkers like Nooyi and Holmes, who dared to rethink their products in order to align them better with shifts in customers' food and beverage tastes. Nooyi and Holmes did not allow themselves to be thwarted by the bureaucracy they inherited or to stagnate within existing organizational structures.

Perhaps all human resources departments should make original thinking a mandatory job qualification when hiring a new manager or executive.

Organizational Climate vs. Culture

Organizational climate is usually defined as the shared perceptions that workers have about the organization that employs them. It is different from (but still related to) *organizational culture*, which is defined as an organization's shared behavioral expectations (teamwork, accountability, etc.).

Former MIT Sloan School of Management professor Edgar Schein is perhaps the most well-known academic credited with a deep exploration of corporate culture and how culture is linked to an enterprise's success. Schein's concepts were first widely popularized in his 1985 book, *Organizational Culture and Leadership*.[138]

In the book, Schein describes three levels of influencers that help determine how external observers perceive an organization's overall culture. These factors include the basic assumptions that employees have (largely unconscious ones) about expected behaviors in an organization. Then there are espoused values, typically what an organization says publicly and promotes as its values and expected behaviors—team oriented, respect for others, for example. Finally, there are the externally facing cultural indicators that Schein called artifacts and symbols, which includes an organization's physical building, furniture, expected dress code, and so on.

Changing an organization's culture is a long-term commitment that must have, at a minimum, the full, wholehearted commitment from not only the CEO but also upper and middle management. In my experience, most major culture change efforts fail for many reasons (including lack of leadership commitment), which are well documented in both academic and popular literature. The problem is that many leaders seek to change their organization's culture to better compete in the marketplace (increase productivity, reduce costs, strengthen execution, be faster to market). While these are important and necessary goals, leaders often do not appreciate that culture change should never be thought of as a "quick fix" solution. Barring a major crisis with tremendous upheaval, it is often a longer-term process.

However, it is possible to change the work climate in an office, department, or several departments even when the predominant culture of the larger organization can't be rapidly changed. I believe this because I've done it in departments and divisions I've led where the larger organization is change adverse, bureaucratic, or content to rest on its laurels. Changing the behaviors and attitudes of specific parts of an organization is sometimes more manageable since assessing and implementing changes to improve climate at this level allows more direct management of the outcome.

Of course, improving perceptions about an organization's climate piecemeal without a connection to an ongoing culture change process can create problems in some organizations, especially if other areas of the enterprise become jealous or resentful of another functional area with a much better work environment than their own. ∎

In my leadership roles at Blue Shield, Stanford University, the United States Navy, and two "top 10" community hospital/health systems, I have long advocated that key organizational functions, like HR, must adopt an outside-in mindset, in which they actively seek perspectives from outside the core management team, such as from customers. Here are some suggestions to help with that proposal: [139]

1. Reward those who offer interesting, novel, and creative ideas, even when you have doubts about the practicality of such ideas. Never stifle originality and enthusiasm.
2. Strive to unleash the strengths of others. Effective leadership is not about amassing personal power.

3. Never be fearful of hiring someone because you feel they might outshine you or are more intelligent than you—after all, their accomplishments will reflect well on you.

4. Seek out those who believe in serving others, not themselves. Look for those who know how to check their egos at the door, and are humble, and likely to work well with others—but aren't reticent about expressing their views.

5. Identify open-minded people who can listen attentively, conceptualize and synthesize well, and function both independently and in a team setting.

6. Avoid those who seem to enjoy blaming or belittling others, have difficulty admitting their own mistakes, and/ or who shun personal accountability.

7. Be leery of "yes men" and "yes women."

8. Look for problem solvers, as they typically have a rich array of fresh ideas and approaches. Remember that no one size fits all.

9. Avoid the "limelight seekers" and instead search for those who are never too busy to extend a helping hand and go the extra mile.

10. Find those who embrace change, realizing that rapid adaptation in today's global economy can often be the difference between success and failure.

11. Seek people who have passion, who inspire others, who care about results but also value people highly, and who aren't likely to "sweat the small stuff" (get their knickers in a knot!).

Immersion

Immersion is a business practice often associated with intensive training programs designed to build a language skill rapidly or instill cultural awareness quickly in participants. For example, the State Department's Critical Language Scholarship Program is focused on encouraging more Americans to be fluent in languages it considers essential to national security and global competitiveness.

Many businesses and their supporting consulting firms have adapted this idea to help them cope with today's rapidly changing marketplace and its shifting customer expectations. In a business context, immersion is a structured learning event featuring executives from a variety of industries and sectors who work with participants to challenge conventional thinking and provide outside perspective along with vital networking experience.

Companies see this experience as a proactive way to develop new kinds of leaders who are adaptable and open to change and can think strategically and predict tomorrow's business trends, which can include the impact of emerging technology such as artificial intelligence (AI) and augmented reality (AR) on business models. The most successful of these programs move leaders out of their comfort zones and give them new and innovative perspectives. A few examples of these programs include:

- **Yale School of Management's** three-day Behavioral Economics Immersion program focuses on marketing and product development. This program is grounded in the latest behavioral research aimed at understanding customer drivers and how to align these drivers to a company's value position amid changing customer expectations.

- **Northwestern Kellogg Executive Education** offers intensive programs on how to lead through an understanding of big data and analytics. The program is designed to help executives build new, disruptive business models and increase innovation.

- **Silicon Valley Innovation Center** uses leaders of the most innovative companies in Silicon Valley to help participants connect with emerging trends and spot the next disruptive technologies that might impact a participant's business. Program offerings are directed at a wide range of industry sectors, including banking, transportation, manufacturing, the oil and gas business, retail industry, and the venture capital business.

The rationale for a company to think beyond traditional and entrenched ways of leadership thinking was recently highlighted in a study conducted by IE Universidad's Business School, a Spain-based private university, in Segovia. The study of the S&P 500 CEOs found that direct experience in an industry does not necessarily mean that such experience transfers to the next job. In fact, the study showed a "negative learning transfer" because the related experience created "knowledge corridors" that kept the CEOs from acting differently or adapting.[140] ∎

Safety Is Not an Option

The current political climate has prompted some college campuses to create "safe zones," places where students can go and speak freely among like-minded people only and not be challenged. While well-meaning, the approach is naïve and sends the wrong message about free speech and the importance of both courage and civility when challenging opposing ideas. If these students wish to be tomorrow's leaders, they will need courage and civility and strength of character.

You can't lead if you can't respect another person's opinion, defend your own, or challenge the status quo. It's important that colleges and universities prepare students for the challenges they will most assuredly face as future leaders.

You can't lead if you can't respect another person's opinion, defend your own, or challenge the status quo.

Instead of setting up safe zones, here are three ways to teach future leaders about dealing with ideas that might not mirror their own: [141]

- Embrace challenges to your thinking with excitement and anticipation. Don't bury your head in the sand and pretend they don't exist.
- Learn how to expand the boundaries of mutual respect. Accept differences. Build consensus.
- What you believe now may change later, so become a champion of the free expression of ideas (even when you disagree with those ideas), and treasure human dignity in everything you do.

Key Concepts

> Too many companies are focused on short-term results and not on long-term, sustainable outcomes. You can begin changing this focus by reducing your emphasis on quarterly results, revising unreasonable expectations and performance goals, rewarding top performance, and providing appropriate support.

> The marketplace and the products and services consumers want change often. The most sustainable companies are the ones that adapt quickly and effectively to changes in customer demand.

> Creativity and adaptability are needed characteristics of today's global leaders; therefore, human resources departments should include these traits as top requirements when hiring.

> Embrace challenges, accept civil debate, and learn to listen to others.

~

"In the long run, we shape our lives, and we shape ourselves. The process never ends until we die. And the choices we make are ultimately our own responsibility."

—ELEANOR ROOSEVELT

CHAPTER 8

Assume Responsibility

IN THIS CHAPTER

> **Real Leaders Take Responsibility**
> **What Great Leaders Say About Responsibility**
> **Trust and Responsibility**
> **Whining Leaders Need to Go**
> **Key Concepts**

INTRODUCTION

Harry S. Truman (1884–1972), who ascended to the presidency after the death of Franklin D. Roosevelt in April of 1945, is credited with popularizing the phrase "The buck stops here." This leadership principle guided all the decisions Truman made during his two terms in office (1945–1953). Truman famously kept a plaque of the quote on his Oval Office desk, strategically angling it toward the door so that no visitor could miss seeing it.[142] Taking the message to heart, Truman left behind a record of personal responsibility that includes the still-controversial decision to end World War II by unleashing the terrible power of an atomic bomb on the civilian populations of Hiroshima and Nagasaki.

Unfortunately, the current administration has made a mockery of this essential leadership characteristic. Late-night comedians regularly make jokes about the president's habit of blaming others, and editorial cartoonists, often using variations of Truman's famous plaque to make their point, have feasted on the fact that our current commander-in-chief takes no responsibility for anything that happens on his watch.

Of course, to some media the blame-shifting behavior is completely consistent with the modus operandi of all bullies, narcissists, and adolescent children. When challenged about their lies or their failure to deliver on a promise or claim, bullies—and children—simply shift the blame. While it may be understandable (even cute) when children exhibit this behavior, it is unacceptable in the extreme when the president of the United States does it. In my opinion, it's an embarrassment to the nation, and it tarnishes the legacy of all those who have held the office.

Here are a few of the media's cited examples of the president's blame-deflecting behavior. After the Senate was unable to ram a vindictive replacement for the Affordable Care Act through, his tweeted response was "We're not going to own it. I'm not going to own it." On numerous other issues, from more restrictive immigration and travel policies to building a border wall, the administration has blamed its failure on a cabal of outside forces (the Obama administration, Hillary Clinton, the Democratic Party, to name a few).

If this chapter had a subtitle it would be "Show Me a Flawless Leader." Clearly, no such leader has ever existed. True leaders understand this fact of life and take responsibility for their actions when they fall short. This chapter discusses how failing to take responsibility undermines the respect a leader needs to inspire and motivate a workforce. It also points out why leaders who are not firmly committed to taking responsibility unwittingly set up a dynamic that impacts the long-term viability of the organization.

Real Leaders Take Responsibility

If you've seen the 2013 movie about the life of baseball legend Jackie Robinson, titled after his jersey number, *42*, you might recall the movie's depiction of how Jackie learned to respond to the spiteful challenges he faced on and off the field. He did so by taking responsibility for his own behavior and adopting a heroic level of self-restraint. Few athletes are as supremely gifted as Robinson, and fewer still can match his incredible courage, discipline, and strength of character. (I write in more detail about Robinson in the final chapter.)

When an organization experiences a failure, the quickest way to judge whether the person in charge is a real leader or just a boss is by watching what happens next. Real leaders understand that setbacks are temporary and respond with action; they seek input from their team, admit failure, resolve to learn from the mistakes, and then move forward with renewed vigor.

Real leaders understand that setbacks are temporary and respond with action; they seek input from their team, admit failure, resolve to learn from the mistakes, and then move forward with renewed vigor.

Former President Obama followed this leadership playbook repeatedly during his eight years in office. In 2010, after an intelligence failure on Christmas Day nearly resulted in a tragic bombing attack, Obama paraphrased President Truman's famous mantra, saying, "The buck stops with me." Earlier, in 2009, under criticism for allowing AIG Insurance Company executives to keep their bonuses even after receiving a government bailout, Obama said, "Ultimately, I'm responsible. I'm the President of the United States."[143]

Presidents George W. Bush and Bill Clinton also took responsibility for their failures: Bush for not responding appropriately to the Katrina disaster in New Orleans, and Clinton, after initial denials, for the relationship with intern Monica Lewinsky that nearly ended his presidency.

What Great Leaders Say About Responsibility

I have always been intrigued by the issue of leadership responsibility and have written about it extensively. However, I wanted a fresh perspective for this book, so I assembled a panel of bright, successful, and thoughtful leaders from the C-suite, academia, law enforcement, journalism, foreign affairs, and athletics to download their thoughts on taking responsibility. Here are some highlights from those interviews.

David A. Brandon, the board chairman of Domino's Pizza and chairman and CEO of Toys "R" Us, told me, "Just because someone is in a leadership position doesn't mean they are a true leader. A true leader won't put his or her personal goals ahead of building trust and a strong, positive relationship with members of the team. Finger-pointing and blaming is not what true leaders do."

Brandon went on to say, "True leaders make themselves vulnerable. This requires them to accept responsibility, admit mistakes, accept criticism and coaching, and not adopt the old 'I am the boss, so I always have to be right' attitude. Effective leaders think of themselves as the 'captain of the team' versus allowing themselves to become isolated from the team."

Michael D. Bradbury, who served with distinction as district attorney of Ventura County, California, for twenty-four years, offered his perspective: "'Leadership' is one of those somewhat ephemeral qualities that is part learned but also part innate or 'You're born with it.' Although perhaps counterintuitive, there are some aspects of leadership that you simply don't learn. You either have it, or you don't. 'Character' is the broad-brush [term] normally used to describe these qualities that must be inherent. But there are many aspects to character. You rarely find an effective leader who doesn't have great character."

Harold Edwards, president and CEO of Limoneira, the leading agribusiness and real estate company I've referred to, believes, "Leaders that blame others really aren't leaders. I view leadership as the act of selfless consensus building.... [L]eaders that blame others position themselves as either victor (if all goes as planned) or victims (if they aren't able to accomplish some of their goals). Leaders that blame others in the face of failure really aren't team players and statistically show a lower probability of accomplishing goals versus team-playing leaders who selflessly commit themselves to executing goals. Leaders who are known winners typically take complete accountability and responsibility for their important goals. If they come up short, they dig deeper and work harder. This behavior tends to motivate and inspire teams, elevate performance, and sharpen execution."

Edwards went on to say, "In my experience, the best leaders foster teamwork. The worst leaders act as individuals and blame others for their lack of performance. Leaders who demonstrate these tendencies typically experience shorter careers."

Professor Stephen A. Stumpf, PhD, the Fred J. Springer Chair in Business Leadership and professor of management and operations at Villanova University School of Business, suggested, "Humans are hardwired to defend themselves—a primal instinct. Defensiveness is automatic. The difference between those that blame and those that do not is that [the latter] can self-acknowledge their need to blame, and then [refrain from doing] it. Once 'there is no blame,' it is possible to look for new options, alternatives, and actions. Creativity kicks in. Exploring others' perspectives becomes worthy of thought. The future becomes the focus, not reconciling the past with one's ego."

Stumpf also offered this further insight: "For the 'non-blamers,' [failure to meet goals] is a temporary situation in their minds. Goals get redefined, timeframes are altered, and whatever progress was made (or lessons learned) [becomes] the inspiration for the next round of effort."

Larry Ames, former *Boston Globe* assistant sports editor, retired *Ventura County (CA) Star* sports editor, and author of *Never Dull*, whom I quoted earlier, told me, "In any business, whether a small company or a corporation, there are hundreds and often thousands of decisions made every day. Not all decisions are the right ones, nor can one expect them to be; therefore, laying blame is never the right approach." Ames added, "It serves no purpose to analyze, dissect or criticize a wrong. In any situation, the correct approach is to find a solution and move forward rather than rehash what went wrong. Looking back, as opposed to moving forward, can only make matters worse and also create ill will."

When I do teach, I often remind my students that real leaders aren't loners; they are builders of strong, diverse teams. They set up a work climate of integrity, intellect, trust, and safety, wherein all members of the team are highly respected, their dignity is reinforced, and their efforts and selflessness are recognized. Real leaders lift your spirits and place a premium on high morale. As Dr. Clifton R. Wharton Jr., noted African American "pioneer" and highly distinguished leader in four different fields (foreign economic development, philanthropy, higher education, and business), said, "The best leader understands the power of unleashing individual talent by offering persons the opportunity to learn, to be enterprising, and to make a contribution."

Wharton and his spouse, Dolores D. Wharton, an esteemed corporate director (she has served on some thirty corporate boards of directors) and arts advocate, are great exemplars of leaders who teach. Such leaders encourage and mentor new leaders by exposing them to how organizations really work and by giving them opportunities to use their creativity.

Leaders encourage and mentor new leaders by exposing them to how organizations really work and by giving them opportunities to use their creativity.

Again, the wisdom of Howdy Holmes is worth citing. "You find those that accept responsibility for their own actions and those that blame others for their mistakes in every walk of life," he told me. "To some extent, I think it is in your DNA," he said, but also pointed out that your orientation is, in part, a function of how you were raised. He also believes we can learn a great deal by observing others and modeling the best of those behaviors we admire.

"Some business systems," he added, "make it easier to blame others for our mistakes, and CEOs need to ensure their egos don't get in the way." Finally, this distinguished, plain-speaking, down-to-earth leader who has successfully blended the latest management practices with cherished, traditional values, said, "One of the most important lessons I've learned is the importance of differentiating between what is best for the company versus what is best for the CEO. If you can't consistently make this distinction, it is impossible to develop trust throughout your organization."[144]

An anonymous source of mine said it best, "Unpredictability may be a useful tool with adversaries, but with allies it creates uncertainty and irritation."

Trust and Responsibility

I couldn't agree more with Holmes's focus on consistency, which is particularly important during times of organizational crisis, such as when someone in management is caught up in a public scandal or if the company is having financial struggles. During such difficult periods, an organization's track record of trustworthy behavior and taking responsibility for its actions is often the only line of defense against dire consequences.

So, how does an organization set itself up to be one of these resilient enterprises with a sustaining and positive reputation? Here are three survival conditions the best leaders must work to create:

1. **Consistent performance over time.** Customers, employees, and community members judge leaders by their consistent and unfaltering ethical behavior. Institutions truly committed to trustworthy behavior know that pursuing transparency is vital. Accordingly, leaders of these institutions create a process for transparency and disclosure that works for both current and future operations. They also speak candidly, both with employees and with the community the company serves, about the company, its strategy, and the values that underpin it.

2. **A supportive internal culture.** Organizations must build an internal culture that fosters trust and responsibility. All employees hired must be evaluated not only on their

technical competencies and/or scholastic achievements, but also on their ability to thrive in a culture of high accountability. By hiring and keeping this type of employee, such organizations create a class of ambassadors that build a strong market brand based on trust and responsibility. Some organizations make ethics training a requirement or ask new hires to sign a letter agreeing to the company's ethical values and other important business principles.

Some conduct a "culture audit" to ensure that all employees understand the organization's guiding principles. Building an internal culture of trust and responsibility requires top-to-bottom involvement, including the leadership team and the support of an internal communication program that reinforces these values.[145]

3. **Unwavering leadership commitment.** Leaders must believe fervently in the principles of honesty, integrity, and taking responsibility even in trying times. Organizations and their leaders must never sacrifice these values for short-term gain or to avoid conflict or embarrassment. How an organization responds in its darkest moments will have a far more telling effect on its reputation than what it does when the sun is shining.

True leaders can be counted on to do the right thing, even when it is unpleasant or costly. For example, Senator John McCain again broke rank with his party on October 31, 2017, when he warned an audience at the U.S. Naval Academy that it was time to "wake up" and recognize the dangers of the present administration's direction. "We have to remind our sons and daughters that we became the most powerful nation on earth by tearing down walls, not building them," he said, among other things. McCain was no doubt aware that his remarks would alienate him from many in his own party, but he was willing to speak the truth as he perceived it.[146]

True leaders never lie or deceive. They are sincere, candid, and forthright. Enterprises guided by such leaders have an advantage over their competitors because the trust they form with stakeholders allows them to reap the sometimes essential benefit of the doubt. And in today's atmosphere of leadership distrust, that edge is a powerful one indeed.

Whining Leaders Need to Go

Unlike the effective leaders noted in this chapter, the president spends an inordinate amount of time whining and blaming others for his failures. Anyone who disagrees is either "dishonest" or "crooked." Whether behind a podium or on Twitter, his steady stream of deflective claims in reaction to perceived slights and indignities is both embarrassing and destructive to the authority of the office.

As I was writing this book, the way the president deals with media, especially his tendency to discredit all news media accounts critical of his actions, got the attention of the United Nations High Commissioner for Human Rights, Zeid Ra'ad al-Hussein. The commissioner commented at a news conference in Geneva that President Trump's continuing denunciations of the media outlets as "fake news" was having dangerous consequences outside the U.S.

"It's really quite amazing when you think that freedom of the press, not only a cornerstone of the Constitution but very much something the United States defended over the years, is now itself under attack from the president himself," Mr. al-Hussein said. "It's a stunning turnaround."[147]

The "Fake News" Phenomenon

Undermining the truthfulness and integrity of the free press is a well-known strategy of every despotic, corrupt, or bullying political leader's playbook. From the outside, it's such an obvious power play that we find it hard to believe that anyone living under such a repressive regime would buy the leader's lies. However, if our own recent political experience has taught us anything, it surely must be empathy for these countries. As Eugene Robinson noted in a December 2017 editorial for the *Washington Post*, "Imagine that the legislature of some other country—Brazil, say, or Mozambique, or Thailand—decided to rewrite the tax code, with no public hearings or expert testimony, in a way that benefited the rich overall, with maximum financial gain for businesses like that of the sitting head of government. What would you say?"[148]

A recent piece in the *New York Times* highlighted the destructive ripple effects that dishonest leadership can create worldwide. As the article noted, Syria's president, Bashar al-Assad, recently proclaimed, "We are living in a fake news era," in response to an Amnesty International report about prison abuses in his country. In Venezuela, a country where democracy is losing its foothold, President Nicolás Maduro has lashed out at the global media, saying, "This is what we call 'fake news' today." And in Russia, the Foreign Ministry's website now stamps the word "FAKE" in red letters over any news story it wishes to disparage. Other countries—Turkey, China, Russia, Libya, and Somalia, to name a few—are also using this truth suppression tactic when any news organization shines a light on any corrupt or potentially unpopular practice.[149]

To be fair, *some* false news stories certainly do indeed exist on the Internet and sometimes even the best, most careful news outlets report incorrect information and deserve to be called out on that. However, constantly challenging the veracity of all news outlets is another matter altogether. Yet, despite the lessons of history, nations continue to hop on board this well-traveled "alternate reality" train, and once onboard it is hard to stop. Sadly, tragically, it's a journey that won't end well for a nation or its people.

As Supreme Court Associate Justice Oliver Wendell Holmes Jr. wrote, "If there is any principle of the Constitution that more imperatively calls for attachment than any other, it is the principle of free thought—not free thought for those who agree with us but freedom for the thought that we hate." ∎

As someone who has spent a career working with military, health care, higher education, and agricultural leaders on the importance of fair, open, and *honest* communications, I have experienced firsthand what happens when people fail to take responsibility for their actions. Credibility is lost. Morale drops. Productivity comes to a standstill.

When leaders take to casting blame on others for anything that does not go according to plan and handily take credit for results they had little or nothing to do with, it is seen as classic bully and narcissist behavior. In this administration's case, when a flawed executive immigration ban was put on hold by a U.S. judge, it was the judiciary system that was said to have failed. The administration even tried to insulate itself from potential blame by claiming that any future terrorist attack would be the judge's fault. If any CEO showed such behavior, he or she would hear the immortal words "You're fired" (echoing a popular reality television show's catchphrase).

Hubris, on its own, is a dangerous vice; when combined with naïveté and narcissism, it is lethal. As President George H. W. Bush once told his sons (according to Mark Updegrove, author of *The Last*

Republicans, speaking on *Face the Nation*), "Understand that power accompanied by arrogance is very dangerous." He was speaking at the time about former President Nixon, but then he added on a prescient note, "It is particularly dangerous when men with no experience have it, for they can abuse our great institutions."[150]

As I began to prepare my book for publication, the *Washington Post* published a piece for the one-year anniversary of Trump's inauguration. At the time, they counted that Trump had not named nominees for about 245 jobs, from director of the Office on Violence Against Women at Justice to commissioner of the Social Security Administration to ambassador to South Korea. When asked about these open spots, Trump did not let on that he would even be filling all of the positions and later admitted that he will intentionally be leaving them open, as he doesn't feel it's necessary to fill the spots. Leaving these spots open and without any clarity on when/if they will even be filled can lead to distrust among those left in the office.[151] A *New York Times* article reported that the White House staff has a 34% turnover rate, which is said to be the highest it's been in decades.[152] There are twelve positions that are seen as the most important to the president and it was recently reported that of the White House staff, only five of those twelve positions are still held by the same person that took the spot when the president took office. Many of the open positions have actually never been filled from the start. What he may be forgetting is that building a team is a careful effort—it takes time for people to get to know each other, understand how to work together, and find a "groove." The longer this goes on, the more of a toll it can take on him and those around him.

Unfortunately, some leaders don't seem to grasp the difference between leading in a democracy and ruling by fiat. It's easy to find contemporary examples of what can happen when leaders allow their narcissism to take over and forget that the electorate is in charge. Leading can sometimes be a lonely and frustrating experience because not everyone is going to agree with you. As David Brinkley once said, "A successful man is one who can lay a firm foundation with the bricks others have thrown at him." Real leaders understand that sage comment and accept it as a challenge. And they do the right thing.

Leading can sometimes be a lonely and frustrating experience because not everyone is going to agree with you.

I sometimes remind myself and others that Naval Academy Midshipmen in Annapolis are allowed three answers when they address an upperclassman:

"Yes sir."

"No sir."

"No excuse, sir."

The word *but* is not allowed, so blame is not possible. This is the first leadership lesson plebes learn, in addition to a strictly enforced honor code: "We will not lie, cheat, or steal." Our nation's leaders would benefit from this uncompromising approach to responsibility-taking. After all, if the leader does not accept responsibility for his or her actions, then neither will anyone else.[153]

Key Concepts

> A leader's failure to take responsibility for many of his actions and decisions sends the wrong message to his or her organization, community, or nation. Leaders who refuse to accept responsibility are neither trusted nor respected and are ultimately ineffective.

> When leaders refuse to take responsibility for their actions, credibility is lost, morale drops, and productivity comes to a standstill.

> When leaders are quick to blame others around them, they set the tone for other people in powerful positions to feel as if it is okay to do the same. This behavior should be an example of how NOT to lead.

~

"No man will make a great leader who wants to do it all himself or to get all the credit for doing it."

— ANDREW CARNEGIE

CHAPTER 9

Seek Win-Win Solutions

IN THIS CHAPTER

> **Five Reasons Teamwork Works**
> **The Five Ws of a Winning Team**
> **Alleviating Workplace Loneliness: A Great Example of a Win/Win Solution**
> **The Gift of Loyalty**
> **Too Much Loyalty**
> **Key Concepts**

INTRODUCTION

In **Real Leaders Don't Boss**, I outline eight essential characteristics of effective leadership.[154] Beginning with the book's title trait (non-bossiness), I list several other ethical and behavioral guideposts that leaders should embrace, including honesty, clarity, support for people, passion for the corporate mission, accessibility, and humility.

Finding win-win solutions, the topic of this chapter, might easily be added to the list as the ninth characteristic, or perhaps even as a substitute for the other eight. After all, a leader who values compromise and fair interchange is likely to be a leader who also exhibits honesty, integrity, respect for people at all levels; humility; and a passion for achieving the goals of the organization.

A bullying leader, on the other hand, is NOT focused on solutions achieved through compromise and respectful communications, or on solutions that satisfy most stakeholders. Such narcissistic leaders follow an "either you're with me or against me" agenda—a way of doing business that is consistently used by some of our national leaders.

This chapter will focus on the benefits of dialogue, compromise, respectful conversation, and finding ways to move a shared goal forward. This approach is a much more effective way to run an organization, or a country for that matter, but leaders need the right skills and temperament to pull it off. For those who succeed, the rewards are clear: you, your organization, and all other stakeholders in the enterprise are winners.

Five Reasons Teamwork Works

Watching a crew team glide across a calm patch of water with machine-like precision is a beautiful, even mystical, sight to witness. Guided by a trusted coxswain, rowers must drop all individual desires and thoughts in order to achieve "oneness" with their shell and the other crew members. Perhaps more than any other sport, crew embodies the true meaning of teamwork.

What it means to be a crew team member was explored in fascinating detail in Daniel James Brown's 2013 best-seller, *The Boys in the Boat: Nine Americans and Their Epic Quest for Gold at the 1936 Olympics.* As the title suggests, the book follows the journey of an extraordinary crew team (and their coach and boat builder) as they overcome countless roadblocks to win an Olympic race in Berlin and shame an emerging tyrant. It was a feel-good story that reinforced American resolve during an especially dark period in humanity's history.

George Yeoman Pocock, the crew's master boatbuilder, coach, and frequent spiritual advisor, constructed the sleek, glass-smooth boats raced by the University of Washington crew team (and several other U.S. teams at the time) in a loft above the shell-house on the Spokane River. As part of an English family boatbuilding enterprise extending back to his grandfather, Pocock had a reverential regard for the art of shell-building and the sport of rowing. Here is how he described the sport and the teamwork needed to win: "It's the finest art there is. It's a symphony of motion. And when you're rowing well, why it's nearing perfection. And when you near perfection, you're touching the Divine."[155]

Last fall, my wife and I were visiting several historical locations in New York—FDR's Presidential Library and Museum in Hyde Park, the Roosevelt family cottage, and Val-Kill Cottage, as well as Eleanor Roosevelt's retreat. I had read Brown's book and was inspired by its leadership message, so we decided to see if we could find any historical remnants of this proud rowing past. Our quest took us to the banks of the Hudson River and Marist College in Poughkeepsie to see where "The Boys" had launched their boat during the famed Poughkeepsie IRA Regattas, which were held at that location from the late nineteenth century through the 1940s.

It was here that the University of Washington crew honed its competitive skills. For the better part of a century, regattas, such as the one in Poughkeepsie, were among the country's most followed sporting events. The Poughkeepsie race pitted long-time university rivals—Penn, Columbia, Cal, Navy, and, of course, the Ivy League schools of Cornell, Princeton, Yale, and Harvard—against one another. Thousands of ardent fans lined both sides of the Hudson River to watch the races. Today, historical markers along Poughkeepsie's riverfront mark the spot where the races were held. Cornell's original boathouse (restored) is still in use on the Marist College campus.

Standing on the banks of the nearly half-mile-wide Hudson River, with the elegant Railroad Bridge spanning the water in the distance, I was inspired by these young men and by the strong leadership model that rowing offers us all.

Clearly, if any organization or project team could achieve this level of synchronization, it would be unstoppable. Pocock's observations about teamwork are still relevant to today's organizations and teams seeking solutions that move both individual players and the organization itself toward the same goal.

My experience in multiple industries has consistently reinforced one of my core beliefs about leadership: the best leaders know how to get everyone rowing in the same direction. Sure, sometimes an individual or a group may "lose" a battle, but that loss doesn't mean they'll walk away feeling like "losers." If that is the case, the solution may not have been a favored team-based effort from the start.

The best leaders know how to get everyone rowing in the same direction.

The Five Ws of a Winning Team

My formula for creating and sustaining a cohesive team is straightforward and based on my decades of leadership experience seeking positive solutions that serve both individual stakeholders and their organizations. Here are my Five Ws of building a winning team:[156]

> **Winning mentality**—Each carefully selected team member is passionate about results and highly motivated, but also knows how to subordinate himself or herself to "The Team."

Each member strives to succeed 100 percent of the time and goes the extra mile to get the work done. Winning teams must have players who will "kick the tires and light the fires."

> **Wear-well**—This is a term my father used to refer to someone who is congenial, cooperative, and shares ideas naturally. This is a person who "wears well," one whose presence you will enjoy for the long term.

> **Weather-resistant**—Someone who is not easily frustrated and won't obsess when faced with obstacles. Weather-resistant team members are unfailingly determined; they persevere no matter what. They have great gumption and staying power.

> **Window-of-opportunity watcher**—Someone who is highly alert, agile, flexible, and can quickly analyze opportunities—and is not afraid to take calculated risks.

> **Worthiness**—Individuals of integrity, self-control, probity, wholesomeness, and high moral principles. They watch out for their colleagues, and they never lie, cheat, or steal to achieve individual or team goals.

Alleviating Workplace Loneliness:
A Great Example of a Win-Win Solution

There are many *lose-lose* situations in the modern workplace that cause both the employee *and* the company to suffer. A good leader must develop sensitivity to these issues and try to turn them into positive solutions. For example, loneliness in the workplace is a seldom-discussed issue that hurts both the individual and the organization.

Loneliness is rarely a good thing, and it certainly has negative impacts on productivity and happiness in the workplace. Research has shown that loneliness can lead to mental and physical illnesses that cause workers to take more sick days than the average worker. A growing number of studies have also found it leads to problems like reduced organizational commitment among hotel workers, school principals, medical workers, and others, according to a recent article in the *Harvard Business Review* by Vice Admiral Vivek H. Murthy, our nation's surgeon general from 2014 to 2017. "Loneliness at work even affects the boss, with half of CEOs reporting that they feel lonely in their jobs," Murthy wrote.[157]

Feeling alone and tired at work has also been found to seriously impact burnout, which doesn't just affect individuals but can have serious consequences for organizations too. When Emma Seppälä researched for her book *The Happiness Track*, she found that 50 percent of people across professions are burned out.[158] Experts and companies have struggled to figure out how to counter this growing level of burnout. Many recommendations focus on relieving stress, teaching mindfulness, or reducing workload—all of which treat burnout as an individual condition. But its link to loneliness suggests that greater human connection at work may also be key to solving the burnout problem. Leaders and managers can play a key role in helping people feel less lonely and, therefore, less burned out at work by promoting a workplace of empathy and inclusion, encouraging employees to build networks that can provide emotional support, celebrating collective success that fosters a sense of belonging, and listening to ideas and feedback they receive from their employees.[159] The United Kingdom has already recognized their own citizens' loneliness and has appointed an official position—Minister of Loneliness—to confront it and establish policies surrounding the issue.[160]

For most Americans, the workplace is much more than just a place you go to earn a paycheck. It's an important part of many people's social lives, especially for those who are unmarried and don't have families or children at home. The workplace is a key place to meet friends. Most people spend eight or more hours a day at their place of work—a third of their lives on any given workday—and they spend more time interacting with coworkers than with their spouses or kids. But there are many aspects of the modern workplace that discourage, rather than encourage, social interaction.

Maybe it's because of the physical way offices are often set up, with people working in walled-off cubicles. Maybe it's because more people are working remotely or from home. Maybe it's because people like to surf their mobile phones and tablets on their breaks instead of chatting with coworkers at the water cooler like we used to. There are many reasons people feel isolated at work, but more important is the issue of how to fix it.

Here are six ways employers, CEOs, human resources folks, and others in leadership positions at work can help alleviate workplace loneliness:

1. Provide a pleasant physical space at work for employees to eat lunch, get coffee, or share breaks together. You can't force people to eat in your office break room, but if you set up a nice space that is decorated with green plants and artwork and has a clean fridge and microwave, I'm betting that's where people will congregate. Bring in a high-quality food truck a few days a week and watch the social interaction explode.

2. Offer team-building exercises that get workers together on a monthly basis to brainstorm, catch up, and share

what they have been working on. Ask HR to set up a format whereby everyone can share ideas with coworkers, in writing. "Escape Rooms" continue to increase in popularity around the globe and can be used as an off-site team-building exercise. These rooms are also great for family bonding—two of our grandchildren and their parents have participated in these joint puzzle-solving sessions in Berlin, Prague, Munich, and most recently in Thousand Oaks, California, where my wife and I joined them at Nodus805 in January 2018.

3. Bring remote workers together by starting an activity on social media that they can participate in, such as a fitness challenge or a game with prizes.

4. Organize social events for workers after work, such as a pizza party, ice cream social, holiday potluck, hot dog barbecue, jogging club, or museum excursion. Start a Secret Santa gift exchange at the holidays.

5. Encourage coworkers to help one another or to help people in need in the community, maybe by volunteering to assist lonely seniors or to mentor teens. "Giving and receiving help freely is one of the most tangible ways we experience our connections with each other," Murthy said in his article.

6. Celebrate job successes together. Each time an employee lands a new contract, signs up a new client, sells another vehicle, or reaches a significant achievement in the office, acknowledge the worker's success in a public way company-wide. Recognition can be done with a shout-out during a department meeting or a notice in the company newsletter.

Even Mother Teresa commented on the hurt that loneliness can bring to society, saying, "Loneliness and the feeling of being unwanted is the most terrible poverty." Taking steps to bring people together not only benefits individuals, it also benefits the company by virtue of reducing sick time, increasing team bonding, building commitment to the job, and fostering the exchange of creative ideas, among other things. This is a situation that is beneficial for all involved!

The Gift of Loyalty

When great teams and organizations work together toward win-win solutions, they engender another powerful competitive advantage: loyalty to each other and the company that supports them.

> When great teams and organizations work together toward win-win solutions, they engender another powerful competitive advantage: loyalty to each other and the company that supports them.

Great leaders know that loyalty directly affects behavior. In the business world, we see evidence of this every day. Employees who are loyal are the most likely to execute the company's strategy, go the extra mile to please a customer, and trust their employer in time of crisis. Historically, in fact, a loyal person stays with the object of their loyalty, such as an employer, even when it may be disadvantageous to do so. "All teams as well as organizations hang together or fall apart because of loyalty," says author and speaker Tom Krause. "Loyalty, trust, and commitment are truly the glue that holds relationships together."[161]

Loyalty is something that most people inherently want to give if presented with the right environment, motivation, and inspiration. Of course, today's definition of loyalty has changed dramatically and no longer describes only those committed to a lifetime of service to one organization. Today's yardstick of loyalty is the *quality* of service, not the *duration*.

Employees now consider themselves loyal if they do excellent work, treat their company with respect, and leave the company in good stead. Under this new rubric, longevity is no longer a necessary bedmate of loyalty, meaning that leaders must now find new ways of quantifying just what makes an employee loyal.

Today's leaders must adapt to this new definition of loyalty. They must throw away their tidy assumptions and certainties about loyalty and instead realize that loyalty, as the cliché goes, starts at the top. And, importantly, they need to realize that loyalty, like trust, must be earned. Here's how:

1. Understand that trust is a prerequisite for loyalty, making it essential that successful leaders practice three key elements of trust: integrity, honesty, and promise-keeping.
2. Exhibit leadership by solving problems, being a calming influence in troubling times, and having the courage to make and stand by tough decisions. Leadership also means being fair, consistent, and transparent. The days of secret handshakes are over.
3. Show genuine care and concern for workers. Treat every employee as an individual and look for ways to demon-

strate your caring at every opportunity. Forget the old employee rules and look for new ones. Consider adopting flextime, child care, telecommuting, in-house gyms, and concierge service. In short, find ways to tune in to employees' needs.

4. Show appreciation for employees' ideas and input. Promote debate and be willing to listen attentively.

5. Invest in your employees' future by providing development, training, and opportunities for advancement, ideally within the company, even if that means a future star in your company decides to pursue greater opportunities elsewhere.

6. Have the right values and hammer them home every day through words and deeds.

7. Understand that loyalty is a sentiment, but acknowledge that it is often rationally motivated as well. Appeal to employees on both levels.

8. Be fair.

Too Much Loyalty

While loyalty is a virtue in many cases, sometimes extreme loyalty does great harm, especially when it clouds good judgment. In his book *Police Unbound*, former Minneapolis police chief Anthony Bouza describes the damage and injustice caused by the unspoken agreement among police officers not to report wrongdoing committed by one of their own.[162] Those who follow this "blue code of silence" believe they are being loyal to the force, but as Bouza points out, such loyalty is misplaced, and those involved should instead be bound to a higher loyalty: to the public they have sworn to serve and protect.

Perhaps nowhere is loyalty more fundamental than in the military, where faithful performance of your duties—even to the point of giving your life—is an expectation. However, even in that context, loyalty has its limits. The Holocaust Museum in Washington, D.C., is a required destination for those attending the United States Naval Academy. Midshipmen are given this experience so they may see firsthand the results of misplaced loyalty and blind obedience. According to the museum's website, "The Museum's programs and resources for military personnel encourage reflection and discussion on leadership, decision making, and genocide prevention. Through examination of the Holocaust and in particular the German military, military members gain fresh insight into their own professional and individual responsibilities and explore ways in which they can work to prevent mass atrocities today."[163] Topics of the program include critical factors that influence ethical decision making and command responsibility in complex environments, changing cultural and professional contexts influencing military operations, and the dynamics of genocide and mass atrocities.[164]

The lessons here are clear: loyalty is an attribute laced with nuance, and there are not always easy answers as to where it lies, how it is earned, and how it is kept. However, the ability to build loyalty is an essential component of good leadership.

Key Concepts

> The Five Ws of a winning team include a *winning mentality* based on passion for the mission that goes the extra mile; a congenial and cooperative group that gets along and shares ideas naturally, that is, they *wear well*; a team that is *weather resistant*, meaning they overcome obstacles and are not easily deterred; team members who actively look for a *window of opportunity* in which to take action and are not risk adverse; and members who exhibit *worthiness*, that is, are people of integrity, self-control, probity, and high moral principles.

> Traditional definitions of loyalty no longer apply. Today's team members see loyalty in terms of *quality* of service and psychological commitment, not length of employment.

> Blind loyalty to a leader can be just as destructive to an organization or a country as disloyalty and is a sure path to organizational failure and even tyranny.

"Think of yourself as an athlete. I guarantee you it will change the way you walk, the way you work, and the decisions you make about leadership, teamwork, and success."

—MARIAH BURTON NELSON

CHAPTER 10

Look to Sports for Models and Mentors

IN THIS CHAPTER

> **Leadership Lessons From Arnold Palmer**
> **The Courage of Jackie Robinson's Convictions**
> **Lessons for Millennials**
> **A Personal Connection to Sports**
> **Key Concepts**

INTRODUCTION

Here's a word association quiz that might surprise you. What do Walter Robb (former Whole Foods CEO), Meg Whitman (former Hewlett Packard CEO), Samuel Palmisano (former IBM CEO), Jeffrey Immelt (chairman and former CEO of General Electric), Brian Moynihan (Bank of America CEO and chairman), Brian Roberts (chairman and CEO of Comcast), Indra Nooyi (PepsiCo CEO and chairwoman), and Lynn Elsenhans (former Sunoco CEO and chairwoman) have in common?

OK, maybe a bit too easy given the context of this chapter. Yes, they were all once top-performing athletes![165]

- *Robb led the Stanford University soccer team.*
- *Whitman played lacrosse, tennis, and basketball when she was at Princeton. She was also on the swim team.*

- *Palmisano was a top offensive center for Johns Hopkins University's football team.*
- *Immelt played football at Dartmouth.*
- *Moynihan played football and rugby at Brown University.*
- *Roberts won a gold medal playing squash at the 2005 Olympics.*
- *Nooyi played cricket when she was in college.*
- *Elsenhans played on Rice University's first women's basketball team.*

Of course, it's not surprising that someone who excels in sports might also excel in business because the leadership skills learned on the football field or basketball court directly transfer to the C-suite. A widely quoted statistic from Fortune *magazine's annual Fortune 500 survey is that 95 percent of all Fortune 500 CEOs played some type of college sport.[166]*

Although it's hard to definitively verify that statistic, the notion that a significant, perhaps even overwhelming, percentage of C-suite executives took part in sports rings true. A 2013 Ernst & Young survey of 821 high-level executives found that upwards of 70 percent took part in sports activities. Interestingly, fully 90 percent of the women sampled in the Ernst & Young research said they had a competitive sports background.[167]

Here are five key leadership attributes offered by sports:[168]

Athletes...

1. *Know how to achieve goals and stay strong and focused no matter what*
2. *Are adaptable and not intimidated by striving to meet any metrics of success*
3. *Learn teamwork and what it means to work toward common goals*

4. *Understand the work mandated to get results and do what it takes to win*

5. *Are comfortable with the stress and pressure needed to achieve peak performance*

This chapter echoes these benefits and adds a few more to the list as it explains the many ways that sports participation enhances business enterprises and drives leaders to succeed.

Leadership Lessons From Arnold Palmer

Real leaders inspire; they don't demean and demand. Perhaps no one illustrated that character lesson better than the iconic golfer, the late Arnold Palmer.

In my book *Truth, Trust + Tenacity*, I cite Palmer as an outstanding example of a real leader. Palmer, who died in 2016 at the age of eighty-seven, was known for his aggressive golf swing, easy smile, matchless charisma, unstinting generosity, and high business acumen.[169]

Palmer the Businessman

During his fifty-two years playing on the PGA Tour and Champions Tour, Arnold Palmer took home about $3.6 million in prize money, but it was his smart endorsement and licensing deals, speaking and appearance fees, and golf course design work that really made him rich. When he died in 2016, he had spun his prize money into a career earnings total of about $875 million (or $1.3 billion on an inflation-adjusted basis, according to a *Forbes* magazine accounting of his earnings).[170]

Palmer's reputation as a good businessman is well deserved. After he won the 1954 U.S. Amateur at the Country Club of Detroit, he signed his first equipment endorsement deal with Wilson Sporting Goods. Soon, his picture accompanied advertisements for the company's Dyna-Weight irons. He won his first Masters in Augusta, Georgia, and twelve other major golfing events, using Wilson clubs. He eventually left Wilson and began marketing his own brand in 1963 when he formed the Arnold Palmer Golf Company. He continued to endorse equipment made by other companies through the mid-1990s.

Palmer signed with Callaway Golf in 2000 and kept that relationship the rest of his life, despite some controversy about the initial failure of the driver he endorsed to meet a technical standard enforced by United States Golf Association. Just a few years before his death, he was still playing golf, charming audiences, promoting his product and brand, and making money.[171] ∎

Palmer had an uncanny ability to relate to all people, regardless of their position. He understood the power of respect and civility. He appreciated his fans and treated them well, selflessly signing autographs for hours when asked. Palmer built such a large fan base that the press gave his fans a name: Arnie's Army.

Arnold Palmer never forgot his modest Pennsylvania roots or the discipline he learned through his enlistment in the United States Coast Guard. Nearly everyone loved and respected him—I confess I was one of them. I closely followed Palmer's career, first in the gallery when I was fresh out of the Navy and later as a PGA Tour marshal. When I met him, I, like countless others, felt like I was the most important person in his world.

His genuine humility and strength of character are relevant today, especially in the business community. Too many so-called business "leaders" don't lead. They boss. They demean. They disparage. They fail to motivate, and they lack personal integrity. Real leaders inspire rather than demand. They encourage risks without punishment for failure, and they treat everyone with dignity and respect, just as Arnold Palmer did with his fans and later with his business associates.

Too many so-called business "leaders" don't lead. They boss. Real leaders inspire rather than demand.

Here are three critical lessons we can learn from Palmer:

1. **Treat people decently, and you will be rewarded with appreciation, business, and loyalty.** Being successful in the sports world is a two-way street—just as it is in the business world. Treat people well, and they will return the favor. Palmer understood this more than anyone and became a role model for the right way to treat others. He showed great patience with his fans as he stopped to shake their hands, make eye contact, and sign autographs. He was never too busy to acknowledge the little guy who adored him. Palmer's fans appreciated this and, as a result, supported him throughout his career. It may be a cliché, but the golden rule is just as relevant today as it ever was.

2. **Remember your roots and appreciate them.** Even though Palmer was astonishingly successful and achieved wealth beyond his wildest dreams, he never forgot his roots. Though he won sixty-two PGA Tour events and seven major championships, and was the first pro golfer to break the million-dollar mark in earnings, he piloted his

own airplane to tournaments, a practice not common at the time. Thanks in part to his efforts to democratize the game, the majority of golf courses are public, and everyone is welcome.

3. **Inspire others through your personal acts.** Palmer was awarded the Presidential Medal of Freedom and the Congressional Gold Medal, America's highest civilian awards. His charity, the Arnie's Army Charitable Foundation, continues to provide financial support to organizations that help children, families, and important causes. A few years ago, my wife, Joan, and I toured the Arnold Palmer Hospital for Children in Orlando, a truly remarkable facility that we won't forget. Real leaders understand the importance of giving back to their employees and their communities.

Palmer may not go down in history as the planet's best golfer—that title may eventually be given to Tiger Woods, Jack Nicklaus, Jordan Spieth, Rory McIlroy, Dustin Johnson, or an emerging player as yet unknown. My guess is that Palmer would be okay with that. In fact, he would no doubt tell you it's more important to be remembered as one of the world's best citizens than its best golfer. As he once said, "Success in this game depends less on strength of body than strength of mind and character." Arnold Palmer certainly exuded both, on the links and in the boardroom.[172]

The Courage of Jackie Robinson's Convictions

Jackie Robinson, like Arnold Palmer, came from humble beginnings. He was the grandson of a slave and son of a sharecropper and became known as the athlete who broke the color barrier in Major League Baseball when the Brooklyn Dodgers put him on the field at first base on April 15, 1947.

Robinson was a natural leader who, despite being confronted with racism and bigotry, understood the importance of working with others, being true to yourself, and balancing personal and professional commitments. Although it has been more than seventy years since Robinson's groundbreaking accomplishment, this athlete from a past generation can teach today's workers a thing or two about hitting a home run in the workplace:

> **Focus on results.** While racism and bigotry still exist today, they were worse in the United States of the 1940s. Robinson overcame the odds by focusing on results—scoring runs and winning games. Very few, if any, welcomed him as an equal when he joined the Dodgers, but he still succeeded because his fellow players couldn't argue with success. He was an MVP for six consecutive years and played in six World Series, including the Dodgers' 1955 championship game. Eventually, his focus on results enabled him to break records and barriers.

> **Accept challenges.** Robinson knew he was changing the game; while he could have stayed in the Negro League, he made the bold move to the majors. He wasn't afraid of taking chances and accepted the challenges that faced him. Robinson was ridiculed, even physically abused, by players from other teams. However, other players from both the Dodgers and competing teams eventually spoke up and defended him. Because Robinson received support,

he overcame the challenges confronting him, leading to the success of the entire team. It's important to accept challenges and look for support mechanisms to help you meet those challenges. It's also crucial to confront racism, sexism, or xenophobia when you see it, rather than look the other way.

> **Don't settle for less.** Jackie Robinson didn't stop when his baseball career ended. His commitment to lifelong learning and the entrepreneurial spirit led to many other firsts for him, including being the first African American to serve as a TV analyst for Major League Baseball, the first African American to serve as vice president of a major American corporation (Chock full o' Nuts), and the first black cofounder of a successful New York bank. Embrace curiosity and use it to move forward. Resist the temptation to settle for less (and complain), and instead channel your ideas into constructive change.

> **Balance work and life.** Robinson knew that having a life outside of work was essential. He had a dedicated support system in his wife, Rachel; she kept him grounded. It's easy to get caught up in work at the expense of life. Don't let that happen to you. Even if you are working long hours, be sure to find balance. Turn off your smartphone and have a real dialogue with a friend, spouse, or relative. You'll be surprised at how energizing true conversation can be. Studies have shown that a break from work improves productivity, proving that less can be more.

> **Support a community organization you care about, even if only for a few hours a month.** You will broaden your range

of friends, your horizons will be extended, and your work-life balance will be enhanced. To be in service to a cause larger than yourself is vital.

Robinson was much more than a celebrated athlete who crossed the color barrier in pro sports generations ago. He lives on as a symbol of the human spirit and a true leader. He never let fear shut his mouth or close his mind. He understood the importance of results, challenges, goals, and balance. Seven decades later, those lessons in leadership from this giant in baseball are still relevant to new generations.[173]

Lessons for Millennials

Millennials, whom generation demographers place as being born somewhere in the early 1980s to early 2000s, were the first generation to come of age during the digital revolution. They grew up in an expanding economy with few of the obvious challenges of earlier generations, such as economic upheaval, wars, and national strife. As a result, they are sometimes labeled as more narcissistic than other generations. Even if this self-centered assumption were true—and many would argue it is not—the great recession of 2009 may have served as this generation's "wake-up" call.

While the name Jackie Robinson is more familiar to baby boomers than to millennials, Robinson shared many traits with young people entering the workforce today: confidence, tolerance, and civic-mindedness. So, his legacy of leadership and courage has much to teach this generation and others that follow (the so-called Y and Z generations). Here are six Robinson-inspired leadership principles that strike me as particularly noteworthy for this group:[174]

1. **Excel.** Strive to do the very best job you can. Even if there is no welcome mat, keep your head down, focus on the requirements of your job, and eventually your associates will realize your efforts are helping the firm succeed and they will "come around."

2. **Be courageous.** Speak up when you see a wrong being committed in your workplace, such as bullying, discrimination, sexual harassment, fraud, or abuse. Turning a blind eye or a deaf ear is detrimental to all.

3. **Offer a helping hand.** Get to know your associates and learn everything you can about your company. When a coworker is struggling with a work issue, express a genuine willingness to help. With success comes the responsibility to advance your colleagues' and your organization's goals.

4. **Never stop learning.** Jackie Robinson acknowledged that his athletic skills were natural, but realized he had "to go to school" to learn about business once his baseball career had ended. His zest for learning, coupled with dedication, entrepreneurial spirit, and staunch backing from his wife, UCLA alumnus Rachel Isum, led to numerous ventures, many of which were "firsts" for African Americans.

5. **Champion change.** Every effective leader I've known has encouraged followers to try to improve the lives of others and to better the organizations of which they are a part. Resist the temptation to complain, and instead channel your creative energies to constructive ends. I learned early in life: "never bitch about a problem without pitching a solution."

6. **Make a difference.** To paraphrase President Harry Truman, history teaches us that our country wasn't built on fear but rather on courage, imagination, and an unbeatable determination.

A Personal Connection to Sports

When I was a kid, the Dodgers and the Giants still played in New York. To see a professional baseball game meant a trip from my home in Marysville, California, to Sacramento, where the Solons, who were part of the old Pacific Coast League, played. But the trips were well worth the ride because I gained much inspiration from watching the pro athletes of my era perform.[175] Some ended up "in the bigs" while others had previously been to "the show." Now that the Dodgers are in Los Angeles, attending a game is much easier for me, especially thanks to one of my best friends, Ross Goldberg. Ross is president of Kevin Ross Public Relations, a top notch Westlake Village firm and a longtime fan. He often asks me to accompany him to the stadium where we have a great time watching Dodger Blue.

Today, the Chavez Ravine canyon in the city of Los Angeles is home to the iconic Dodger Stadium, so my travel to see a game is a much shorter distance. Many highly accomplished baseball players, including former standouts Gary Matthews of the Phillies, Doug DeCinces of the Orioles, and Dwight Evans of the Red Sox, live in the region. Jackie Robinson, my childhood hero, grew up in nearby Pasadena. Having a personal connection to sports figures has always been important to me as a developing leader.

Growing up, one of the most inspirational figures to me personally was Pancho Segura, the famously bow-legged tennis player who rose from poverty in Ecuador to become one of the greatest pro tennis players of the '40s and '50s and later the coach of Jimmy Connors. Segura not only had to rise above the challenges of a physical condition caused by malnutrition, but he also had to teach himself how to play, rather than rely on coaches and pros. As he once said, "It doesn't take more than a racket and a heart to play this game. It's a great test of democracy in action. Me and you, man, in the arena. Just me and you, baby. Doesn't matter how much you have, or who your dad is, or if you went to Harvard or Yale, or whatever. Just me and you."[176]

As a self-taught tennis player myself, I identified strongly with Segura. I often found myself playing against kids who received lessons from tennis pros or who belonged to swim and tennis clubs or country clubs, which I did not. Playing against kids from privileged families made me want to win even more! It was my way of making a statement that you didn't have to come from any special background in order to succeed.

I carried that "badge" with me as a young man and probably still do. Segura helped shape my democratic philosophy of leadership, in which it's all about what you bring to the table today, not about what your pedigree is.

Sports are a powerful incubator for future leaders. If you don't believe me, just ask your boss.

Key Concepts

> ❯ Arnold Palmer was an athlete and a leader who displayed extraordinary strength of character. He stayed humble throughout his career and never forgot his roots. Beyond his abilities as a golfer, he was successful because he treated everyone with respect, never believed his own press, and inspired others with his generosity.

> ❯ Jackie Robinson was a natural leader who, despite being confronted with racism and bigotry, succeeded at balancing personal and professional commitments. He did so by focusing on results, accepting challenges, refusing to settle for less, living a balanced life, and serving others.

> ❯ Robinson's life is an inspiration to every generation, from the baby boomers to the Millennials and the following Z generation. The leadership principles exemplified by his life remain undiminished and stand as inspiration for today's emerging leaders.

~

"The challenge of leadership is to be strong, but not rude; be kind, but not weak; be bold, but not bully; be thoughtful, but not lazy; be humble, but not timid; be proud, but not arrogant; have humor, but without folly."

—JIM ROHN

CHAPTER 11

Conclusion

IN THIS CHAPTER

> **Are Leaders Born That Way?**

> **The DNA of True Leaders**

> **Today's Politics—The Upside**

> **How to Stay Ahead of the Curve**

> **The Take-Away Lessons**

Are Leaders Born That Way?

Vince Lombardi, the iconic football coach, once said that he thought leaders were not born with leadership abilities, but were made through "hard effort, which is the price all of us must pay to achieve any goal that is worthwhile." Lombardi is correct, at least in my estimation, but the question of whether leaders are born or made is still very much an open one among researchers and among other leaders.

In 2012, the Center for Creative Leadership (CCL) tackled this question, not so much to settle it but because the answer could have a profound impact on how an organization promotes, recruits, and develops its leaders. To answer the question, CCL surveyed 361 chief executives, operating officers, and company presidents as part of a CCL World Leadership Survey.

The respondents from fifty-three countries strongly supported Lombardi's views. More than 50 percent thought that leaders were made (52.9 percent). Only 19.1 percent thought leaders were born with the ability to lead, and 28.5 percent gave equal weight to innate talent and effort. While this is an interesting statistic, how these beliefs about the origins of leadership impact leadership style is even more significant. According to the report:

Understanding how top-level leaders believe people become leaders can help you to be more effective in how you work with those leaders and how you lead within the organization. If top managers think that leaders are more born than they are made, those executives may embrace a dominant and authority-focused approach to leadership. Asking for many opinions, deflecting authority, or seeking consensus may be interpreted as weak or ineffective leadership.

On the other hand, if you are working in an organization where C-suite executives believe that leaders are more made than they are born, those executives may believe that a more collaborative approach is most successful. Being dominant and focused on rules and formal leadership may be less effective with them. In both cases, being a person who is participative, team oriented, engaging and humane is likely to be viewed positively and contribute to your success as a leader.[177]

The DNA of True Leaders

I believe that leadership skills can be developed in the vast majority of people and that both new and experienced leaders can always learn how to advance their own skillsets. It is my hope that by providing the research I've collected and sharing my own leadership stories, you can feel as if you have the beginnings of a leadership roadmap.

Leadership skills can be developed in the
vast majority of people and both new and
experienced leaders can always learn
how to advance their own skillsets.

It's important to note, though, that the CCL study mentioned above does acknowledge the role of natural abilities, experience, and training as well in the development of leaders. As you might expect, those respondents who subscribed to the "born leader" point of view gave less weight to the importance of training and experience than those who thought leaders were "made." Still, to give at least some weight to the "born" side of the debate is valid, for some people, because of personality, preferences, or abilities, are not ideally suited for the role.

In any case, for those who wish to pursue a leadership role, I believe *Leadership CPR* is a helpful resource for your journey toward becoming an accomplished leader. The values-based leadership principles I've talked about in the preceding pages are essential guideposts in our hypercompetitive global marketplace. These values include pursuing human connection; balancing strength and decisiveness against compassion, empathy, and fairness; and developing the skills of consistent execution and an ability to "see around the corner."

Today's Politics—The Upside

I cannot predict as to how or when the virulent, destructive national political climate will end. I believe many more of our elected officials and captains of industry—and everyday citizens—must stand up.

At the time of writing this book, I saw this in the way first responders and ordinary citizens responded to the twin national disasters of the Thomas Fire and Hurricane Harvey. The Thomas Fire, which began on December 4, 2017, consumed nearly 290,000 acres of forest and brushlands in Ventura and Santa Barbara Counties along with hundreds of homes and businesses.[178] After these fires came devastating mudslides—with all the vegetation burned down, the rain had nothing in its path and it barreled through the counties. However, the rescue efforts have been astounding—rescuers have been tearing through mounds of mud, furniture, and fallen trees to search for those trapped.[179] Hurricane Harvey's disastrous route through the Gulf Coast states of Louisiana and Texas in August of 2017 flooded thousands of homes and put huge swaths of Houston, Texas, under water.

The core human decency and altruism demonstrated by first responders and ordinary citizens does give me hope for the future. Thousands of firefighters and police along with hundreds of volunteers and the coordinated efforts of other disaster relief organizations and governmental agencies such as the Red Cross and the Federal Emergency Management Agency (FEMA) stepped in to help in any way they could. The divisive politics of the day took a back seat to the more important work at hand of saving lives and helping people. It was nothing short of inspiring to see such revealed generosity of spirit.

While this book does highlight leadership and ethical failures of a number of political figures, such emphasis should not be viewed as thinly veiled political commentary. Rather, these comparisons were simply used as the most current and effective benchmark to separate productive leadership characteristics from those that are less so. Rather than provide made-up stories or case studies from unknown individuals, I've tried to use real examples to show how certain behaviors stack up against the model behaviors of the "possible" boss discussed in this book's introduction.

You should also not assume that all is doom and gloom or that an upside does not exist! Clearly, the issue of sexual harassment and assault has finally found a much overdue foothold in our national conversation. Participation and engagement in political institutions and the established structure's potential to drive change is on the upswing. The national conversation about the undoubtable contribution of our immigrant population has also been elevated. Positive changes in many our business schools are also happening as a direct response of national politics.

As reported in the *New York Times*, a growing number of educational institutions are focusing on ensuring that our future business leaders enter the workforce with a real appreciation of the ethical boundaries that must guide their behavior. The article notes that business schools around the country are upgrading their curriculums to include topics that are "ripped straight from the headlines." Pressure to include more social justice and ethics training is coming not only from students, but also from shareholders and other stakeholders that support these schools.

Prestigious schools such as Harvard, Stanford, Vanderbilt, Carnegie Mellon, Georgetown, UVA, and others now include courses on sexual harassment, the ethical conduct needed by leaders, and the importance of appreciating diversity, among other non-business topics. Business schools do not need to look far to see the consequences of leaders who ignore these important norms—for example, Wells Fargo's willingness to put profit over ethical behavior and Uber's seemingly shameless disregard towards sexual harassment claims in 2017.[180]

The Trump administration's stance on the Affordable Care Act and immigrants also has given us an opportunity to focus on these critical issues. Legendary newsperson Tom Brokaw recently highlighted the vital role that immigrants play both in our society and in our health care system.

In an opinion piece for the *New York Times*, Brokaw catalogs the many immigrant medical professionals who have treated his medical issues in recent years. He expertly notes the origins of many doctors who have treated him—Russia, Ecuador, China, Kazakhstan, India, Argentina, Pakistan, and Kenya—and reminds us just how much we all rely on their expertise and talents. "When the president's emissaries meet with Congress and the insurance and pharmaceutical industries to negotiate health care," Brokaw concludes, "our caregivers, in all their diverse and compassionate glory, should be there too."[181]

Again, I don't wish you to finish this book feeling as if we are spiraling into a dark abyss. Yes, the leitmotif of deceit and fabrication of facts seems endless in the top echelons of the executive branch, but fortunately, there are many members of the commentariat who are diligent in the pursuit of truth and who are standing up to the injustice.

Leon Panetta, who served as secretary of defense from 2010 to 2013, has penned an article reminding his readers that he, like almost every one of us, came from a family of immigrants and that's how the country was born. His call to action was to argue that it is important that the world knows that, "although he may be President, Donald Trump does not speak for the overwhelming majority of Americans. This is not who we are."[182]

U. S. Senator Jeff Flake (R-AZ) has stepped out and openly challenged the current treatment of the media, reminding us all that when we begin to distrust the news and stifle the voices and opinions of the free press, we run the risk of losing the very democracy our country was built on. Senator Flake has called on the administration to remember that these values aren't just heard in America but are heard worldwide, and are affecting how other countries treat their own press and journalists.[183] Tammy Duckworth, junior United States Senator for Illinois and retired U.S. Army Lieutenant Colonel, recently criticized Trump for calling Democrats "treasonous" after they did not applaud him at his 2018 State of the Union address. Tammy reminded us all that she (and others in the government) are not in their positions to serve as an on screen audience and clap on command, but rather, are there to, "...preserve, protect and defend the Constitution of the United States."[184]

And finally, Republican Senator John McCain has stepped in and voiced his concerns, noting that the work being done to undermine the press will continue to make it more difficult to hold governments accountable. He has called on Congress to commit to protecting freedom of the press, and defend the rights we all have to freedom of opinion and expression.[185]

It's not that these leaders look forward to speaking out against the president—I am positive it isn't a fun thing for them to do. TV commentator John McLaughlin explained it best when he said, "If you have a genuine conviction that the country is endangered, you can't help but speak out about it. No one from the intelligence community who speaks out about a president does it with joy or satisfaction. It's against the grain of the culture we've grown up with."[186] These are just some of the leaders out there who are stepping up to the plate, and it is these reactions that continue to give me hope. If these leaders continue to fight for our right to freedom of speech, and challenge the administration, it will hopefully remind us to continue to question certain decisions and actions and to stand up for our own rights, either at home or at work.

How to Stay Ahead of the Curve

I began playing baseball at about age four and switched to softball later in life. I loved it, so please pardon the metaphor.

Let me answer a question I've often been asked during my professional life: "What steps can I take to advance in my career?" While each of us is different from one another and no one response fits all, here is a short list of ten tips I find useful.

First and foremost, never lie, cheat, and steal to get ahead! Remember Mark Twain's words: "If you tell the truth, you don't have to remember anything."

> Make sure you excel in executing your current responsibilities before you jump at other opportunities. A CEO I reported to in my thirties told me, "If you exceed expectations, new opportunities will often present themselves." And they did.

> Be resourceful and know where to go to get answers. Learn how other departments and divisions in your organization work to increase your knowledge and constantly expand your network of advisers, associates, and friends. Your curiosity will pay important dividends if you carve out some time each week to do this.

> Keep your sense of humor and always remain positive. There are more than enough naysayers around; don't become one of them.

❭ Never be afraid to write handwritten notes of thanks to people who help you along your path to success. Personal notes of gratitude are much more meaningful than Instagram postings, Facebook messages, texts, e-mails, and more.

❭ Remember, larger organizations look for people who they believe can successfully handle positions of increasing responsibility; have budgets that have more impact on the firm's revenue, productivity, and market position; have larger spans of control; and will build bridges across and not walls around cross-functional teams.

❭ When you're offered a promotion you're genuinely interested in, check out your likely supervisor before you accept. While it's flattering to be recognized for past performance, the last person you want to report to in your quest for advancement is someone who is known "to put his or her associates in a box," that is, who limits their horizons or micromanages them.

❭ Never stop learning. As a naval reservist, I recall one promotion I received where the admiral reminded me that what I had accomplished was much less important than what I was now expected to achieve.

❭ Don't burn bridges! Avoid being one of those opportunists who consciously steps over or on others while climbing up the ladder to success.

❭ Keep it classy. Be honorable, honest, thoughtful, encouraging, and humble, and champion the underdog. Always look to ensure no one is left behind or marginalized. Don't be afraid to show your humanity, and always be kind and respectful to all.[187]

The Take-Away Lessons

Over the course of my career, I promise you that I have not been perfect in my leadership practice. I learned to accept the imperfection that comes with the desire to grow, and I have been fortunate to be surrounded by many wonderful and highly skilled people who have helped me all along the way. I believe you can learn only so much in a classroom setting and that real leadership growth comes from doing in the field, where you are exposed to a variety of increasingly challenging leadership experiences, including some in which you'll make mistakes. And I firmly believe the real leaders are those who make time to share their own leadership achievements and their failures with younger people anxious to make a difference in their world. After forty years of working in four industries, the very best executives I worked with developed roles as teachers, mentors, coaches, constructive critics, and yes, cheerleaders, for their staffs.

> The real leaders are those who make time
> to share their own leadership achievements
> and their failures with younger people
> anxious to make a difference in their world.

My purpose in writing this book is simply to pass on what I've learned about both leading and following others effectively. And one of the main ways I have sought to inspire and engage others is by showing clearly defined behavioral and ethical boundaries. These boundaries include:

> ❭ Unquestioned trustworthiness and integrity
> ❭ A celebration of diversity
> ❭ Respect, empathy, and compassion for others
> ❭ Taking responsibility for my decisions
> ❭ Never blaming others
> ❭ "Going to bat" for others
> ❭ Always working toward compromise and solutions from which all will benefit

These are the key principles that have guided my professional career, and they apply to every category of leader, whether they're heading a Fortune 500 company, a small nonprofit organization, a large governmental agency, or their local church group.

Of course, these principles have wider applications as well. You can employ them even if you don't consider yourself a leader at all because the fact is we all play both leader and follower in the various roles we assume in day-to-day life—within our family, within our community, within our groups of friends and coworkers, and even when interacting with strangers. As I said earlier, whenever you seize the opportunity to influence or guide someone toward a more successful, productive, and happy life, then you *are*, in that critical and perhaps life-changing moment, a TRUE leader. As Ralph Waldo Emerson famously said, "What lies behind us and what lies before us are tiny matters compared to what lies within us."

Good Luck and Happy Leading.

"A ship in port is safe, but that's not what ships are built for."

—GRACE HOPPER

A Contribution from Paul Grossgold

Followership is often a missing element from many leadership books. That's an unfortunate omission since leaders who have experience following others arrive at their leadership positions with key leadership attributes already highly developed, including humility, cooperation, collaboration, respect, and other competencies discussed in this book.

Paul Grossgold, retired navy captain and former director of the General Services Agency for the County of Ventura (California), argues that in the concepts of leadership and followership, we find two sides of the same coin.

What makes one person want to follow another's lead?

Why are some people able to garner wide support and inspire many to action and others aren't?

How, when we find ourselves in the role of counselor and advisor to senior leaders, can we find the moral courage and wisdom to serve them well?

To help answer these questions, I asked Paul to conduct a short analysis of three acknowledged military leaders, Generals James Mattis, John Kelly, and H. R. McMaster, as a closing statement to my book.

Mattis

In a recorded interview published on October 13, 2016, and available on YouTube, retired Marine General James Mattis recalled one night in combat when the enemy was attacking at one end of the compound. Where was the general at that moment? He was walking the perimeter at the opposite end of the compound. Asked by a baffled soldier why he was doing that, he answered that he feared the attack might be a feint, while the real attack might be coming from the other direction.

In this brief interchange between leader and follower, much is revealed. First, during the heat of battle, the soldier saw that his general was not ensconced in a command center, but rather patrolling the compound in full view and sharing risk with his troops. Second, the soldier felt comfortable enough to ask his general a question about what he was doing at that location. Mattis had clearly created a command atmosphere in which such inquiry was encouraged. Finally, in answering the soldier's question, Mattis was also taking advantage of a teaching moment. Not only did that soldier learn an important lesson, but also the lesson, no doubt, went viral when he shared the experience with his comrades.

Kelly

Unlike General Mattis's one-on-one encounter described above, the leader-follower equation often involves communication to many. Retired Marine General John Kelly often uses storytelling, among other tools, as a powerful way of trying to create unity of purpose and mission buy-in.

Few stories could be more effective than the one Kelly often tells of an incident that took place in Ramadi, Iraq, on April 22, 2008, while he was commander of all U.S. and Iraqi forces. Two young Marines were guarding the entrance gate of a barracks housing fifty Marines and a hundred Iraqi police. The general tells how these two men came from vastly different backgrounds, "but they were Marines, combat Marines, forged in the same crucible of Marine training, and because of this bond they were brothers as close, or closer, than if they were born of the same woman."

Their orders were simple: let no unauthorized personnel or vehicles pass. So, when a large truck approached at high speed, they stood their ground and opened fire before the truck exploded catastrophically, killing the two Marines instantly. The only eyewitnesses were Iraqi policemen, who had run to safety while the Marines did their duty. In an emotional statement, one of the Iraqis said, "Sir, in the name of God, no sane man would have stood there and done what they did. They saved us all."

General Kelly has told this story many times, to many different audiences, military and civilian. In doing so, he has captured and communicated the very essence of heroism—selfless sacrifice, commitment to duty, and devotion to country—and inspired thousands to follow the two Marines' example.

McMaster

In the leader-follower relationship, we most often think of the leader as the senior. On occasion, however, those roles must be reversed, and the junior must provide leadership to the senior. For the subordinate, such "leadership from below" can be fraught with risk and must be conducted carefully. The junior's leadership must come in the form of sound, well-reasoned advice, delivered convincingly yet respectfully.

In his 1979 book *Dereliction of Duty: Lyndon Johnson, Robert McNamara, the Joint Chiefs of Staff, and the Lies That Led to Vietnam*, then U.S. Army Major H. R. McMaster laid the blame for the disaster of the Vietnam War squarely at the feet of President Lyndon Johnson and severely condemned his military and civilian advisors for failing to provide proper counsel to the commander in chief.

Now, serving as national security advisor in the tumultuous Trump administration, Lieutenant General McMaster finds himself in the very role of the senior advisors he so harshly criticized in his book. In assessing his suitability for this position, a brief review of his Army career is instructive.

Despite outstanding combat credentials, McMaster was twice passed over for general officer rank, likely owing to his reputation as a maverick who was never afraid to speak truth to power. With help from General David Petraeus, however, he was finally promoted to Brigadier General, Major General, and, ultimately, Lieutenant General. To quote Lieutenant General Dave Barno, "H. R. is also the rarest of soldiers, one who has repeatedly bucked the system and survived to join its senior ranks."

McMaster's relationship with the president has not always been smooth, and the ultimate success of his tenure as national security adviser cannot yet be known. Owing to the moral courage he has demonstrated in the past, however, we can be certain that he is providing his president with his best and most unvarnished advice. (*Editor's Note:* Unfortunately, at the time of printing, McMaster has been fired from his post.)

•••

American combatant commanders enjoy great latitude in how they employ the forces provided. Tradition also dictates that senior military officers who serve in government roles provide their civilian leadership with their candid, honest and unvarnished opinions.

Some former senior military leaders express misgivings about their former colleagues serving in such posts for fear it can erode the vital trust between the American public and the military, and we have also seen prominent retired officers speaking critically of presidents, current and past.

What is the proper behavior, then, of retired senior officers when they disagree with their former civilian masters? While they certainly have the right to go public with their opposition—in keeping with the etiquette of the profession, this is not traditionally appreciated.

About the Author

Throughout his lifetime, Ritch K. Eich's reach has gone far beyond one community, industry, or state. As a business leader, author, tireless volunteer, and former military officer, Eich's approach to life can be summed up in these words: "Let's not rest on our laurels. Let's make things better for all."

Eich was born in San Francisco and raised in the Sacramento Valley's Gold Rush community of Marysville. He is a fourth-generation Californian who worked in the peach orchards of Yuba and Sutter Counties every summer from his teen years through college. While at Sacramento State College, Eich lettered in varsity tennis and was a member of the Far Western Conference championship team; he also served as vice president of the student body and was a member of Sigma Phi Epsilon fraternity and Blue Key National Men's Honorary, and he received the Associated Students Distinguished Service Award at graduation. With the Vietnam War raging during college, Eich enlisted in the U.S. Naval Reserve as a seaman recruit. He later rose steadily through the ranks and retired as a captain after serving more than twenty-eight years.

Eich received various commendations and medals, including a Meritorious Mast from the Commanding Officer of Marine Barracks while on duty at a major military brig, the Indiana National Guard Commendation Medal from the Adjutant General, the Military

Outstanding Volunteer Service Medal and the Navy's Meritorious Service Medal, among others. He served overseas at NATO South, the Joint Chiefs of Staff at the Pentagon, the Pacific and Atlantic Fleets, the Central Command, the Naval War College, and numerous other joint commands during his Naval Reserve career.

The U.S. Naval Academy recognized Eich for many years of service as a Blue and Gold Officer, recruiting outstanding young men and women to attend the Naval Academy in Annapolis. In addition, Eich served on the Service Academy Selection Committees for U.S. Senators Carl Levin and Dan Coats and Congressmen Dan Burton and Marvin Esch. He also enjoyed a successful civilian career in several industries including healthcare, public relations, and higher education. Eich's peers often recognized Eich for his work ethic, sound judgment, goodwill, experience, and savvy. He served as:

> Vice president, St. Joseph Mercy Hospital, Ann Arbor
> Senior vice president, Butterworth Hospital, Grand Rapids
> Associate director of hospitals, Indiana University Medical Center, Indianapolis
> Chief of public relations, Blue Shield of California Headquarters, San Francisco
> Chief of public affairs, Stanford University Medical Center, Palo Alto
> Vice president for marketing and communications, California Lutheran University, Thousand Oaks
> President and cofounder, Eich Associated, Thousand Oaks

Eich has served on more than a dozen boards of directors and trustees including founding board member of the Ronald McDonald House of West Michigan; founding board member of the USS

INDIANAPOLIS MEMORIAL (CA-35); University of Michigan Alumni Association Board; Journal, National Association of Hospital Development; VCEDA (Ventura County Economic Development Association); Strategic Health Care Marketing; *Journal of Values-Based Leadership*; Kingsmen Shakespeare Festival; Santa Barbara and Ventura Colleges of Law; among others. He has also chaired his regional hospital's board of trustees (Los Robles Hospital and Medical Center). Ritch is a graduate of Leadership San Francisco and Opportunity Indianapolis, two Chamber of Commerce–sponsored programs. He has been a member of two Rotary Clubs: Downtown Indianapolis and Downtown Ann Arbor.

Eich has also distinguished himself as an author and prolific writer. He has published three other books on leadership and has donated proceeds from the sale of his books to charities as follows: *Real Leaders Don't Boss* (Career Press, 2012), to nonprofit organizations caring for military men and women wounded in Iraq or Afghanistan; *Leadership Requires Extra Innings* (Second City Publishing, 2013), to the Jackie Robinson Foundation for minority scholarships; and *Truth, Trust + Tenacity* (Second City Publishing, 2015), to children's hospitals and the Ronald McDonald House.

Eich has also penned scores of articles on leadership and business that have appeared in many publications including:

> *Bloomberg Business*
> *Forbes*
> *CEO* magazine
> *Fast Company*
> *Investors Business Daily*
> *The Globe & Mail*
> Fox News

> *Leadership Excellence*
> *Directors & Boards*
> *Monster.com*
> The Naval Institute's *Proceedings*
> *Pacific Standard* magazine
> *Trusteeship* magazine
> *Stanford University Report*
> *Modern Healthcare*
> *Marine Corps Gazette*
> *Santa Barbara News Press*
> *Ventura County Star*
> *Pacific Coast Business Times*
> *Training* magazine
> *Communication Quarterly*
> *Journal of Values-Based Leadership*
> *Corp!* magazine
> *San Jose Mercury News*
> *The Hill*
> *Strategic Health Care Marketing*
> *CASE Currents*
> *Costco Connection*
> *Los Angeles Daily News*
> *Los Angeles Business Journal*
> *San Fernando Valley Business Journal*
> American Management Association publications

Despite a busy executive management career, Eich has made time to teach once a year as an adjunct professor. He has taught courses in organizational behavior, leadership, marketing, and strategic planning.

He has lectured at the University of Michigan; Eastern Michigan University; Indiana University-Purdue University, Indianapolis; and California Lutheran University. He is a firm believer that managers and executives learn much from regular interactions with university students.

Eich has always striven to improve every organization and community of which he has been part. As such, he has been integrally involved in or primarily responsible for several "firsts," including:

> The first multi-year corporate sponsorship executed between Blue Shield of California and the San Francisco Giants at AT&T Park (which has since been renewed several times). The focus of the first agreement was on programs to prevent domestic violence, a significant problem in sports and elsewhere.

> The first million-dollar endowed chair at the University of Michigan (the John G. Searle Pharmaceutics Professorship), through his role as director of the Pharmacy Advancement Program

> The first to set up a Corporate Leaders Breakfast/Speaker Series for Ventura, Santa Barbara, and Los Angeles Counties

> The first to create parity for California Lutheran University's men's and women's athletic teams' identity and logotypes (Kingsmen and Regals), bringing equality to campus athletics

> The first naval reservist to lend his fundraising expertise to the founding president of Washington, D.C.'s U.S. Navy Memorial to raise construction funds and an endowment.

Charity and giving back to the community have always been important to Eich and his wife, Joan. They have made several gifts to their alma maters: Sacramento State, Michigan State, and the University of Michigan, where Eich received his PhD. They established a scholarship program at Leadership San Francisco for applicants with financial need, and the Eichs were the first to establish a trustee scholarship at the University of California, Merced, where Ritch served as a founding trustee on the university's foundation board.

The Eichs have additionally volunteered for many civic organizations, including United Way, March of Dimes, Farm and Garden, Crossroads Rehabilitation, Boy Scouts and Girl Scouts, and many others. For the past two decades, they have served as volunteer marshals at more than a dozen major PGA Tour stops; the charitable proceeds from these golf tournaments benefit nonprofit organizations in many U.S. communities across several states.

Ritch and Joan, a former teacher and guidance counselor, live in southern California. They have two sons, Geoffrey and Edward (Ted), two daughters-in-law, Nancy and Mary, and four grandchildren. Geoff is an executive director at Amgen, Inc., and Nancy Sun, MD, is an emergency physician. Ted is an attorney with PricewaterhouseCoopers and Mary is a CPA with KPMG.

Author biography written by A. S. Bentley.

U.S. Senate Tribute to Ritch Eich, by Senators Dan Coats and Richard G. Lugar

http://capitolwords.org/date/1998/09/11/S10247_tribute-to-ritch-k-eich-upon-his-retirement-as-us-/

Volume 144, Number 120, pages s1024, senate, Fri, Sept. 11, 1998

Tribute to Ritch K. Eich
Upon His Retirement as U.S. Navy Representative to the Adjutant General, Indiana National Guard

Senator Dan Coats

Mr. President, on behalf of Senator Richard G. Lugar and myself, I am pleased to offer this tribute to Captain Ritch K. Eich, United States Naval Reserve. Captain Eich retires in September after 30 years as a reservist, the last three of which he spent on active duty, representing the Navy in the Office of the Adjutant General of the Indiana National Guard.

Ritch Eich has been a valued member of the Indiana team since 1989, when he started work for me as a member of my Service Academy Selection Committee, screening and recommending promising Hoosier high school students as candidates for our nation's Service Academies. Three years ago, he took on the additional responsibility of serving as the U.S. Navy's Liaison Officer for the State of Indiana, working in the office of Indiana's

Adjutant General. During that time, Ritch made substantial contributions to readiness planning in Indiana. He completed Disaster Preparedness Operations Plans for Indiana Naval, Marine Corps and Coast Guard facilities and ensured a close working relationship between the Indiana National Guard and the State Emergency Management Office.

Ritch Eich's civilian job during this period was as the chief marketing, public affairs and physician relations officer for Indiana University Medical Center, where, over the course of a decade, he has helped to build a vibrant and effective health care environment for Hoosiers. According to one health care executive, Ritch had helped "define our vision, map our strategies, deliver on our promises and guide our affiliations." And for Ritch, "helping Hoosiers access the best healthcare in the mid-west" was what it was all about.

In all his endeavors, Ritch Eich has demonstrated a skill and dedication that reflect great credit upon himself, the State of Indiana and the United States Navy. I feel privileged to offer this tribute to Ritch on the occasion of his retirement from the Naval Reserve. We wish him well. ∎

Quotes by Which
to Lead Your Life

Dear Reader,

As you've read my book, you've probably made note that each chapter has started with a quote.

It was difficult selecting just one quote to place before each section, but the goal was to find a quote from a well-known leader, a successful businessperson, or a respected individual that best fit with the contents of that particular section. In addition, I also did not want to repeat names.

With only eleven chapters, I was left with a number of quotes that still spoke to me in one important way or another.

I believe that remaining a constant student of leadership is one of the best ways you will achieve success. That is why I am constantly reading, researching, and talking at length with those around me about the important topics of trust, integrity, quality of service, climate, and respect. When you stop learning, you stop growing.

That being said, I'd like to use this part of the book to provide you with a list of powerful quotes (in addition to the ones inserted before each section) that only further support the importance of leading with all the values I've discussed in this book.

They are in no particular order below, but I do hope that some (if not all) of these make an impact in how you continue forward on your path to leadership.

"I've learned that people will forget what you said, people will forget what you did, but people will never forget how you made them feel."

—MAYA ANGELOU

"Honesty is the first chapter in the book of wisdom."

—THOMAS JEFFERSON

"If we have no peace, it is because we have forgotten that we belong to each other."

—MOTHER TERESA

"A leader...is like a shepherd. He stays behind the flock, letting the most nimble go out ahead, whereupon the others follow, not realizing that all along they are being directed from behind."

—NELSON MANDELA

"Excellence is a better teacher than mediocrity. The lessons of the ordinary are everywhere. Truly profound and original insights are to be found only in studying the exemplary."

—WARREN BENNIS

"Sometimes you win. Sometimes you lose. And sometimes it rains."

—BULL DURHAM

"Execution is a specific set of behaviors and techniques that companies need to master in order to have competitive advantage. It's a discipline of its own."

—RAM CHARAN and LARRY BOSSIDY, Execution

"Be more concerned with your character than with your reputation, because your character is what you really are, while your reputation is merely what others think you are."

—JOHN WOODEN

"Building a visionary company requires one percent vision and 99 percent alignment."

—JIM COLLINS and JERRY PORRAS, *Built to Last*

"Simplicity is the ultimate sophistication."

—LEONARDO DA VINCI

"The signs of outstanding leadership appear primarily among the followers."

—MAX DE PREE (1924–2017), former chairman of Herman Miller, Inc.

"Do I not destroy my enemies when I make them my friends?"

—ABRAHAM LINCOLN

"Pile up enough tomorrows and you'll find you've collected nothing but a lot of empty yesterdays."

—MEREDITH WILSON

"Few of us will have the greatness to bend history itself. But each of us can work to change a small portion of events. And in the total of those acts will be written the history of this generation."

 —ROBERT KENNEDY

"Power isn't control at all—power is strength, and giving that strength to others. A leader isn't someone who forces others to make him stronger; a leader is someone willing to give his strength to others that they may have the strength to stand on their own."

 —BETH REVIS

"If you're ridin' ahead of the herd, take a look back every now and then to make sure it's still there."

 —WILL ROGERS

"Few things can help an individual more than to place responsibility on him, and to let him know that you trust him."

 —BOOKER T. WASHINGTON

"Anyone can hold the helm when the sea is calm."

 —PUBLILIUS SYRUS

"Do, or do not. There is no try."

 —YODA

"The noblest art is that of making people happy."

 —P. T. BARNUM

"Effective leadership is not about making speeches or being liked. Leadership is defined by results not attributes."
—PETER DRUCKER

"One of the best tests of leadership is the ability to recognize a problem before it becomes an emergency."
—ARNOLD GLASOW

"You do not lead by hitting someone over the head—that's assault, not leadership."
—DWIGHT D. EISENHOWER

"The first responsibility of a leader is to define reality. The last is to say thank you. In between, the leader is a servant."
—MAX DEPREE

"Leadership is lifting a person's vision to higher sights, the raising of a person's performance to a higher standard, the building of a personality beyond its normal limitations."
—PETER DRUCKER

"Leadership is a potent combination of strategy and character. But if you must be without one, be without the strategy."
—NORMAN SCHWARZKOPF

"Never doubt that a small group of thoughtful committed citizens can change the world. Indeed, it is the only thing that ever has."
—MARGARET MEAD

"Leaders go first."
—JAMES KOUZES & BARRY POSNER

"To lead people, walk beside them."
—LAO-TSE

"Great leaders are almost always great simplifiers who can cut through argument, debate, and doubt to offer a solution everybody can understand."
—COLIN POWELL

"At the end of the day, you bet on people, not on strategies."
—LARRY BOSSIDY, retired CEO at Allied Signal, formerly at Honeywell and GE

"It's always hard until it's done."
—NELSON MANDELA

~

"The single best way a leader can learn and grow is through reading."

—JAMES STAVRIDIS

Ritch's Marysville Union High School Commencement Speech

When I began writing this book, I stumbled across a copy of my high school graduation speech. As I was reading it again, I realized that this message is still current. I hope you can read this and perhaps find some inspiration and/or direction as you continue to forge your own path!

AS INDIVIDUALS

NOW IS THE TIME OF YEAR WHEN MANY
YOUNG PEOPLE THROUGHOUT THE WORLD
PARTICIPATE IN COMMENCEMENT EXERCISES--
FROM HIGH SCHOOL,--COLLEGE-AND GRADUATE
SCHOOL. THE QUALITY OF THEIR FUTURE
LIVING DEPENDS UPON WHETHER THIS
GRADUATION ESTABLISHES A NEW BEGINNING
FOR THEM,-OR MARKS AN END OF SYSTEMATIC
DISCIPLINED CULTIVATION OF THE MIND.

EXACTLY WHAT WE INDIVIDUALS ARE,-AND
WHAT WE WILL BE,-DEPENDS MUCH ON OUR
OWN DETERMINATION TO LIVE BY THE
BELIEFS AND THE CODE OF HONOR SUPPORTED
BY OUR HOMES, CHURCHES, AND SCHOOLS.
THESE INSTITUTIONS CANNOT LIVE OUR LIVE
FOR US-NOR CAN THEY DECIDE HOW WE SHALL

<u>ACT</u> IN EACH SITUATION. EACH OF US (2)

MUST SOLVE HIS OWN PROBLEMS. *HER*

NOW IS THE TIME WHEN WE,-<u>AS INDIVID-</u>
<u>UALS</u>,- ARE ON <u>OUR</u> OWN, AND WHEN REAL
CHARACTER IS APPARENT. THIS CHARACTER
SHOWS IN THE DECISIONS WE MAKE AND THE
WAY IN WHICH WE FOLLOW THROUGH.

AS INDIVIDUALS,-AS GRADUATES,-WE
SHOULD BE <u>CREATIVE</u> AND <u>ACTIVE.</u> WE
PRESERVE OUR <u>INTEGRITY</u> BY BEING <u>RESPON-</u>
<u>SIBLE</u> FOR OUW ACTIONS. WE REACH OUR
GREATEST POINT OF ACHIEVEMENT BY
CO-OPERATING WITH OTHERS — FREEDOM
TO ACT RESPONSIBLY AS EXHIBITED BY
COMPETITION AND THROUGH CO-OPERATION
WITH OTHERS,-IS TRUE LIBERTY OF THE
INDIVIDUAL.

Slow down!!

(3)

LET US PAUSE FOR A MOMENT AND CONSIDER SOME OF THE FRONTIERS WHICH LIE BEFORE US. SCIENCE POSES MANY QUESTION MARKS. WHEREAS, WE HAVE MADE TREMENDOUS PROGRESS IN THE FIELD OF MEDICINE,-DREAD DISEASES STILL TAKE THEIR TOLL. WE HAVE MADE GREAT STRIDES IN THE FIELD OF COMMUNICATIONS-BUT THE POSSIBILITIES FOR EVEN GREATER ACHIEVE- MENTS ARE UNLIMITED. WE HAVEN'T SCRATCH ED THE SURFACE-OF WHAT MAY BE THE MOST IMPORTANT FRONTIER OF ALL- - SPACE!

OUR CONQUEST OF SPACE WILL AFFECT OUR VITAL DEFENSES, AND MAKE COMMUNICATION AMONG NATIONS MORE EFFECTIVE.

PARTICIPATION IN AFFAIRS OF OUR GOVERNMENT OFFERS A CHALLENGE* * * *

(4)

OUR LOCAL,-STATE,-AND NATIONAL GOVERN-
MENTS NEED YOUNG MEN AND YOUNG WOMEN
OF INTEGRITY-TO PLAY ACTIVE ROLES IN
MAKING AND ENFORCING OUR LAWS. THESE
OPPORTUNITIES ARE ONLY A FEW WHICH LIE
BEFORE THE ALERT AND INQUIRING MINDS OF
OUR GENERATION.

SIGNIFICANT AND HAPPY LIVES-GROW OUT
OF IDEALS-THAT GO BEYOND THE TRIVIAL AN
COMMONPLACE. THEY DEMAND OUR BEST
EFFORTS. JOY IN LIFE IS NOT AN ACCIDEN
IT IS THE END PRODUCT OF A CONSCIOUS XX
EFFORT TO PERFECT THE ART OF LIVING.
THE LINE OF LEAST RESISTANCE SOME-
TIMES SEEMS THE MOST DESIRABLE,-BUT THE
INDIVIDUAL WHO STRIVES TO CORRECT UN-
DESIRABLE CONDITIONS-AND WHO ACHIEVES

THE BEST OF WHICH HE IS CAPABLE--HAS

THE SATISFACTION OF--A JOB WELL DONE!

Bibliography

Alda, Alan. *If I Understood You, Would I Have This Look on My Face.* New York: Random House, 2017.

Amidon, Jim. "Leadership Starts With Integrity." *Wabash Magazine,* Summer/Fall 2003.

"Armed Forces: Zinging Zumwalt, U.S.N." *Time Magazine,* November 9, 1970.

Badaracco, Joseph L., Jr. *Leading Quietly.* Boston: Harvard Business School Press, 2002.

———. *Questions of Character.* Boston: Harvard Business School Press, 2006.

Baker, James A, III. *The Politics of Diplomacy.* New York: G. P. Putnam's Sons, 1995.

Baker, William F., and Michael O'Malley. *Leading With Kindness.* New York: AMACOM, 2008.

Balboni, John. *Lead With Purpose.* New York: AMACOM, 2012.

Barner, Robert. *Bench Strength.* New York: AMACOM, 2006.

Bennis, Warren. *Harvard Business Review on Developing Leaders.* Boston: Harvard Business School Press, 2004.

———. *On Becoming a Leader.* Reading, MA: Addison-Wesley, 1989.

Bennis, Warren, and Patricia Ward Biederman. *Organizing Genius.* Reading, MA: Addison-Wesley, 1997.

Bennis, Warren, and Burt Nanus. *Leaders*. New York: HarperCollins, 1985.

Bennis, Warren, and Robert J. Thomas. *Geeks and Geezers*. Boston: Harvard Business School Press, 2002.

Benton, D. A. *How to Think Like a CEO*. New York: Warner Books, 1996.

Bergman, Barrie. *Nice Guys Finish First*. Self-published, 2009.

Betof, Ed. "Leaders as Teachers." *T+D*, May 2004.

Blanchard, Ken, and Spencer Johnson, MD. *The One Minute Manager*. New York: William Morrow, 1981.

Bossidy, Larry, and Ram Charan. *Execution: The Discipline of Getting Things Done*. New York: Random House, 2002.

Bracey, Hyler. *Building Trust: How to Get It! How to Keep It!* Self-published, 2002.

Brinkley, Douglas. *Cronkite*. New York: HarperCollins, 2012.

Brokaw, Tom. *The Greatest Generation*. New York: Random House, 1998.

Brooks, David. *The Road to Character*. New York: Random House, 2015.

Bryant, Adam. "He Wants Subjects, Verbs and Objects." *New York Times*, April 26, 2009.

Brzezinski, Zbigniew. *Strategic Vision: America and the Crisis of Global Power*. New York: Basic Books, 2012.

Buffett, Warren. "Stop Coddling the Super Rich." *New York Times*, August 14, 2011.

Burrell, Brian. *The Words We Live By*. New York: Free Press, 1997.

Cannon, Jeff, and Jon Cannon. *Leadership Lessons of the Navy Seals*. New York: McGraw-Hill, 2003.

Carrick, Moe, and Cammie Dunaway. *Fit Matters: How to Love Your Job*. Palmyra, VA: Maven House Press, 2017.

Carroll, Stephen J., and Patrick C. Flood. *The Persuasive Leader: Lessons From the Arts*. San Francisco: Jossey-Bass, 2010.

Carter, Louis, David Giber, Marshall Goldsmith, Richard F. Beckhard, W. Warner Burke, Edward E. Lawler III, Beverly L. Kaye, Jay Alden Conger, and John Sullivan. *Best Practices in Organization Development and Change: Culture, Leadership, Retention, Performance, Coaching*. San Francisco: Jossey-Bass, 2001.

Carter, Louis, Marshall Goldsmith, and Warren G. Bennis. *Linkage Inc.'s Best Practices in Leadership Development Handbook: Case Studies, Instruments, Training*. San Francisco: Jossey-Bass, 2000.

Catmull, Ed. *Creativity, Inc.* New York: Random House, 2014.

Charan, Ram. *Leadership in the Era of Economic Uncertainty*. New York: McGraw-Hill, 2009.

Chernow, Ron. *Grant*. New York: Penguin Press, 2017.

Choudhury, Uttara. "Wharton's Leadership Program Is at the Heart of MBA Life." *Braingainmag.com*, July 16, 2011.

Cialdini, Robert. *Influence*. New York: William Morrow, 1984.

Ciampa, Dan. "Almost Ready." *Harvard Business Review*, January 1, 2005.

Coey, Nancy. *Finding Gifts in Everyday Life*. Raleigh, NC: Sweetwater Press, 1995.

Cohen, Adam. *Nothing to Fear*. New York: Penguin, 2009.

Cohen, Eli, and Noel Tichy. "How Leaders Develop Leaders." *Training & Development*, May 1997.

Collins, Jim. *Good to Great*. New York: HarperCollins, 2001.

———. *How the Mighty Fall*. New York: HarperCollins, 2009.

Conaty, Bill, and Ram Charan. *The Talent Masters*. New York: Crown Business, 2010.

Covey, Stephen M. R. *The Speed of Trust*. New York: Free Press, 2006.

Crockett, Roger O. "How P&G Finds and Keeps a Prized Workforce." *BusinessWeek*, April 9, 2009.

Deal, Terrence E., and Allen A. Kennedy. *Corporate Cultures*. Reading, MA: Addison-Wesley, 1982.

DePree, Max. *Leadership Is an Art*. New York: Currency, 1989.

———. *Leadership Jazz*. New York: Currency, 1992.

DeVos, Rich. *Ten Powerful Phrases for Positive People*. New York: Center Street, 2008.

Drucker, Peter F. "The American CEO." *Wall Street Journal*, December 4, 2004.

———. *The Effective Executive*. New York: HarperCollins, 2002.

———. *Managing the Non-Profit Organization*. New York: Harper-Collins, 1990.

Eich, Ritch K., and William E. Wiethoff. "Toward a Model of Hierarchical Change: Admiral Elmo R. Zumwalt and Naval Innovation." *Communication Quarterly* 27, no. 1 (Winter, 1979): 29–37.

Eisner, Michael D., and Tony Swartz. *Work in Progress*. New York: Hyperion, 1998.

Ellis, Joseph. *American Sphinx: The Character of Thomas Jefferson*. New York: Random House, 1996.

Erskine, Carl. *What I Learned From Jackie Robinson*. New York: McGraw-Hill, 2005.

Erwin, Dan. "Why Is Defense Secretary Gates So Successful?" *Dan Erwin* (blog), February 9, 2010.

Farnham, Alan. *Forbes Great Success Stories*. New York: John Wiley & Sons, 2000.

Friedman, Thomas L. *Hot, Flat, and Crowded*. New York: Farrar, Straus and Giroux, 2008.

Fulmer, Robert M., and Marshall Goldsmith. *The Leadership Investment: How the World's Best Organizations Gain Strategic Advantage Through Leadership Development.* New York: AMACOM, 2001.

Gagne, Matt. "A Fine Vintage." *Sports Illustrated,* February 7, 2011.

Gates, Robert M. *Duty: Memoirs of a Secretary of War.* New York: Vintage Books, 2014.

———. *Duty: A Passion for Leadership: Lesson on Change and Reform From Fifty Years of Public Service.* New York: Vintage Books, 2017.

George, Bill. *True North.* San Francisco: Jossey-Bass, 2007.

Gerstner, Lewis V., Jr. *Who Says Elephants Can't Dance.* New York: HarperBusiness, 2002.

Gibbs, Nancy, and Michael Duffy. *The Presidents Club.* New York: Simon & Schuster, 2013.

Goethals, George R., Georgia J. Sorenson, and James MacGregor Burns. *Encyclopedia of Leadership,* Vols. 1–4. Thousand Oaks, CA: Sage, 2004.

Goldblatt, Joe Jeff. *Special Events: Best Practices in Modern Event Management.* New York: John Wiley & Sons, 1997.

Goldsmith, Marshall. *Succession: Are You Ready? (Memo to the CEO).* Boston: Harvard Business School Press, 2009.

———, John Baldoni, and Sarah McArthur. *The AMA Handbook of Leadership.* New York: AMACOM, 2010.

———, and Mark Reiter. *Triggers: Creating Behavior That Lasts— Becoming the Person You Want to Be.* New York: Crown Business, 2015.

Goodwin, Doris Kearns. *Team of Rivals.* New York: Simon & Schuster, 2005.

Gordon, Jon. *The Energy Bus: 10 Rules to Fuel your Life, Work, and Team With Positive Energy.* Hoboken, NJ: John Wiley & Sons, 2017.

Graham, Katharine. *Personal History.* New York: Alfred A. Knopf, 1997.

Grant, Adam. *Give and Take: Why Helping Others Drives Our Success.* New York: Penguin, 2014.

Greenfield, Jeff. *Then Everything Changed.* New York: G. P. Putnam's Sons, 2011.

Greenleaf, Robert K. *Servant Leadership.* Mahwah, NJ: Paulist Press, 1977.

Harari, Oren. *The Leadership Secrets of Colin Powell.* New York: McGraw-Hill, 2002.

Harth, Marjorie L. *Pomona College: Reflections on a Campus.* Claremont, CA: Pomona College, 2007.

Hartmann, Susan M. *The Other Feminists.* New Haven, CT: Yale University Press, 1998.

Harvard Business Review on Developing Leaders. Boston: Harvard Business School Press, 2004.

Hayden, Michael V. *Playing to the Edge: American Intelligence in the Age of Terror.* New York: Penguin, 2016.

Heath, Chip, and Dan Heath. *Made to Stick.* New York: Random House, 2007.

Heifetz, Ronald A. "Leadership in a (Permanent) Crisis." *Harvard Business Review,* July 2009.

———, Alexander Grashow, and Marty Linsky. *The Practice of Adaptive Leadership.* Boston: Harvard Business Press, 2009.

Hesselbein, Frances, Marshall Goldsmith, and Richard Beckhard. *The Leader of the Future.* San Francisco: Jossey-Bass, 1996.

Howard, Carole M., and Wilma K. Mathews. *On Deadline.* Prospect Heights, IL: Waveland Press, 2000.

Hoyle, Leonard H. *Event Marketing.* New York: John Wiley & Sons, 2002.

Hughes, John Emmet. *The Ordeal of Power: A Political Memoir of the*

Eisenhower Years. New York: Atheneum, 1963.

Iacocca, Lee. *Where Have All the Leaders Gone?* New York: Scribner, 2007.

Issacson, Walter. *Steve Jobs*. New York: Simon and Shuster, 2011.

Johnson, W. Brad, and David Smith. Athena Rising: How and Why Men Should Mentor Women. New York: Bibliomotion, Inc., 2016.

Kelleher, Herb. "Business of Business Is People." YouTube video, October 14, 2008.

Kelling, George L., and James Wilson. "Broken Windows: The Police and Neighborhood Safety." *The Atlantic*, March 1982.

Kennedy, Caroline. *Profiles in Courage for Our Time*. New York: Hyperion, 2002.

Kennedy, Edward M. *True Compass*. New York: Twelve, 2009.

Kethledge, Raymond, and Michael S. Erwin. *Lead Yourself: Inspiring Leadership Through Solitude*. New York: Bloomsbury, 2017.

Knowledge@Wharton. "A Bias Against 'Quirky'? Why Creative People Can Lose Out on Leadership Positions." *Leadership and Change*, February 16, 2011. http://knowledge.wharton.upenn.edu/article. cfm?articleid=2713.

Komisarjevsky, Chris. *The Power of Reputation*. New York: AMACOM, 2012.

Kotter, John P. *A Force for Change*. New York: Free Press, 1990.

———. *A Sense of Urgency*. Boston: Harvard Business Press, 2008.

Kouzes, James M., and Barry Z. Posner. *The Leadership Challenge*. San Francisco: Jossey-Bass, 2007.

Lafley, A. G., and Ram Charan. *The Game-Changer*. New York: Crown Business, 2008.

Lamb, Brian, and Susan Swain. *Abraham Lincoln*. New York: Public Affairs (Perseus Books), 2008.

Lannon, Judie, and Merry Baskin. *A Master Class in Brand Planning:*

The Timeless Works of Stephen King. West Sussex, England: John Wiley & Sons, 2007.

Laymon, Rob, and Kate Campbell. "Learning to Lead, Marine Style." *Wharton Alumni Magazine,* Summer 2001.

Lowney, Chris. *Heroic Leadership.* Chicago: Loyola Press, 2003.

Lucas, James R. *The Passionate Organization.* New York: AMACOM, 1999.

Lutz, Bob. *Icons and Idiots.* New York: Portfolio/Penguin, 2013.

Machiavelli, Niccolo. *The Prince.* New York: Mentor Books, 1952.

Maxwell, John C. *The 17 Essential Qualities of a Team Leader.* Nashville, TN: Thomas Nelson, 2002.

———. *The 21 Indispensable Qualities of a Leader.* Nashville, TN: Thomas Nelson, 1999.

———. "Create a Winning Team." *Success Magazine,* May 3, 2011.

———. *No Limits: Blow the Cap Off Your Capacity.* New York: Hachette, 2017.

———. *Sometimes You Win, Sometimes You Learn.* New York: Center Street, 2013.

McCann, Greg. *Who Do You Think You Are? Aligning Your Character and Reputation.* DeLand, FL: McCann & Associates, 2012.

McCullough, David. *The Path Between the Seas.* New York: Simon and Schuster, 1977.

McGrath, Rita Gunther. *The End of Competitive Advantage.* Boston: Harvard Business Review Press, 2013.

McIlvaine, Andrew R. "GE Opens the Doors to Crotonville." *Human Resource Executive Online,* November 23, 2009.

Mellon, Liz. *Inside The Leader's Mind.* Harlow, England: Pearson, 2011.

Miroff, Nick. "In Latin America, John Kelly Trained for a Job Serving Trump." *Washington Post,* January 7, 2018.

"Nation: Humanizing the U.S. Military." *Time*, December 21, 1970.

Norwood, Stephen H., and Harold Brackman. "Going to Bat for Jackie Robinson: The Jewish Role in Breaking Baseball's Color Line." *Journal of Sports History*, Spring 1999.

O'Reilly, Charles A., III, and Jeffrey Pfeffer. *Hidden Value.* Boston: Harvard Business School Press, 2000.

Ornstein, Norman J. "Ted Kennedy: A Senate Giant, Partisan Hero and Legislative Master." *Roll Call,* May 21, 2008.

Pfeffer, Jeffrey. *What Were They Thinking?* Boston: Harvard Business School Press, 2007.

Pink, Daniel H. *Drive: The Surprising Truth About What Motivates Us.* New York: Riverhead Books, 2011.

Prahalad, C. K., Rosabeth Moss Kanter, and Lawrence H Summers (eds.). "In Search of Global Leaders." *Harvard Business Review on Leadership in a Changed World.* Boston: Harvard Business Review Press, 2004.

Reeves, Richard. *Infamy: The Shocking Story of the Japanese-American Internment in World War II.* New York: Henry Holt, 2015.

Reynolds, Cynthia Furlong. *Jiffy: A Family Tradition.* Chelsea, MI: Chelsea Milling, 2008.

Ricks, Thomas E. *The Generals: American Military Command From World War II to Today.* New York: Penguin, 2012.

Rucker, Philip. "Kennedy's 'Farm System' Now Wields Power." *Washington Post*, August 28, 2009.

Sandberg, Sheryl. *Lean In.* New York: Alfred A. Knopf, 2013.

Schembechler, Bo, and John U. Bacon. *Bo's Lasting Lessons.* New York: Business Plus, 2007.

Schieffer, Bob. *Bob Schieffer's America.* New York: G. P. Putnam's Sons, 2008.

———. *This Just In.* New York: G. P. Putnam's Sons, 2003.

Seidman, Dov. *How: Why HOW We Do Anything Means Everything.* New York: John Wiley & Sons, Inc., 2007.

Senor, Dan, and Saul Singer. *Start-Up Nation: The Story of Israel's Economic Miracle.* New York: Hachette, 2009.

Slater, Robert. *Jack Welch and the G. E. Way.* New York: McGraw-Hill, 1999.

Smith, Bill, and Larry ten Harmsel. *Fred Meijer: Stories of His Life.* Grand Rapids, MI: William B. Eerdmans, 2009.

Sparks, Dennis. "Explain, Inspire, Lead: An interview With Noel Tichy." *National Staff Development Council*, Spring 2005.

Stavridis, James G. *The Accidental Admiral: A Sailor Takes Command at NATO.* Annapolis, MD: Naval Institute Press, 2014.

Stavridis, Adm. James, and R. Manning Ancell. *The Leader's Bookshelf.* Annapolis, MD: Naval Institute Press, 2017.

Sutton, Robert I. *The No Asshole Rule.* New York: Warner Business Books, 2007.

———. *Good Boss, Bad Boss.* New York: Business Plus, 2010.

———. *Scaling Up Excellence With Huggy Rao.* New York: Crown Business, 2014.

Thomas, Helen. *Front Row at the White House.* New York: Scribner, 1999.

Tichy, Noel M. "GE's Crotonville: A Staging Ground for Corporate Revolution." *The Academy of Management EXECUTIVE* III, no. 2 (1989).

———, and Warren G. Bennis. *Judgment: How Winning Leaders Make Great Calls.* New York: Portfolio, 2007.

———, and Eli Cohen. *The Leadership Engine.* New York: Collins Business Essentials, 2007.

———, and Andrew R. McGill. *The Ethical Challenge.* San Francisco: Jossey-Bass, 2003.

Vance, J. D. *Hillbilly Elegy: A Memoir of a Family and Culture in Crisis.* New York: HarperCollins, 2016.

Vogel, Steve. "Saluting the Admiral Who Steered the Navy." *Washington Post,* January 11, 2000.

Walsh, Bill, Steve Jamison, and Craig Walsh. *The Score Takes Care of Itself.* New York: Portfolio, 2009.

Weick, Karl E. "Small Wins: Redefining the Scale of Social Problems." *American Psychologist,* January 1984.

———, and Kathleen M. Sutcliffe. *Managing the Unexpected.* San Francisco: Jossey-Bass, 2001.

Welch, Jack. *Winning.* New York: HarperCollins, 2005.

———, and Suzy Welch. "Emotional Mismanagement." *BusinessWeek,* July 16, 2008.

Wharton, Clifton R., Jr. "Reflections on Leadership, Diversity and Human Capital." Speech delivered at the American Agricultural Economic Association Annual Meeting, July 26, 2005.

Whitaker, Catherine J. *A Tradition of Mercy: The History of St. Joseph Mercy and Mercywood Hospitals, Ann Arbor, Michigan, 1911–1979.* Ann Arbor, MI: Catherine McAuley Health Center, 1983.

Wilson, George C. *Super Carrier.* New York: Macmillan, 1986.

Woodall, Marian K. *Thinking on Your Feet.* Bend, OR: PBC, 1996.

Wooden, John, and Steve Jamison. *Wooden: A Lifetime of Observations and Reflections On and Off the Court.* Chicago: Contemporary Books, 1997.

Woodward, Bob. *State of Denial.* New York: Simon & Schuster, 2006.

Zehnder, Egon. "Interview With General Colin Powell." *The Focus Magazine,* May 2006.

Zenger, John H., and Joseph Folkman. *The Extraordinary Leader.* New York: McGraw-Hill, 2002.

Endnotes

Note to My Readers

[1] Eich, Ritch K. *Real leaders Don't Boss: Inspire, Motivate, and Earn Respect From Employees and Watch Your Organization Soar.* Pompton Plains, NJ: Career Press, 2012.; Eich, Ritch K. *Leadership Requires Extra Innings: Lessons on Leading from a Life in the Trenches.* New York, NY: Second City Publishing, 2013.; Eich, Ritch K. *Truth, Trust + Tenacity: How Ordinary People Become Extraordinary Leaders.* Madison, WI: Second City Publishing, 2015.

[2] Miller, Jake. "What traits and attributes make an effective president?" Face the Nation. November 03, 2016. Accessed August 28, 2017. https://www.cbsnews.com/news/what-traits-and-attributes-make-an-effective-president-election-2016/.

[3] Jargon, Julie, and David Benoit. "How a Shareholder Coup at Olive Garden's Owner Sparked a Turnaround." Markets. The Wall Street Journal. April 05, 2016. Accessed August 14, 2017. https://www.wsj.com/articles/activists-reap-olive-garden-bounty-1459902161.

[4] Christensen, Clayton M. *The Innovator's Dilemma: When New Technologies Cause Great Firms to Fail.* Cambridge, MA: Harvard Business Review Press, 2016.

[5] A World in Disarray: American Foreign Policy and the Crisis of the Old Order, Richard Haass, New York, NY. Penguin Press, 2018.

[6] Dickerson, John. "Donald Trump is an Impossible Boss." *Atlantic Magazine*, June 08, 2017.

[7] Eich, Ritch K. "Here's a wish list for leadership in 2017." Guest Commentary. Pacific Coast Business Times. January 14, 2017. Accessed August 30, 2017. https://www.pacbiztimes.com/2017/01/13/heres-a-wish-list-for-leadership-in-2017/.

[8] Eich, Ritch K. "Being In Charge Doesn't Make You A Leader." Leadership, IndustryWeek. April 18, 2017. Accessed December 30, 2017. http://www.industryweek.com/leadership/being-charge-doesn-t-make-you-leader.

[9] Jacobson, Louis. "Trump and pardoning Arpaio; a look at the pardon process." PolitiFact. August 22, 2017. Accessed January 15, 2018. http://www.politifact.com/truth-o-meter/article/2017/aug/22/trump-says-considering-pardoning-arpaio/.

[10] Cornwell, Paige. "Mercer Island student newspaper lands interview with U.S. Defense Secretary Mattis." Education. The Seattle Times. July 11, 2017. Accessed August 21, 2017. http://www.seattletimes.com/education-lab/mercer-island-student-newspaper-lands-interview-with-us-defense-secretary-mattis/.

Chapter 1 – Lead With Values

[11] Eich, Ritch K. *Real leaders Don't Boss: Inspire, Motivate, and Earn Respect From Employees and Watch Your Organization Soar.* Pompton Plains, NJ: Career Press, 2012.

[12] Miller, Jake. "What traits and attributes make an effective president?" Face the Nation. November 03, 2016. Accessed August 28, 2017. https://www.cbsnews.com/news/what-traits-and-attributes-make-an-effective-president-election-2016/.

[13] Budhos, Marina. "Donald Trump's childhood in Queens can explain his obsession with borders." Insider-Outsider. Quartz. October 20, 2016. Accessed January 24, 2018. https://qz.com/814851/donald-trumps-childhood-in-queens-can-explain-his-obsession-with-borders/.

[14] Baker, Peter, Michael S. Schmidt, and Maggie Haberman. "Citing Recusal, Trump Says He Wouldn't Have Hired Sessions." Politics. The *New York Times*. July 19, 2017. Accessed December 15, 2017. https://www.nytimes.com/2017/07/19/us/politics/trump-interview-sessions-russia.html.

[15] Shear, Michael D., and Maggie Haberman. "Trump Defends Initial Remarks on Charlottesville; Again Blames 'Both Sides'." The *New York Times*. August 15, 2017. Accessed January 24, 2018. https://www.nytimes.com/2017/08/15/us/politics/trump-press-conference-charlottesville.html.

[16] Feser, Claudio, Fernanda Mayol, and Ramesh Srinivasan. "Decoding leadership: What really matters." McKinsey Quarterly. January 2015. Accessed August 21, 2017. http://www.mckinsey.com/global-themes/leadership/decoding-leadership-what-really-matters.

[17] Eich, Ritch K. "Being In Charge Doesn't Make You A Leader." Leadership. IndustryWeek. April 18, 2017. Accessed December 30, 2017. http://www.industryweek.com/leadership/being-charge-doesn-t-make-you-leader.

[18] Eich, Ritch K. *Truth, Trust + Tenacity: How Ordinary People Become Extraordinary Leaders*. Madison, WI: Second City Publishing, 2015.

[19] Eich, Ritch K., and Michael D. Bradbury. "Help wanted: Leaders who will actually lead." The Hill. January 22, 2016. Accessed

December 30, 2017. http://thehill.com/blogs/congress-blog/politics/266602-help-wanted-leaders-who-will-actually-lead.

[20] Eich, Ritch K. "Here's a wish list for leadership in 2017." Guest Commentary. Pacific Coast Business Times. January 14, 2017. Accessed August 30, 2017. https://www.pacbiztimes.com/2017/01/13/heres-a-wish-list-for-leadership-in-2017/.

[21] Albright, Madeleine K. "Opinion | The national security emergency we're not talking about." Opinion. The *Washington Post*. November 29, 2017. Accessed December 15, 2017. https://www.washingtonpost.com/opinions/the-national-security-emergency-were-not-talking-about/2017/11/29/9fddd7ba-d53b-11e7-a986-d0a9770d9a3e_story.html?tid=ss_mail&utm_term=.2af228cba610.

[22] https://www.census.gov/prod/cen2010/briefs/c2010br-03.pdf.

[23] The Lugar Center. Accessed December 15, 2017. http://www.thelugarcenter.org/about.html.

[24] Hunt, Albert R. "Some Blessings in a Bad Year." The Wall Street Journal, December 27, 2001.

Chapter 2 – Show Compassion and Respect for All

[25] Eich, Ritch K. *Real leaders Don't Boss: Inspire, Motivate, and Earn Respect From Employees and Watch Your Organization Soar*. Pompton Plains, NJ: Career Press, 2012.

[26] Kiely, Eugene, and Robert Farley. "Trump vs. Comey." Articles. FactCheck.org. May 17, 2017. Accessed January 24, 2018. https://www.factcheck.org/2017/05/trump-vs-comey/.

[27] Stracqualursi, Veronica, and Tom Liddy. "Comey gave Trump assurances about investigation, but questions

remain." ABC News. June 8, 2017. Accessed January 24, 2018. http://abcnews.go.com/Politics/comey-testify-trump-asked-loyalty-drop-flynn-investigation/story?id=47893899.

28 Age and Sex Composition: 2010. May 2011. Accessed August 30, 2017. https://www.census.gov/prod/cen2010/briefs/c2010br-03.pdf.

29 Zarya, Valentina. "The Percentage of Female CEOs in the Fortune 500 Drops to 4%." Fortune. Accessed August 30, 2017. http://fortune.com/2016/06/06/women-ceos-fortune-500-2016/.

30 Linda-Eling Lee, Ric Marshall, Damion Rallis, and Matt Moscardi. "Women on Boards: Global Trends in Gender Diversity on Corporate Boards (MSCI, November 2015): p. 3 (Data from MSCI global director reference universe)." Accessed December 14, 2017. https://www.msci.com/documents/10199/04b6f646-d638-4878-9c61-4eb91748a82b.

31 "Fortune 500 Executive Officer Positions Held By Women." Catalyst. December 10, 2013. Accessed August 30, 2017. http://www.catalyst.org/knowledge/fortune-500-executive-officer-positions-held-women.

32 "Chapter 1: Women in Leadership." Pew Research Center's Social & Demographic Trends Project. January 14, 2015. Accessed August 30, 2017. http://www.pewsocialtrends.org/2015/01/14/chapter-1-women-in-leadership/.

33 Ibid.

34 Quackenbush, Casey. "The World Health Organization Just Picked Its New Leaders. Most of Them Are Women." World. Time Magazine. October 04, 2017. Accessed August 30, 2017. http://time.com/4968413/world-health-organization-women-leadership/.

35 Eich, Ritch K. "Women deserving of more respect in the workplace." Pacific Coast Business. June 16, 2017. Accessed December 29, 2017. https://www.pacbiztimes.com/2017/06/16/women-deserving-of-more-respect-in-the-workplace/.

36 Eich, Ritch K. "How Trainers Can Help Spot Sidelined Employees And Return Them To The Starting Lineup." Training Magazine. November 11, 2016. Accessed December 30, 2017. https://trainingmag.com/how-trainers-can-help-spot-sidelined-employees-and-return-them-starting-lineup.

37 Lang, Davison, and Kausik Rajgopal. "Working across many cultures at Western Union." Insights. McKinsey & Company. January 2018. Accessed January 27, 2018. https://www.mckinsey.com/industries/financial-services/our-insights/working-across-many-cultures-at-western-union?cid=other-eml-alt-mkq-mck-oth-1801&hlkid=ca59333ee5e348cea6aef43436c5707d&hctky=9396576&hdpid=fa77941b-81a0-43d6-a733-b251a39b52cb#0.

38 Adkins, Amy. "Employee Engagement in U.S. Stagnant in 2015." Gallup News. January 13, 2016. Accessed August 30, 2017. http://www.gallup.com/poll/188144/employee-engagement-stagnant-2015.aspx.

39 Steelcase Inc. "Engagement and the Global Workplace." *Engagement and the Global Workplace*, 2016, 1-12. Accessed August 30, 2017. http://cdn2.hubspot.net/hubfs/1822507/2016-WPR/Americas/Final_Executive_Summary_PDF.pdf?_hssc=130454992.1.1504120270786&_hstc=130454992.dacd90e00360f1d406e0e83ez91e06061.1504120270785.1504120270785.1504120270785.1&_hsfp=272369572&hsCtaTracking=66a4e-6be-c464-49a4-8a48-50ef3a9cb-d49%7C08ef6620-295c-45e8-9b38-dd8884bba72c.

40 Hakobyan, Margarita. "Are You Treating Your Employees Like

People Or Processes." Business. Huffington Post. December 21, 2016. Accessed August 30, 2017. https://www.huffingtonpost.com/margarita-hakobyan/are-you-treating-your-emp_b_8854416.html.

41 Eich, Ritch K. "Bringing Marginalized Employees Back Into The Fold." Engagement. IndustryWeek. May 23, 2016. Accessed December 30, 2017. http://www.industryweek.com/engagement/bringing-marginalized-employees-back-fold.

42 Eich, Ritch K. *Truth, Trust + Tenacity: How Ordinary People Become Extraordinary Leaders.* Madison, WI: Second City Publishing, 2015.

43 Eich, Ritch K. "The Real Cost of Rudeness." Leadership. IndustryWeek. September 01, 2016. Accessed December 30, 2017. http://www.industryweek.com/leadership/real-cost-rudeness.

44 Sherwin, Bob. "Why Women Are More Effective Leaders Than Men." Business Insider. January 24, 2014. Accessed August 30, 2017. http://www.businessinsider.com/study-women-are-better-leaders-2014-1/.

45 Mochari, Ilan. "The Leadership Qualities That Made Angela Merkel 'Time' Magazine's Person of the Year." Great Leaders. Inc. com. December 05, 2017. Accessed December 29, 2017. https://www.inc.com/ilan-mochari/time-person-of-year-angela-merkel.html.

46 News, CBS. "Face the Nation Transcript: November 26, 2017." CBS News. November 26, 2017. Accessed December 10, 2017. https://www.cbsnews.com/news/face-the-nation-transcript-november-26-2017.

47 Robb O'Hagan, Sarah. "Can Great Leaders Be Both Tough and Nurturing?" Forbes Woman/#LikeABoss. Forbes.

April 13, 2017. Accessed November 15, 2017. https://www.forbes.com/sites/forbes-summit-talks/2017/04/12/can-great-leaders-be-both-tough-and-nurturing/#71aac4e11c8e.

[48] Eich, Ritch, K. "Why Patience Is a Virtue in Leaders." Leadership. IndustryWeek. August 16, 2016. Accessed December 30, 2017. http://www.industryweek.com/leadership/why-patience-virtue-leaders.

[49] Eich, Ritch K. "How a personal touch stands out in the digital age." Leadership Lab. The Globe and Mail. February 18, 2015. Accessed March 25, 2017. https://www.theglobeandmail.com/report-on-business/careers/leadership-lab/why-a-personal-touch-stands-out-in-the-digital-age/article23024070/.

Chapter 3 – Reward Service

[50] Sloan, Tom. "Camp Pendleton has lead role in honoring President Reagan." Marine Corps Base Camp Pendleton. February 16, 2006. Accessed January 24, 2018. http://www.pendleton.marines.mil/News/News-Article-Display/Article/536100/camp-pendleton-has-lead-role-in-honoring-president-reagan/.

[51] Burgess, Rebecca. "Veterans in the 115th Congress." Veterans in the 115th Congress. November 18, 2016. Accessed August 30, 2017. http://www.aei.org/publication/veterans-in-the-115th-congress/.

[52] Bump, Philip. "Thirty-seven administration officials who've resigned or been fired under Trump." Politics: Analysis. The *Washington Post*. February 8, 2018. Accessed February 9, 2018. https://www.washingtonpost.com/news/politics/wp/2018/02/08/thirty-seven-administration-officials-whove-resigned-or-been-fired-under-trump/?utm_term=.3191ccdd41b8.

53 Eich, Ritch K. "Why Military Training Will Benefit the New Trump Administration." Leadership. IndustryWeek. January 11, 2017. Accessed December 30, 2017. http://www.industryweek.com/leadership/why-military-training-will-benefit-new-trump-administration?utm_test=redirect&utm_referrer.

54 Eich, Ritch K. *Leadership Requires Extra Innings: Lessons on Leading from a Life in the Trenches*. Chicago, IL: Second City Publishing, 2013.

55 Eich, Ritch K. *Truth, Trust + Tenacity: How Ordinary People Become Extraordinary Leaders*. Madison, WI: Second City Publishing, 2015.

56 Pophal-Grensing, Lin. "Cracking the Code on Military Resumes." Human Resource Executive Online. March 17, 2014. Accessed December 29, 2017. http://www.hreonline.com/HRE/view/story.jhtml?id=534356840&ss=ritch.

57 Eich, Ritch K. "The real reason to hire a veteran." Veterans. Fox News. March 04, 2016. Accessed December 27, 2017. http://www.foxnews.com/opinion/2016/03/04/real-reason-to-hire-veteran.html.

58 Senor, Dan, and Saul Singer. *Start-up Nation: The Story of Israel's Economic Miracle*. New York, NY: Hachett Book Group, 2011.

59 Ibid.

60 "Rambam Health Care Campus Underground Hospital." Verdict Designbuild. Accessed January 3, 2018. http://www.designbuildnetwork.com/projects/rambamhealthcarecamp/.

61 Segal, David, and Isabel Kershner. "'Nobody Thought It Would Come to This': Drug Maker Teva Faces a Crisis." Business Day.

The *New York Times*. December 27, 2017. Accessed December 29, 2017. https://www.nytimes.com/2017/12/27/business/teva-israel-layoffs.html.

[62] Chalabi, MonaChalabi. "What Percentage Of Americans Have Served In The Military?" Dear Mona. FiveThirtyEight. May 25, 2015. Accessed August 21, 2017. https://fivethirtyeight.com/datalab/what-percentage-of-americans-have-served-in-the-military/.

[63] Eich, Ritch K. "What Can American Business Leaders Learn from the Israelis?" Leadership. IndustryWeek. June 14, 2016. Accessed December 27, 2017. http://www.industryweek.com/leadership/what-can-american-business-leaders-learn-israelis.

[64] The Peace Corps. Accessed August 29, 2017. https://www.peacecorps.gov/about/history/founding-moment/.

[65] Swanbrow, Diane. "Empathy: College students don't have as much as they used to." Michigan News. May 27, 2010. Accessed August 21, 2017. http://ns.umich.edu/new/releases/7724-empathy-college-students-don-t-have-as-much-as-they-used-to.

[66] Eich, Ritch K. *Real Leaders Don't Boss: Inspire, Motivate, and Earn Respect from Employees and Watch Your Organization Soar.* Pompton Plains, NJ: Career Press, 2012.

[67] https://www.findagrave.com/cgi-bin/fg.cgi?page=gr&GRid=20677.

[68] Eich, Ritch K. "Candidates Can Learn From Zumwalt." Opinion. VC Star. September 24, 2016. Accessed December 29, 2017. http://www.vcstar.com/story/opinion/columnists/2016/09/24/ritch-eich-candidates-can-learn-zumwalt/90913328/.

Chapter 4 –Build a Better Board

[69] Langstaff, David H. "Rethinking 'Shareholder Value' and the Purpose of the Corporation."Llogg School of Management – Northwestern University, March 08, 2013, 1-12. doi:https://assets. aspeninstitute.org/content/uploads/files/content/upload/Tomor-row%27s%20Corporation-March%207%202013.pdf.

[70] Eich, Ritch K. *Leadership Requires Extra Innings: Lessons on Leading from a Life in the Trenches.* Chicago, IL: Second City Publishing, 2013. Page 102.

[71] Eich, Ritch K. "Tapping young expertise: Time for a new generation in hospital boardrooms." Hospitals. Modern Healthcare. July 4, 2011. Accessed December 27, 2017. http://www.modernhealthcare. com/article/20110704/MAGAZINE/307049990.

[72] Browning, Peter C., and William L. Sparks. *The Director's Manual: A Framework for Board Governance.* New York, NY: Wiley, 2016.

[73] "The CS Gender 3000: The Reward for Change." Credit Suisse. September 2016. Accessed August 31, 2017. http:// publications.credit-suisse.com/tasks/render/file/index. cfm?fileid=5A7755E1-EFDD-1973-A0B5C54AFF3FB0AE.

[74] "Women On Corporate Boards Globally." Catalyst. March 16, 2017. Accessed August 31, 2017. http://www.catalyst.org/ knowledge/women-corporate-boards-globally.

[75] "Women in the Boardroom." Deloitte. 2015. Accessed August 31, 2017. https://www2.deloitte.com/women-in-the-boardroom.

[76] "The CS Gender 3000: The Reward for Change." Credit Suisse. September 2016. Accessed August 31, 2017. http:// publications.credit-suisse.com/tasks/render/file/index. cfm?fileid=5A7755E1-EFDD-1973-A0B5C54AFF3FB0AE.

77 Lantry, Lauren. "Women in the Lead: One Milestone on the Path to Equity, Justice, and Inclusion." The Planet. July 13, 2017. Accessed August 31, 2017. http://sierraclub.org/planet/2017/07/women-lead-one-milestone-path-equity-justice-and-inclusion?utm_source=insider&utm_medium=email&utm_campaign=newsletter.

78 Williams, Vanessa. "Analysis | 'Unbought and unbossed': Shirley Chisholm's feminist mantra is still relevant 50 years later." The Washington Post. January 26, 2018. Accessed February 13, 2018. https://www.washingtonpost.com/news/post-nation/wp/2018/01/26/unbought-and-unbossed-shirley-chisholms-feminist-mantra-is-as-relevant-today-as-it-was-50-years-ago/?utm_term=.d76b29e21c18.

79 Drysdale, Jennifer. "Jennifer Aniston on How Society Views Women: 'If We Don't Have a Baby or a Husband Then We're Useless'." News. ET. December 1, 2016. Accessed August 31, 2017. http://www.etonline.com/news/204075_jennifer_aniston_on_how_society_views_women.

80 "Women On Board: A Catalyst Initiative." Catalyst. July 31, 2017. Accessed August 31, 2017. http://www.catalyst.org/knowledge/women-board-catalyst-initiative.

81 Eich, Ritch K. "CEO Alert: Better Boards for Better Outcomes." Leadership. IndustryWeek. December 21, 2016. Accessed December 29, 2017. http://www.industryweek.com/leadership/ceo-alert-better-boards-better-outcomes.

82 "New Study Finds Little Age Diversity Within Corporate Boards." IRRC Institute. March 21, 2017. Accessed January 15, 2018. https://irrcinstitute.org/news/new-study-finds-little-age-diversity-within-corporate-boards/.

83 Eich, Ritch K. "Bringing PR to the Boardroom." Strategic Health Care Marketing, January 2012, 11-12.

84 Svriuga, Susan, and Donna St.George. "Helen Dragas: The leader who forced out U-Va.'s president." Education. *Washington Post.* June 21, 2012. Accessed August 31, 2017. https://www.washingtonpost.com/local/education/helen-dragas-the-leader-who-forced-out-u-vas-president/2012/06/21/gJQA4ds5sV_story.html?utm_term=.949b01fdbd9f.

85 Eich, Ritch K. "Top 10 Reasons for Not Selecting Someone as Board Chair." Directors & Boards. High Beam Research. September 22, 2013. Accessed January 03, 2018. https://www.highbeam.com/doc/1G1-347407338.html.

Chapter 5 – Invest in the Arts

86 Segran, Elizabeth. "Welcome To The Brave New World Of The Corporate-Sponsored Artist." My Creative Life. Fast Company. October 3, 2015. Accessed August 31, 2017. https://www.fastcompany.com/3043276/welcome-to-the-brave-new-world-of-the-corporate-sponsored-artist.

87 "What is Amtrak Residency?" Accessed August 31, 2017. http://blog.amtrak.com/general-faqs/.

88 Eich, Ritch K. *Truth, Trust + Tenacity: How Ordinary People Become Extraordinary Leaders.* Madison, WI: Second City Publishing, 2015.

89 Horrocks, Heather. "How incorporating art into workplace design can affect employee wellness, job performance, and best represent your brand." Momentum. CUInsight. October 07, 2013. Accessed January 04, 2018. https://www.cuinsight.com/

how-incorporating-art-into-workplace-design-can-affect-employ-
ee-wellness-job-performance-and-best-represent-your-brand.html.

90 Bailey, Melissa. "Harvard joins growing trend of arts education in medical schools." Stat. Boston Globe. November 2, 2015.
Accessed August 31, 2017. https://www.bostonglobe.com/busi-
ness/2015/11/02/harvard-joins-growing-trend-arts-education-med-
schools/nra9CQHb1h0Zfmz3x8bPNO/story.html.

91 Kaimal, Girija, Kendra Ray, and Juan Muniz. "Reduction of
Cortisol Levels and Participants' Responses Following Art Making." Art Therapy Journal of the American Art Therapy Association
33, no. 2 (May 23, 2016). Accessed August 31, 2017. http://www.
tandfonline.com/doi/full/10.1080/07421656.2016.1166832.

92 Hendrix, Drew. "Can Office Artwork Influence Employee Productivity?" Entrepreneurs. Forbes. January 12, 2015. Accessed
August 31, 2017. https://www.forbes.com/sites/drewhen-
dricks/2015/01/12/can-office-artwork-influence-employee-produc-
tivity/#367df2d71884.

93 Eich, Ritch K. "5 Creative Ways To Use Art To Boost
Employee Morale." Fast Company. December 12, 2014.
Accessed December 29, 2017. https://www.fastcompany.
com/3039773/5-ways-to-invigorate-your-employees-with-art.

94 McGregor, Jane. "Why Amazon built its workers a mini rain forest inside three domes in downtown Seattle." On Leadership. The
Washington Post. January 29, 2018. Accessed January 30, 2018. www.
washingtonpost.com/news/on-leadership/wp/2018/01/29/why-am-
azon-built-its-workers-a-mini-rainforest-inside-three-domes-in-
downtown-seattle/?utm_term=.53a91edb1e0d.

95 A Historical Overview." Kelloggs. Accessed August 31, 2017.
http://www.kellogghistory.com/history.html.

96 Eich, Ritch K. "5 Creative Ways To Use Art To Boost Employee Morale." Fast Company. December 12, 2014. Accessed December 29, 2017. https://www.fastcompany. com/3039773/5-ways-to-invigorate-your-employees-with-art.

97 Eich, Ritch K. "Why business leaders should trumpet the arts." Op/eds. Pacific Coast Business Times. January 30, 2015. Accessed January 04, 2018. https://www.pacbiztimes.com/2015/01/30/ oped-why-business-leaders-should-trumpet-the-arts/.

98 Sentz, Rob. "What Can You Do With That (Useless) Liberal Arts Degree? A Lot More Than You Think." Business/#IfIOnlyKnew. Forbes. October 19, 2016. Accessed December 28, 2017. https://www.forbes.com/sites/emsi/2016/10/19/what-can-you-do-with-that-useless-liberal-arts-degree/#41e8186141b8.

99 "IT TAKES MORE THAN A MAJOR: Employer Priorities for College Learning and Student Success." Hart Research Associates. April 10, 2013. Accessed August 31, 2017. http://www.aacu.org/ sites/default/files/files/LEAP/2013_EmployerSurvey.pdf.

100 Phillips, Lisa. *The Artistic Edge: 7 Skills Children Need to Succeed in an Increasingly Right Brain World*. New York, NY: The Artistic Edge, 2012.

101 Linshi, Jack. "10 CEOs Who Prove Your Liberal Arts Degree Isn't Worthless." Business: Workplace & Careers. Time Magazine. July 23, 2015. Accessed August 31, 2017. http://time.com/3964415/ ceo-degree-liberal-arts/.

102 Eich, Ritch K. "How the arts vitalize business and the bottom line." VC Star. May 07, 2016. Accessed December 29, 2017. http:// www.vcstar.com/story/opinion/columnists/2016/05/07/ritch-eich-how-the-arts-vitalize-business-and-the-bottom-line/88725976/.

103 Isaacson, Walter. *Steve Jobs*. New York, NY: Simon and Schuster, 2011.

104 Eich, Ritch K. "Op/ed: Cultivating leadership through the arts." Opinion. Pacific Coast Business Times. October 17, 2014. Accessed December 30, 2017. https://www.pacbiztimes.com/2014/10/17/oped-cultivating-leadership-through-the-arts/.

105 Ibid.

106 "An Innovative New Children's Hospital Uses a Mix of Technology, Nature and Playtime to Help Patients Heal." T Brand Studio. The *New York Times*. February 13, 2018. Accessed February 13, 2018. https://paidpost.nytimes.com/stanford/an-innovative-new-childrens-hospital-uses-a-mix-of-technology-nature-and-playtime-to-help-patients-heal.html?tbs_nyt=2017-jan-nytnative_ribbon&cpv_dsm_id=188726832.

107 Barber, Mary. "'I've always been thinking big, but getting to work this big is something that happens gradually.' --Norman Hines : Artwork the Size of Texas." LAT Home. October 16, 1986. Accessed August 31, 2017. http://articles.latimes.com/1986-10-16/news/ga-5924_1_sculpture.

108 Pattison, Don. "The Rebirth of Caelum Moor." *Pomona College Magazine*, 2010, 38-42.

Chapter 6 – Trust Is Non-negotiable

109 "In 218 days, President Trump has made 1,094 false and misleading claims." *Washington Post*. August 25, 2017. Accessed August 31, 2017. https://www.washingtonpost.com/graphics/politics/trump-claims-database/?tid=a_inl&utm_term=.e63bd7ba9d27.

110 Leonhardt, David, and Stuart A. Thompson. "Trump Lies." Opinion. New York Times. July 21, 2017. Accessed August 31,

2017. https://www.nytimes.com/interactive/2017/06/23/opinion/trumps-lies.html?ref=opinion.

[111] Barabak, Mark A. . "There's a long history of presidential untruths. Here's why Donald Trump is 'in a class by himself'." Los Angeles Times. February 06, 2017. Accessed January 24, 2018. http://www.latimes.com/politics/la-na-trump-presidential-lies-2017-story.html.

[112] Chernow, Ron. *GRANT*. New York, NY: Penguin Press, 2017.

[113] Eich, Ritch K. "5 Ways Leaders Can Build A Culture Of Trust." Leadership. Playbook, AMA Net. February 24, 2016. Accessed December 29, 2017. http://playbook.amanet.org/5-ways-leaders-can-build-a-culture-of-trust/.

[114] Eich, Ritch K. *Truth, Trust + Tenacity: How Ordinary People Become Extraordinary Leaders*. Madison, WI: Second City Publishing, 2015.

[115] Eich, Ritch K. "UC Davis' troubles offer lessons on character, reputation." Opinion. VC Star. July 09, 2016. Accessed January 04, 2018. http://www.vcstar.com/story/opinion/columnists/2016/07/09/ritch-eich-uc-davis-troubles-offer-lessons-on-character-reputation/88916062/.

[116] Eich, Ritch K. "Respect Is Not A Given." Take It Personelly. March 13, 2016. Accessed December 29, 2017. https://takeitpersonelly.com/2016/03/13/respect-is-not-a-given/.

[117] Parker, Kathleen. "Trump built a wall. Her name is Sarah." Opinion. The *Washington Post*. November 21, 2017. Accessed January 15, 2018. https://www.washingtonpost.com/opinions/trump-built-a-wall-her-name-is-sarah/2017/11/21/e89a5fe4-cee9-11e7-a1a3-0d1e45a6de3d_story.html?tid=sm_fb&utm_term=.ee03893094fa.

[118] Amanpour, Christiane. "Amanpour: No free press, no democracy." CNN. Cable News Network. November 14, 2017. Accessed November 19, 2017. http://www.cnn.com/2017/11/14/opinions/without-free-press-there-is-no-democracy-opinion-amanpour/index.html.

[119] Eich, Ritch K. "Setting the Record Straight." The Journal of Values-Based Leadership, Summer/Fall 2017, X (II): 21–24. https://issuu.com/valposcholar/docs/00_fullissue_ba254a8bd4a7e6.

[120] Nir, Sarah Maslin. "Where There's Smoke, There Are the Traffic Reporters of Los Angeles." U.S. . The *New York Times*. December 08, 2017. Accessed December 09, 2017. https://www.nytimes.com/2017/12/08/us/la-fires-traffic-reporters.html.

[121] Eich, Ritch K. "Setting the Record Straight." The Journal of Values-Based Leadership, Summer/Fall 2017, X (II): 21–24. https://issuu.com/valposcholar/docs/00_fullissue_ba254a8bd4a7e6.

[122] Hartman, Norman. *The Media and You.* Gold River, CA: Norman S. Hartman, 2009.

Chapter 7 – Balance Short- and Long-Term Strategies

[123] CK Staff. "Celebrating corporate sustainability leadership." *Corporate Knights*. Winter 2017, Global 100 Issue. January 16, 2017. Accessed August 31, 2017. http://www.corporateknights.com/reports/2017-global-100/celebrating-corporate-sustainability-leadership-14846084/.

[124] Ibid.

[125] Hesselbeim, Frances, Marshal Goldsmith, and Richard Beckhard. *The Leader of the Future.* New York, NY: Jossey Bass, 1996.

126 Eich, Ritch K. "The Long-Term Danger of Short-Term Goals." American Machinist Newswire. November 02, 2016. Accessed December 29, 2017. http://www.americanmachinist.com/american-machinist-newswire/long-term-danger-short-term-goals.

127 Friedman, Thomas L. "China Could Sell Trump the Brooklyn Bridge." Opinion. The *New York Times*. November 14, 2017. Accessed December 10, 2017. https://www.nytimes.com/2017/11/14/opinion/china-trump-xi-jinping-trade.html.

128 "The Next Episode." The Atlantic. Accessed January 25, 2018. https://www.theatlantic.com/sponsored/jpmc-2017/the-next-episode/1742/.

129 Friedman, Thomas L. "Need a Job? Invent it." Sunday Review. The *New York Times*. March 30, 2013. Accessed August 31, 2017. http://www.nytimes.com/2013/03/31/opinion/sunday/friedman-need-a-job-invent-it.html?rref=collection%2Fcolumn%2Fthomas-l-friedman&action=click&contentCollection=opinion&ion=stream&module=stream_unit&version=search&contentPlacement=3&pgtype=collection.

130 Limoneira. Accessed August 31, 2017. http://limoneira.com/corporate/our-mission/.

131 Digital. "Consumer Trust in Online, Social and Mobile Advertising Grows." Newswire. April 10, 2012. Accessed September 07, 2017. http://www.nielsen.com/us/en/insights/news/2012/

132 "Number of Jobs Held, Labor Market Activity, and Earnings Growth Among the Youngest Baby Boomers: Results from a Longitudinal Survey Summary." Bureau of Labor Statistics. August 24, 2017. Accessed August 31, 2017. https://www.bls.gov/news.release/nlsoy.nr0.htm.

[133] "A Future That Works: Automation, Employment and Productiviity." McKinsey Global Institute. January 2017. Accessed August 31, 2017. https://www.google.com/url?sa=t&rct=j&q=&esrc=s&source=web&cd=7&ved=0ahUKEwivz8absoLWAhWH7IM-KHbkhAUUQFghAMAY&url=http%3A%2F%2Fwww.mckinsey.com%2F~%2Fmedia%2FMcKinsey%2FGlobal%2520Themes%2F-Digital%2520Disruption%2FHarnessing%2520automa-tion%2520for%2520a%2520future%2520that%2520works%2-FMGI-A-future-that-works_Full-report.ashx&usg=AFQjCNHwYDAyhAeSwGoZH_OVl-36GkE3nA.

[134] Eich, Ritch K. "Staying Ahead in a Global Marketplace." News. San Fernanda Valley Business Journal. January 09, 2017. Accessed December 29, 2017. http://sfvbj.com/news/2017/jan/09/staying-ahead-global-marketplace/.

[135] Deresiewicz, William. *A Jane Austen Education: How Six Novels Taught Me About Love, Friendship, and the Things That Really Matter.* New York, NY: Penguin Press, 2011.

[136] Eich, Ritch (2016) "Where in the Heavens are our Earthly Leaders?," The Journal of Values-Based Leadership: Vol. 9 : Iss. 1 , Article 3. Available at: http://scholar.valpo.edu/jvbl/vol9/iss1/3.

[137] "Unilever sees sustainability supporting growth." Globe-Net. May 5, 2015. Accessed August 31, 2017. http://globe-net.com/unilever-sees-sustainability-supporting-growth/.

[138] Schein, Edgar. *Organizational Culture and Leadership.* San Francisco, CA: Jossey-Bass, Inc., 1985.

[139] HR Imperative for 2015: Hire Original Thinkers", December 2015 issue of HR Strategy and Planning Excellence Essentials.

[140] Hamori, Monika, and Burak Koyuncu. "New CEO: Better Without Prior Experience?" Insights. IE Business

School. January 01, 2017. Accessed December 30, 2017. https://www.ie.edu/corporate-relations/insights/new-ceo-better-without-prior-experience-2/.

141 Eich, Ritch K. "Leaders don't reside in 'safe zones.'" Opinion. VC Star. November 26, 2016. Accessed December 29, 2017. http://www.vcstar.com/story/opinion/columnists/2016/11/26/ritch-eich-leaders-dont-reside-safe-zones/94094548/.

Chapter 8 – Assume Responsibility

142 "Buck passing." Wikipedia. Wikimedia Foundation. July 27, 2017. Accessed September 01, 2017. https://en.wikipedia.org/wiki/Buck_passing.

143 Khanna, Satyam. "FLASHBACK: In October, Obama Said That AIG Executives 'Should Be Fired' For Their Excesses." Climate. ThinkProgress. March 18, 2009. Accessed December 30, 2017. https://thinkprogress.org/flashback-in-october-obama-said-that-aig-executives-should-be-fired-for-their-excesses-b2af8b75074d/.

144 Eich, Ritch K. (2013) "Playing Above the Breaks...," The Journal of Values-Based Leadership: Vol. 6 : Iss. 2 , Article 6. Available at: http://scholar.valpo.edu/jvbl/vol6/iss2/6.

145 Trusteeship Magazine, Association of Governing Boards of Universities, and Colleges, 2006.

146 Vazquez, Maegan. "McCain again takes on Trump, says 'it's time to wake up'." Politics. CNN. October 31, 2017. Accessed December 30, 2017. http://www.cnn.com/2017/10/31/politics/john-mccain-naval-academy-speech/index.html.

147 Brice, Nick Cummings. "U.N. Human Rights Chief Condemns Trump's Attacks on Media." Europe. *New York Times*. August 30, 2017. Accessed September 1, 2017. https://www.nytimes.

com/2017/08/30/world/europe/trump-press-united-nations.
html?emc=eta1&_r=0.

148 Robinson, Eugene. "This tax deal is great for Trump. What
a coincidence!" Opinions. The *Washington Post*. December
21, 2017. Accessed December 22, 2017. https://www.wash-
ingtonpost.com/opinions/a-sweetheart-tax-deal--for-the-
trumps/2017/12/21/17546880-e68b-11e7-ab50-621fe0588340
story.html?utm_term=.646629c198d2.

149 Erlanger, Steven. "'Fake News,' Trump's Obsession, Is Now a
Cudgel for Strongmen." Europe. The *New York Times*. December 12, 2017. Accessed December 22, 2017. https://www.nytimes.
com/2017/12/12/world/europe/trump-fake-news-dictators.html.

150 News, CBS. "Face the Nation Transcript: November 26, 2017." CBS News. November 26, 2017. Accessed
December 10, 2017. https://www.cbsnews.com/news/
face-the-nation-transcript-november-26-2017.

151 Hohmann, James. "Trump has no nominees for 245 important jobs, including an ambassador to South Korea." Analysis. The
Washington Post. January 12, 2018. Accessed January 15, 2018.
https://www.washingtonpost.com/news/powerpost/paloma/dai-
ly-202/2018/01/12/daily-202-trump-has-no-nominees-for-245-
important-jobs-including-an-ambassador-to-south-korea/5a57c-
ce830fb0469e8840085/?tid=ss_mail&utm_term=.de0638d1ab1d.

152 Baker, Peter. "A Whirlwind Envelops the White House, and
the Revolving Door Spins." Politics. The *New York Times*. February 12, 2018. Accessed February 13, 2018. https://www.nytimes.
com/2018/02/12/us/politics/trump-white-house-staff-turnover.
html.

153 Eich, Ritch K. "Message to President Trump:
Stop Whining and Start Leading." Leadership.

IndustryWeek. February 16, 2017. Accessed December 30, 2017. http://www.industryweek.com/leadership/message-president-trump-stop-whining-and-start-leading.

Chapter 9 – Seek Win-Win Solutions

[154] Eich, Ritch K. *Real Leaders Don't Boss: Inspire, Motivate, and Earn Respect from Employees and Watch Your Organization Soar.* Pompton Plains, NJ: Career Press, 2012.

[155] Brown, Daniel James. *The Boys in the Boat: Nine Americans and Their Epic Quest for Gold at the 1936 Berlin Olympics.* New York, NY: Penguin, 2016.

[156] Eich, Ritch K. "50 Years in the Trenches: Five Lessons on Teamwork." Teamwork. IndustryWeek. May 02, 2017. Accessed December 29, 2017. http://www.industryweek.com/teamwork/50-years-trenches-five-lessons-teamwork.

[157] Murthy, Vivek. "Work and the Loneliness Epidemic." The Line-up. *Harvard Business Review.* Accessed December 30, 2017. https://hbr.org/cover-story/2017/09 work-and-the-loneliness-epidemic.

[158] Seppälä, Emma. *The Happiness Track: How to Apply the Science of Happiness to Accelerate Your Success.* San Francisco, CA: HarperOne, 2017.

[159] Seppälä, Emma, and Marissa King. "Burnout at Work Isn't Just About Exhaustion. It's Also About Loneliness." Managing People. *Harvard Business Review.* June 29, 2017. Accessed January 24, 2018. https://hbr.org/2017/06/burnout-at-work-isnt-just-about-exhaustion-its-also-about-loneliness.

[160] Yeginsu, Ceylan. "U.K. Appoints a Minister for Loneliness." Europe. The *New York Times.* January 17, 2018. Accessed January 24, 2018. https://www.nytimes.com/2018/01/17/world/

europe/uk-britain-loneliness.html?mtrref=undefined&g-wh=A094AA2110B2F48109CA84C12E67585A&gwt=pay.

[161] Krause, Tom. "Leadership: Loyalty from Leadership: Holding the Team Together." Getting Better Results Together. Leader Values. 2006. Accessed September 1, 2017. https://www.leader-values.com/article.php?aid=350.

[162] Bouza, Anthony V. *Police Unbound: Corruption, Abuse, and Heroism by the Boys in Blue.* New York, NY: Prometheus Books, 2001.

[163] United States Holocaust Memorial Museum. Accessed December 30, 2017. https://www.ushmm.org/professionals-and-student-leaders/military-professionals.

[164] "Joint Service Academy Mass Atrocity Prevention Symposium." Accessed September 1, 2017. https://www.ushmm.org/professionals-and-student-leaders/military-professionals/jsamaps.

Chapter 10 – Look to Sports for Models and Mentors

[165] Elkins, Kathleen. "These 9 successful CEOs all played sports in college." Careers. Business Insider. February 18, 2015. Accessed September 1, 2017. http://www.businessinsider.com/successful-ceos-who-played-sports-in-college-2015-2.

[166] Carroll, Jack. "95% of Fortune 500 CEOs Were Athletes." Parents. Coach Up Nation. October 28, 2015. Accessed September 1, 2017. https://www.coachup.com/nation/articles/95-of-fortune-500-ceos-were-athletes.

[167] "Women Athletes Business Network." EY.com. Accessed September 1, 2017. http://www.ey.com/br/pt/about-us/our-sponsorships-and-programs/women-athletes-global-leadership-network---perspectives-on-sport-and-teams.

168 Sullivan, James. "9 Reasons Why You Should Hire Athletes." Blog. The Drive. July 19, 2015. Accessed September 1, 2017. https://www.thedrivegroup.com.au/blog/2015/07/9-reasons-why-you-should-hire-athletes.

169 Eich, Ritch K. *Truth, Trust + Tenacity: How Ordinary People Become Extraordinary Leaders.* P. 63. Madison, WI: Second City Publishing, 2015.

170 Badenhausen, Kurt. "How Arnold Palmer Earned $875 Million During Legendary Career In Golf." Business/#SportsMoney. Forbes. September 26, 2016. Accessed September 1, 2017. https://www.forbes.com/sites/kurtbadenhausen/2016/09/26/arnold-palmer-earned-875-million-during-legendary-career-in-golf/#6399095c3e53.

171 Dusek, David. "Arnold Palmer: The king of gear-crazed golfers." Golfweek, September 25, 2016. Accessed September 1, 2017. http://golfweek.com/2016/09/25/arnold-palmer-king-gear-crazed-golfers/.

172 Eich, Ritch K. "What Business Leaders Can Learn from Arnold Palmer." Leadership. IndustryWeek. October 11, 2016. Accessed December 30, 2017. http://www.industryweek.com/leadership/what-business-leaders-can-learn-arnold-palmer.

173 Eich, Ritch K. "5 Modern Leadership Lessons from Jackie Robinson." Leadership. IndustryWeek. February 02, 2017. Accessed December 30, 2017. http://www.industryweek.com/leadership/5-modern-leadership-lessons-jackie-robinson.

174 Eich , Ritch K. "What Jackie Robinson's Leadership Teaches Us: Seven ground rules for millennials." ePubs. HR.com. March 03, 2017. Accessed December 30, 2017. https://www.hr.com/en/magazines/leadership_excellence_essentials/march_2017_leadership/

what-jackie-robinson%E2%80%99s-leadership-teaches-us-seven_iztsb4ax.html.

[175] Eich, Ritch K. "Working from First Base to the Boardroom." News. *San Fernando Valley Business Journal*. July 25, 2016. Accessed December 30, 2017. http://sfvbj.com/news/2016/jul/25/working-first-base-boardroom/?page=2.

[176] Smith, Harrison. "Pancho Segura, bowlegged tennis champion of the 1940s and '50s, dies at 96." Obituaries. The *Washington Post*. November 20, 2017. Accessed November 23, 2017. https://www.washingtonpost.com/local/obituaries/pancho-segura-bowlegged-tennis-champion-of-the-1940s-and-50s-dies-at-96/2017/11/20/ae47250e-ce06-11e7-9d3a-bcbe2af58c3a_story.html?utm_term=.7d0d4c011800.

Chapter 11 – Conclusion

[177] Gentry, William, Jennifer Deal, Sarah Stawiski, and Marion Tuderman. "Are Leaders Born or Made." Center for Creative Leadership. March 2012. Accessed September 4, 2017. https://www.ccl.org/wp-content/uploads/2015/02/AreLeadersBornOrMade.pdf.

[178] "California Statewide Maps." CAL FIRE - Home. December 04, 2017. Accessed January 03, 2018. http://www.fire.ca.gov/current_incidents/incidentdetails/Index/1922.

[179] Karimi, Faith, Jason Hanna, and Steve Almasy. "California mudslides: Evacuation zones expanded as searches continue." CNN. January 12, 2018. Accessed January 13, 2018. http://www.cnn.com/2018/01/11/us/southern-california-mudslides/index.html.

[180] Gelles, David, and Claire Cain Miller. "Business Schools Now Teaching #MeToo, N.F.L. Protests and Trump." Business Day. The

New York Times. December 25, 2017. Accessed January 02, 2018. https://www.nytimes.com/2017/12/25/business/mba-business-school-ethics.html.

[181] Brokaw, Tom. "You Can Find the Entire World Inside Your Hospital." Opinion. The *New York Times.* December 31, 2017. Accessed January 02, 2018. https://www.nytimes.com/2017/12/31/opinion/tom-brokaw-health-care-immigrants.html.

[182] Panetta, Leon. "Leon Panetta: The world needs to know Trump is not who we are." Opinion. CNN. January 17, 2018. Accessed January 24, 2018. http://www.cnn.com/2018/01/17/opinions/leon-panetta-the-world-needs-to-know-trump-is-not-who-we-are/index.html.

[183] Phillips, Amber. "Analysis | 'Our democracy will not last': Jeff Flake's speech comparing Trump to Stalin, annotated." Analysis. The *Washington Post.* January 17, 2018. Accessed January 24, 2018. https://www.washingtonpost.com/news/the-fix/wp/2018/01/17/our-democracy-will-not-last-jeff-flakes-speech-comparing-trump-to-stalin-annotated/?utm_term=.09279740e80a.

[184] Phillips, Kristine. "Sen. Tammy Duckworth: I swore an oath to the Constitution, not to clap when Trump demands." The *Washington Post.* February 06, 2018. Accessed February 06, 2018. https://www.washingtonpost.com/news/checkpoint/wp/2018/02/06/sen-tammy-duckworth-i-swore-an-oath-to-the-constitution-not-to-clap-when-trump-demands/?utm_term=.c823eb7b4f79.

[185] McCain, John. "Opinion | Mr. President, stop attacking the press." *The Washington Post.* January 16, 2018. Accessed January 24, 2018. https://www.washingtonpost.com/opinions/mr-president-stop-attacking-the-press/2018/01/16/9438c0ac-faf0-11e7-a46b-a3614530bd87_story.html?utm_term=.5be4ebf8aef2.

[186] Ignatius, David. 2018. "Ex-Spy chiefs weigh how to say enough about Trump without saying too much." Opinion. The *Washington Post.* January 25, 2018. Accessed January 27, 2018. https://www.washingtonpost.com/opinions/ex-spy-chiefs-weigh-how-to-say-enough-about-trump-without-saying-too-much/2018/01/25/bed73e6a-021b-11e8-bb03-722769454f82_story.html?utm_term=.66fb75088155.

[187] Eich, Ritch K. "Staying Ahead in a Global Marketplace." *San Fernando Valley Business Journal* 22, no. 1 (January 9, 2017): 39.

Index

University of California, Merced, 126
University of Michigan, xviii, 7, 51, 52, 80, 91, 123
University of Virginia, 68-70
University of Washington, 167
USS Amherst, 113
USS Arizona Memorial, 114
USS Carl Vinson, 114

V

Vaughns, Cleopatra, 23
Vietnam War, 96, 207

W

Walt Disney Company, 88
Washington Post, 11, 68, 95, 96, 104, 159, 161
Wells Fargo, 130, 132, 197
Western Union, 26
Wharton, Dolores D., 155
Wharton Jr., Clifton R., 154
Whitman, Meg, 179
Wilson, Bill, 105-106
win-win solutions, xxxi, 165, 169, 173
women on boards, 59, 62-64, 74
World War II, 48, 53, 114, 149

Y

Yale School of Management, 144
Yousafzai, Malala, xxxii, 36

Z

Zumwalt Jr., Admiral Elmo R., 53-55

Ritch K. Eich's other published books can be found on
Amazon.com and **Barnesandnoble.com.**
Please visit the site and search for the title
to purchase in either paperback or digital copy.

Real Leaders Don't Boss
(Career Press, 2012)

Leadership Requires Extra Innings
(Second City Publishing, 2013)

Truth, Trust + Tenacity
(Second City Publishing, 2015)

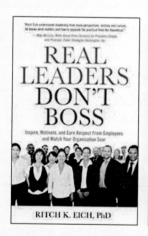 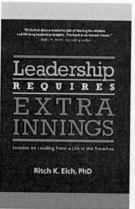 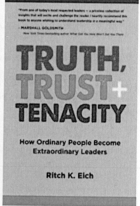

For more information on Ritch's fourth book, *Leadership CPR*,
please visit his website www.leadercpr.com

Praise for *Leadership CPR*

(Redwood Publishing, 2018)

"Ritch Eich has consistently displayed remarkable integrity and authenticity in his public leadership in the United States Navy and with the Indiana University Medical Center. As a Hoosier, I have witnessed Ritch's leadership and I hope, through Leadership CPR, any others will be inspired by his lessons and example."

—RICHARD G. LUGAR, former United States senator; president of the Lugar Center, a nonprofit organization focusing on global food security, WMD nonproliferation, aid effectiveness, and bipartisan governance

"For those who say there are 'born leaders,' Ritch Eich proves there are things to learn about leadership that can help those not genetically endowed. This is a volume for everyone nervous about chairing their first meeting, elected to head the PTA, or interested in stepping up to make a difference."

—MIKE MCCURRY, White House press secretary for President Clinton; principal, Public Strategies Washington, Inc.; distinguished professor *and executive director* of the Center for Public Theology, Wesley Theological Seminary; co-chair, the Commission on Presidential Debates

"The best leaders are those who provide a positive example and inspire those around them. As Ritch Eich explains in his new book with numerous timely examples, no leadership attributes are more important than the moral fiber and integrity that real leaders consistently demonstrate. I strongly recommend this book, especially for younger people aspiring to be effective leaders."

—HOWDY HOLMES, president and CEO, "JIFFY" Mix

"The path to exceptional leadership includes having a clearly defined and consistently executed vision, unyielding ethical principles, and genuine respect and compassion for others, as well as willingness to stick your neck out when necessary, model teamwork, and take responsibility for decisions made. The journey to becoming a successful leader is a difficult one that too few complete. Ritch Eich's book is an essential guidebook for anyone considering embarking on this challenging, highly competitive, but most rewarding journey."

—DAVID A. BRANDON, CEO, Toys "R" Us; chairman of the board, Domino's Pizza

"Ritch Eich has put his finger on many of the common themes shared by true leaders in his book *Leadership CPR*. Demonstrated leadership begins with articulated goals and objectives and an unwavering commitment to achievement. At the same time, this commitment must be backed by the moral compass of an organizational leader's "north star" that is unquestioned. When these traits come together, loyalty and commitment are earned throughout an organization and great things begin to happen. Ritch Eich's stories of these leadership themes resonate loudly and clearly and provide wonderful examples for any reader to take away."

—HAROLD EDWARDS, president and CEO, Limoneira, Inc.

"*Leadership CPR,* Ritch Eich's latest book on leadership, is the capstone of his previous treatments on the subject. The theme of the book is ethical behavior. Virtue is the seminal characteristic of good leadership... how committed leaders are in exhibiting and promoting ethical behavior throughout the organization regardless of type or size. Ritch points out that this behavior must also be consistent regardless of circumstance. Whether dealing with the employees or the board of trustees, the leader's moral compass must overlay whatever decisions need to be made. This is a book that both seasoned leaders and aspiring leaders should read and keep on the corner of their desk."

—MAJOR GENERAL LESLIE M. PALM, USMC (Ret.), president and CEO, Marine Corps Association and Foundation (Ret.)

"In an era where daily newscasts are overwhelming and where groups, peoples, and nation-states appear to be on the brink of self-destructing… leadership—true leadership—is desperately wanting. Ritch Eich, an author and friend, has unfalteringly supplied hope and guidance in such desolate times…. A lifetime of experience in leadership and consultancy roles has uniquely primed him for such a comprehensive effort."

—ELIZABETH GINGERICH, JD, editor-in-chief, *The Journal of Values-Based Leadership*; professor of business law, College of Business, Valparaiso University

"In his new book, Ritch Eich defines the choices a leader makes on the journey to becoming a great leader. It follows my beliefs that great leadership can happen only when all actions are grounded on strong values…. The book is a very good read that covers a lot of new ground, including leadership on boards and learning from sports and arts leaders."

—VERENA KLOOS, CEO, Strategic Design Consulting; former president, BMW Design Works

Praise for *TRUTH, TRUST + TENACITY:*
How Ordinary People Become Extraordinary Leaders
(Second City Publishing, 2015)

"From one of today's most respected leaders—a priceless collection of insights that will excite and challenge the reader, I heartily recommend this book to anyone wishing to understand leadership in a meaningful way."

—MARSHALL GOLDSMITH, *New York Times* best-selling author of *What Got You Here Won't Get You There*

"Ritch Eich gives us a spicy recipe for leadership in *Truth, Trust + Tenacity*, and the ingredients—interesting people, wonderful stories, and keen insights—will help any reader cook up success."

—MIKE MCCURRY, former White House press secretary to President Clinton; principal, Public Strategies Washington, Inc.; distinguished professor and executive director, Center for Public Theology, Wesley Theological Seminary; co-chair, the Commission on Presidential Debates

"Insightful, inspiring, and memorable… a 'must read' for aspiring leaders."

—VERENA KLOOS, former CEO, BMW Design Works

"Ritch understands that great leadership is about personal behavior."

—HOWDY HOLMES, president and CEO, "JIFFY" Mix

"This third volume is leadership expert Ritch Eich's most important book yet."

> —ORA HIRSCH PESCOVITZ, MD, nationally recognized pediatric endocrinologist and researcher; president, Oakland University; former CEO, University of Michigan Health System; former senior vice president, Eli Lilly, Co.; former CEO, Riley Hospital for Children

Praise for Leadership Requires Extra Innings:
Lessons on Leading From a Life in the Trenches
(Second City Publishing, 2013)

"Ritch Eich does a masterful job of sharing his wisdom and life-long leadership insights. The book is an instant classic."

> —NOEL M. TICHY, best-selling coauthor of *Judgment, The Leadership Engine*, and *Control Your Destiny or Someone Else Will*

"You always look to Ritch Eich's next volume on leadership with anticipation that he'll shake up the lineup when it comes to conventional thinking, but this one gives us more. If the need for inspirational thinking for leaders is going extra innings, then Ritch is our 'closer' and ready to bring the argument home."

> —MIKE MCCURRY, former White House press secretary for President Clinton; principal, Public Strategies Washington, Inc.

"In his second book, Ritch Eich communicates essential ingredients of managerial leadership—consistency of message and patient mentoring. No leader 'leads' except by using these fundamental building blocks."

> —EUGENE A. BAUER, MD, Silicon Valley entrepreneur; former CEO, Stanford University Medical Center; former dean, Stanford University School of Medicine; cofounder and chief medical officer, Dermira

"Ritch Eich has a passion for the study of leaders and leadership. In *Leadership Requires Extra Innings*, Ritch explores how successful leaders create high-performance teams capable of accomplishing great things. I recommend this book to anyone who wants to take their leadership competencies to the next level!"

—DAVID A. BRANDON, chairman and CEO, Toys "R" Us

"Successful leadership necessarily warrants respect for, and consideration of, all stakeholder interests. Ritch Eich understands this foundational maxim and encourages those in positions of leadership, and those aspiring to lead, to elicit feedback from others affected by operational decisions and parlay those ideas into meaningful and sustainable action."

—ELIZABETH GINGERICH, editor-in-chief, *The Journal of Values-Based Leadership*

"Ritch Eich has a magical ability—turning the impossible into the possible—as his numerous career accomplishments clearly reveal. At Pomona, Blue Shield, Stanford, the Navy, California Lutheran University, and now with his second book, his rich experiences will be available to all. Ritch is a leader's leader."

—WILLIAM KEARNEY, senior vice president, Merrill Lynch Wealth Management

Praise for *Real Leaders Don't Boss:*

*Inspire, Motivate, and Earn Respect
From Employees and Watch Your Organization Soar*
(Career Press, 2012)

"Ritch Eich is a man of experience. The best leaders are the ones who have taken the high road and now can lift others. Ritch is that leader."

—RICH DEVOS, cofounder, Amway Corporation; owner, Orlando Magic (NBA)

"*Real Leaders Don't Boss* is a 'can't miss' leadership book. Ritch wouldn't write anything less."

—RICHARD G. LUGAR, PRESIDENT, THE LUGAR CENTER; UNITED STATES SENATOR (RET.)

"Books and articles about leadership are not scarce. Insightful books drawn from career-long, successful, hands-on experience are. Ritch Eich brings that experience to his valuable discussion of traits and qualities—some learned, some innate—possessed by the best leaders. His book is careful in describing the difference between leading and managing, a chasm he so clearly understands from his own successful careers."

—JIM FINKELSTEIN, chief of information, Navy Department, Pentagon; rear admiral, U.S. Navy (Ret.)

"Whether you're a new manager or a new executive, Ritch Eich delivers an exceptionally useful pathway to follow for success. Ritch is highly accomplished, incredibly disciplined, and leads by example and with humor and with grace. Don't go to your next staff meeting without reading his book first!"

—MARY D. OLSON, General manager, KCLU Radio, NPR

"Ritch Eich has captured the essence of leadership in his book, *Real Leaders Don't Boss*. People may gain wealth or promotions by the sheer power of their personality and desire; however, the success of the organization fades as soon as they leave.... Real leaders know their trade as well, but they are guided by virtues such as fortitude and temperance. They value those that work for them. They also challenge and mentor them. Real leaders are comfortable in their own skin, which in turn develops the character of those who work for them."

—MAJOR GENERAL LESLIE M. PALM, USMC (Ret.); president and CEO, Marine Corps Association & Foundation (Ret.)

"Ritch Eich's leadership style is part Warren Bennis and Max De Pree, part John Greenleaf and Peter Drucker, and part Jackie Robinson and Colin Powell. Ritch is a change agent and has worked tirelessly to transform the management practices and processes he inherited in each of his positions of increasing responsibility. As a leadership and management consultant, Ritch is continuing to share 'best practices' from the leadership field."

—STEVE GRAFTON, president and CEO, University of Michigan Alumni Association

www.leadercpr.com